Soviet Allies

Also of Interest

Communist Armies in Politics, edited by Jonathon R. Adelman

Civil-Military Relations in Communist Systems, edited by Dale R. Herspring and Ivan Volgyes

**The Armed Forces of the USSR,* Third Edition, Revised and Updated, Harriet Fast Scott and William F. Scott

**The Soviet Art of War: Doctrine, Strategy, and Tactics,* edited by Harriet Fast Scott and William F. Scott

Arms Control and Defense Postures in the 1980s, edited by Richard Burt

Poland Between the Superpowers: Security Versus Economic Recovery, Arthur R. Rachwald

**Politics and Change in East Germany: An Evaluation of Socialist Democracy,* C. Bradley Scharf

Political Cohesion in a Fragile Mosaic: The Yugoslav Experience, Lenard J. Cohen and Paul Warwick

Brezhnev's Peace Program: A Study of Soviet Domestic Political Process and Power, Peter M.E. Volten

**Eastern Europe in the 1980s,* edited by Stephen Fischer-Galati

**National Communism,* Peter Zwick

The Soviet High Command, John Erickson

Communist Nations' Military Assistance, edited by John F. Copper and Daniel S. Papp

East-West Relations in Europe: Observations and Advice from the Sidelines, 1971-1982, Paul E. Zinner

The Future of European Alliance Systems: NATO and the Warsaw Pact, edited by Arlene Idol Broadhurst

The Defense of the West: Strategic and European Security Issues Reappraised, edited by Robert Kennedy and John M. Weinstein

Evaluating Intelligence Estimates of Soviet Naval Intentions, Frank J. Stech

* Available in hardcover and paperback.

Westview Special Studies on the Soviet Union and Eastern Europe

Soviet Allies: The Warsaw Pact and the Issue of Reliability
edited by Daniel N. Nelson

Focusing on the degree to which Warsaw Treaty Organization (WTO) leaders can be assured of non-Soviet military support in hostile circumstances, this book provides empirical guidance for Western assessments of WTO "reliability" (i.e., mobilization potential). The authors specify the variables thought to affect reliability and address the measurement of those variables, then analyze the changing Warsaw Pact alliance structure, the relationship of East European military establishments to the USSR, and the interplay of Soviet and East European security concerns. In case studies of six European countries, the authors assess domestic-level variables (e.g., party-military relations, general domestic political conditions, material and manpower resources, economic performance) and their relationship to the mobilization potential of Eastern Europe.

Daniel N. Nelson is an associate professor of political science at the University of Kentucky. He is author and editor of several books, including *Romania in the 1980s* (Westview, 1981).

Soviet Allies: The Warsaw Pact and the Issue of Reliability

edited by Daniel N. Nelson

Westview Press / Boulder and London

Westview Special Studies on the Soviet Union and Eastern Europe

Published in 1984 in the United States of America by Westview Press, Inc., 5500 Central Avenue, Boulder, Colorado 80301; Frederick A. Praeger, Publisher

Library of Congress Catalog Card Number: 84-50790
ISBN: 0-86531-359-8

Composition for this book was provided by the editor
Printed and bound in the United States of America

10 9 8 7 6 5 4 3 2 1

Contents

Tables

Preface

The Soviet Union's European allies, the six communist party states of the Warsaw Treaty Organization (WTO or Warsaw Pact), have a combined population approaching 120 million and have an annual combined Gross National Product of approximately six hundred billion dollars. As this book was being assembled, the combined militaries of the same six states involved well over a million men and women. Were military and political leaders in the USSR assured beyond any doubt that such nations would commit to the Soviets their civilian and military resources without restraint in a European conflict against NATO forces, the balance of power in Central Europe would weigh heavily in Moscow's favor.

But for many years, Western military planners have thought it would be likely that serious constraints would lessen the effect of East European military performance. Most often, the "reliability" of non-Soviet Warsaw Pact forces was doubted because of, it was thought, morale problems or anti-Soviet sentiment. Western interest in the reliability question has become stronger as the East European forces were up-dated in the 1970s, training with Soviet units increased, and more stress was placed on multilateral actions within the alliance.

These changes, and the obvious need to know what consequences may result from, for example, a Pact offensive in Central Europe, require greater refinement of the concept of reliability. Such an effort necessitates, first, additional comparative studies in which specific observations in six East European cases are used to derive generalizations about the alliance, its cohesion, and likely performance. The same endeavor also demands careful scrutiny of each case and reflection on historical and cultural themes as well as empirical data.

Accordingly, this volume is divided into two sections, the first of which offers conceptual and systemic perspectives regarding Warsaw Pact reliability. In the first chapter in Section I, Daniel N. Nelson argues for the refinement of the term "reliability" through the use of empirical reference points for many of its components.

He suggests that reliability, in fact, connotes the degree to which available forces can be fully mobilized. The "mobilization potential" of a particular regime thus becomes the crux of any assessment of reliability.

Also in Section I are articles by Robin Alison Remington and Christopher Jones. Robin Remington considers the systemic transformations of the Warsaw Pact over its thirty-year existence, with particular attention devoted to the impact of the Polish crisis on the alliance. Christopher Jones views the WTO in terms of its interwoven political administrations, underscoring the political element of the alliance's purpose.

Taken together, these three articles offer to the reader an overview of the complexities inherent in the issue of reliability. Measurement problems are raised by Nelson, longitudinal considerations stressed by Remington's analysis, and ideological and attitudinal aspects discussed by Jones. Put another way, assessments of the reliability of military forces in Eastern Europe are confounded by empirical limitations, changes within the Warsaw Pact over time, and the uncertainties of ideological indoctrination. These articles also point out tendencies not evident from country-specific analysis alone. Variations in the degree to which East European states are integrated into the WTO, or the extent to which their socioeconomic, political, and military conditions could support a regime's mobilization commands, are documented in the Nelson chapter. Remington portrays the WTO's transformation, due in part to crises such as Hungary, Czechoslovakia, and Poland, into a "multipurpose alliance reflecting East European organizational maneuvering as well as Soviet preference." Jones, as well, focuses on conclusions that might not clearly be drawn from individual cases regarding the Soviet effort to "acculturate East European personnel as much as possible to the military ethos of Soviet personnel."

In Section II, Ivan Volgyes, Condoleezza Rice, Henry Krisch, Jan de Weydenthal and Walter M. Bacon investigate the individual cases of East European Warsaw Pact members. Each of these authors was at liberty to adopt the approach he or she felt most appropriate to assess the issue of reliability for the case under examination. Nevertheless, references are made to the concept of "mobilization potential" and its components as introduced by Chapter 1, The Measurement of East European WTO "Reliability." A brief conclusion returns to that concept, and offers a summary of views presented by contributors.

Most of the contributions to this volume were completed by early 1983. That the appearance of this volume was delayed subsequently is the editor's responsibility.

Daniel N. Nelson
Lexington, Kentucky

Acknowledgments

I wish to express my gratitude to Ms. Kim Hayden, who typed this manuscript, as she has many other projects in which I have been involved. Ms. Kathie Golden, a Ph.D. candidate in the Department of Political Science, University of Kentucky, produced the index to this volume and proofed the manuscript. Without the help of both of these individuals, this volume would have been impossible. Neither, of course, bears any responsibility for any remaining errors.

Thanks are also due to Duke University Press for permission to re-print two chapters from a previously published book. The two chapters by Ivan Volgyes appeared as Chapter 3, "Bulgaria: A Faithful Ally" and as Chapter 5, "Hungary: Problematical Performer" in The Political Reliability of The Warsaw Pact Armies: The Southern Tier (Durham, N.C.: Duke University Press) copyright 1982.

D.N.N.

Section I

Conceptual and Systemic Perspectives

1
The Measurement of East European WTO "Reliability"

Daniel N. Nelson

INTRODUCTION

A principal concern to NATO strategists is the relationship between domestic socioeconomic and political conditions of East European states and the use of those countries' military forces in hostile circumstances. This relationship also plays a role in Western negotiating positions for conventional and theatre nuclear force talks, and in discussions among the U.S. and its allies regarding defense expenditures. Among the specific policy questions Western military and civilian planners must consider are:

1. How must our conventional and theatre nuclear force (TNF) planning "factor in" responses to East European forces?

2. To what extent must NATO, specifically our European allies, be prepared for combat with East European forces?

3. Were hostilities to break out, what manpower and material resources could be mobilized to the Soviet effort in East Europe? What ought our expectations be regarding East European compliance with Soviet directives, and the efficiency of compliance, in different scenerios of European hostilities?

4. Were domestic turmoil in an East European state to reach the point of rebellion, and that state's own military were called in to reassert control, what is the likelihood of obedience to such orders? Of refusal?

While many assumptions exist about East European contributions to Soviet European theatre operations in hostile circumstances, few of these assumptions have been subjected to any organized intellectual examination.[1]

We know a great deal about placement of forces, their type and disposition, and armaments; we know little about how general socioeconomic and political conditions affect the degree of assurance with which WTO commanders can view such non-Soviet units.

Speculation, albeit informed about the military capabilities of East European forces, remains widespread regarding the impact of domestic socioeconomic and political conditions.[2] The role assigned to non-Soviet WTO militaries is much more certain than "how reliably... (they) would fulfill that role" in the view of Johnson, Dean and Alexiev. In a "war of attrition", the same analysts suggest, the East European "morale probably would crumble."[3] But in this and other analyses, few domestic data are utilized to support or test hypotheses. Some of the apparent lack of empirical reference points is, of course, a function of necessary deletions when government-sponsored research is "cleansed" of confidential material for public release. Nevertheless, many social scientists and historians have made reference to the reliability of Warsaw Pact militaries without measurement of that quality.[4] Instead, judgments about reliability have been based upon extrapolations from the historical record and assumptions about the effect of various battle scenerios on personnel performance and citizen morale. While we cannot escape entirely the judgmental nature of some evidence--for example, concerning the influence of scenario on reliability as discussed below--we <u>can</u> be more precise about relative judgments and our bases for them while seeking interval-level measurement whenever feasible for other variables. My effort here is to provide a preliminary outline of how we might obtain an empirical basis for Western assessments of the "reliability" of East European military forces.

A "RELIABILITY" MODEL

Reliability is not easily denoted. To be "reliable" is to be dependable, assured, certain and trustworthy. Moreover, reliability often implies a temporal measure of punctuality and the psychological trait of being purposeful or committed. While the list could be made longer, we clearly make judgments about the reliability of others on the basis of expectations regarding distinct qualities of their behavior. The specific forms of behavior about which we have expectations will vary from setting to setting. In a military context, to judge others as "reliable" would mean that we expect certain "behavior" of men and machines, i.e., to have the quality of being dependable, assured, certain, punctual and purposeful. To be judged "reliable" in military terms suggests that troops <u>will</u> obey, that machines <u>will</u>

operate, that tactical plans will be understood and properly implemented, that tasks will be performed without delay, and that behavior in combat will be characterized by dedication and commitment.

None of these are expectations of success, since what we expect in the behavior of others does not mean that their "best" would exceed the maximum effort of others. But the degree of reliability is the degree to which we can expect the behavior of another to be maximally effective, i.e., the proportion of the total military potential likely to be employed. Total reliability, then, means the expectation of an unimpeded application of all available forces to combat when commanded.

As these definitional issues underline, a sizeable part of both a Western and WTO assessment of East European reliability must not be the numbers of troops, their armament, placement or disposition. Instead, given such capabilities (or "force availability" as I shall refer to it below), the question becomes one of the linkages between military performance on the battlefield and what I call "mobilization potential"--a concept in which I subsume many variables which affect non-Soviet Warsaw Pact force reliability. Mobilization potential is an understandable notion if we view it in terms of a political system's ability to ensure efficient compliance when extracting manpower and material resources from its society and economy, only a part of which is the military per se. I see mobilization potential as the principal limitation on force availability, and thus the key determinant of reliability.

Put another way, reliability ("R") can be regarded as the difference between force availability ("fa") and 1.00 minus mobilization potential ("mp") expressed as a proportion, or $R = fa - (1.00 - mp)$. Thus, as mobilization potential (always less than 1.00) decreases, a larger component is subtracted from force availability (fa), thereby reducing reliability. Were $mp=0$, then force availability would be cancelled out, and such military units would be wholly unreliable.

The measurement of mobilization potential, in my view, should be the principal task of analysts seeking to gauge reliability of military forces. The task is a difficult one because mp is not only a composite factor in the above equation, but each of its components confronts the analyst with measurement problems. Military capabilities, the "hardware" of defense establishments, are rather well documented for the Warsaw Pact. We need, however, measures of (to stretch the metaphor) the "software" of this equation. All variables selected to measure mobilization potential must reflect the political system's ability to extract resources from society and economy over time. While some of those variables might tap military expenditures and preparation, all should be indicators of behavior rather than quantities of weapons. Indicators should suggest something of the commitment, efficiency or compliance one could expect from a system called upon to fight under the aegis of the Warsaw Pact. In the following analysis, I introduce and discuss six indicators:

1. Scenario of hostility, which taps such dimensions as offensive vs. defensive mode, combat in homeland vs. in other countries, fighting a "traditional enemy" or not, operating under Soviet command or independently;

2. Duration of involvement in hostile action;

3. Systemic integration, which concerns such dimensions as participation in, and dependence upon, WTO alliance structures for military decisions and actions, Soviet military presence in the country as a proportion of native forces, trade dependence on the USSR, etc.;

4. Domestic socioeconomic conditions, which includes trends in national income and economic performance per capita, the extent of labor unrest, and degree of attitudinal disaffection;

5. Domestic political conditions, which connote the levels of conflict within the polity, and levels of participation in sanctioned institutions vs. behavior directed against the system;

6. and Military preparedness, which refers to policy decisions in the realms of defense expenditures as a proportion of national budget and GNP, modernization of equipment, the extent or frequency of training, the mission for which the military has trained, proportion of conscipts, etc.

Mobilization potential will, then, be a composite of such elements, each of which (in turn) taps several behavioral dimensions. The value of *mp* will vary with scenario, duration, systemic integration, domestic socioeconomic and political conditions and military preparedness.

Although each will be discussed in greater detail below, and will be considered further in subsequent chapters, such components have predicted relationships to *mp*, and therefore to *R*:

-a scenario involving defense of the homeland against a traditional enemy will maximize mp;

-duration will place differential strain on resources and morale of combatant nations, but longer duration will always place more strain on mp than will quick, decisive victory. Short duration, then, will maximize mp;

-a state fully integrated, politically and militarily, into the WTO structures (and thereby into Soviet security planning and wartime command) will maximize mp;

-domestic socioeconomic conditions which are characterized by relative advances in economic indicators, low incidence of work stoppages or slowdowns, and low levels of attitudinal disaffection will maximize mp;

-domestic political conditions which are characterized by infrequent incidents of civil violence, high levels of participation in the Party and other approved channels, and a low degree of alienation among strata such as workers will maximize mp;

-demonstrates a large reservoir of potential power for military use, high levels of military expenditures as a proportion of GNP, high levels of military modernization, and a low proportion of conscripts will maximize mp.

COMPONENTS OF MOBILIZATION POTENTIAL

Scenario

Among the components which most students of Eastern Europe believe influence the reliability of military forces committed to WTO is the scenario of hostilities. It is reasonable to assume, as have others, that military forces in Eastern Europe would perform maximally in defense of their own borders. Regardless of how implausible a NATO offensive may be, defensive operations by East European forces, under WTO command but operating within their own borders, would certainly raise one's expectations that all available forces would be unimpeded when applied to combat. That such a scenario would provide the fewest obstacles to military performance is not a judgment based upon vague cultural or historical allusions, but instead one supported by pragmatic considerations such as ease of supply, proximity to reserves, familiarity with terrain, and the psychology of defending one's family and home. National and ethnic ties are part of that psychology and have been recognized long ago by the USSR's military planners, as discussed by Chris Jones in Chapter 3.

Of the scenarios in which an East European contribution to WTO forces would be most suspect is that of a general conventional/TNF surprise offensive originating through the North German Plain and Fulda Gap. There are, of course, many nuances to this scenario; were there a lengthy period of heightened tension coupled with military incidents in the European theatre, it is possible that an offensive could take on a pre-emptive character. Nevertheless, the command to follow (as certainly they would be) Soviet units into the FRG, or to support such a drive, would necessitate large numbers of casualties for a purpose that would serve only Soviet hegemony. Warsaw Pact planning, of course, recognizes these severe limitations on East European military reliability, and only very select GDR or Polish units would likely be involved in the initial Soviet thrust.

Scenario, then, can be viewed as a continuum along which a variety of environmentally or psychologically-related conditions would affect the maximum application of military forces available. While subject to differing judgmental criteria, one can use an ordinal scale on which to place specific examples distinguishing relatively as to the effect on mobilization potential. Were a rank of 1 assigned to the scenario connoting no obstacles to assured performance of all military personnel and systems, and the rank of 10 assigned to the circumstances which would cause one to doubt entirely the application of all forces available, then I would regard the continuum suggested by Table 1.1 as a reasonable distribution of the effect of various scenarios.

There are many conditions which might alter one's judgments concerning the placement of each case along this scenario continuum. When considering this variable alone, one must, for example, assume that the political leadership would make the commitment to combat. There have been dramatic cases where political commitment was not present, and commands were never given to enter into hostile action. Hungarian military action against the Soviets in 1956, while occasionally effective, was limited to small units because no order was given to make a concerted effort. The Czechoslovak military, for example, was passive in August 1968 notwithstanding the circulation of plans to resist the Soviet-led invasion because, in part, the orders were never given. Historical factors cannot be discounted, of course, since a tradition of military resistance is less firm in Czechoslovakia than elsewhere in Eastern Europe (see the Rice chapter). The political determination to resist

TABLE 1.1
Scenarios of Hostility and the Mobilization Potential of WTO Forces

Scenario	Relative Score	Effect
defensive operations within own borders against external offensive	10	mp increased, fa NOT impeded; positive contribution to R
defensive operations elsewhere in Eastern Europe against external offensive	9	
deployment in another East European state in Soviet-led operation for internal security when resistance unlikely	8	
internal security use when civil resistance unlikely	7	
participation in Soviet-led operation for internal security in another East European state when resistance is likely	6	
internal security use when civil resistance likely	5	mp compromised; fa reduced somewhat; R in question
participation in limited Soviet-led seizure of small territory (e.g., Berlin) in European theatre	4	

TABLE 1.1 (cont'd)

participation in Soviet-led peripheral offensive outside WTO, unlikely to meet NATO response (e.g., in the Baltic)	3	
participation in general Soviet-led conventional TNF offensive through North German Plain/Fulda Gap	2	
participation in Soviet-led retreat/ defensive operations following offensive failure outside WTO	1	mp severely limited; only a fraction of fa will be used maximally; strong negative effect on R

Source: Author's Judgments

invasion, however, has been made clear in Romania as discussed by Walter Bacon in this volume. If such a commitment is made, defensive operations within the national borders is certain to engender the greatest assurance of performance. This does not mean the military forces would succeed, but that they will assuredly try to achieve their objectives.

The principal dimensions of "scenario" incorporated through the above scale are those of defensive vs. offensive, location of operation (and thus likely opponent), Soviet leadership, and presence of resistance when forces are used within the alliance or internally. All of these could be further refined. The defensive/offensive dichotomy is unlikely to be as clear as such terms imply, particularly after a lengthy period of rising tensions and confrontation. Operations may be located in many sectors, on land, sea and air, or simultaneously on the home territory and within Western Europe. Soviet command would likely not be uniform throughout the theatre of operations, with some non-Soviet units directly subordinate and others acting autonomously. Resistance can be military, civilian, para-military, or appear in other forms (e.g., partisan or guerrilla operations). These variations notwithstanding, one may still presume that a defensive operation, conducted in proximity or within the home territory, generates most confidence in military performance. If the operation is to be offensive, then performance as part of the WTO is enhanced with Soviet command. If the operation is to involve internal security duty elsewhere to the region, Soviet oversight may be regarded as critical.

Duration

A second element which must be included in measures of mobilization potential is "duration". All things being equal, the longer militaries of Eastern Europe are required to perform, the more one should doubt the full application of their available forces. The one plausible exception to that rule may be in the defense of national territory, when the exhaustion of manpower and material resources might foster more determined resistance. Once again, the duration of hostilities is not easily measured, for it is not merely the elapsed time of military action but the relative impact of extended conflict on a nation's resources and morale. Other variables will be discussed subsequently which affect mobilization potential reflecting such material and psychological aspects, and therefore need not be included in a measure of duration. Nevertheless, an absolute measure of elapsed time in which hostilities continue is, in and of itself, meaningless. Only as a component of mobilization potential can such a variable as duration be understood. Duration will place differential strain on resources and morale of a combatant nation, but longer duration will always place more strain on mobilization potential than will quick, decisive victory.

Thus, we might again use an ordinal scale to denote elapsed time of hostilities relative to the plausible strain on resources and morale. If we presume the scenario of a general conventional/TNF offensive in Central Europe, forty-eight hours or less of combat would imply that few of the non-Soviet WTO forces would be engaged, save for selected G.D.R., Polish, and perhaps Czechoslovak units. In such brief hostilities, little if any diminution of mobilization potential would take place to (other variables notwithstanding) compromise force availablity. (As Robin Remington states in her chapter's conclusion, warfare in this era may not give East European forces time to be "unreliable".) From a few days through one week of combat, it is likely that East European units would be alerted, mobilized and moved to duty stations. Casualties could be expected, even in rear areas, and those would be heavy in a TNF exchange. Major front-line combat for East European forces, aside from air defense, would still be limited to the Volksarmee, and at most six or seven Polish and four Czechoslovakian divisions in a Central European general offensive scenario.[5] These units would be, from all indications, "corseted" by Soviet divisions. As Ivan Volgyes discussed regarding Bulgarian forces, a thrust into European Turkey might be expected, supported by heavy Soviet involvement.

One to two weeks of full-scale warfare in Europe would increase the likelihood that many non-Soviet formations would be engaged in hostile action beyond their borders, perhaps to guard supply lines or to eliminate pockets of resistance rather than in a front-line capacity. Even category III East European forces, maintained in peacetime at 30 percent of strength, would be filled out and brought to perform such non front-line functions. Were a Soviet-led offensive to reach objectives such as the Rhine or beyond in that time frame (by two weeks) East European forces would nevertheless be exposed to significant levels of combat, and high casualties from conventional or tactical nuclear air strikes, not to mention field casualties.

Beyond two weeks, the regular armed forces would, in all likelihood, require replenishment of personnel and material. Replacements for entire units, as is the typical WTO pattern, would have to accompany the supply of fresh munitions, vehicles, weapons, etc. At that point, given the likely rapidity of technologically advanced warfare to exhaust weapons and personnel (witness the 1973 Yom Kippur War or, more recently, casualty rates in Israeli-Syrian fighting) systemic strains would begin to limit severely the assurance with which WTO commanders could commit such units to combat.

The relative scale thus described might be seen in the following terms:

TABLE 1.2
Duration of Hostilities and Mobilization Potential*

Elapsed Time From First WTO Attack	Relative Score	Effect
under 24 hours	10	except for units of GDR & perhaps Poland, mp unaffected; R unaffected by this variable
24-48 hours	9	
3 thr. 4 days	8	
5 thr. 7 days	7	
8 thr. 10 days	6	
11 thr. 13 days	5	mp compromised; fa reduced somewhat; R in question
2-4 weeks	4	
5-6 weeks	3	
7-8 weeks	2	
beyond 8 weeks	1	mp severely limited; fa highly compromised; strong negative effect on R

*Assumptions: Scenario of General Tactical/TNF Offensive, Central Europe.

Although such a scale is based upon a general offensive scenario, it is reasonable in other contexts as well. Certainly, a Soviet-led WTO invasion of Poland, met by resistance that extended the duration of combat-like conditions for Hungarian or Czechoslovak troops involved would be fraught with doubt about the reliability of such units as time went on. This potential surely weighed heavily in Soviet thinking during 1980-81. Conversely, a quick, unopposed occupation as in August 1968 did not face such severe potential constraints (although Soviet units, one should remember, were the only part of the invading force to face Prague crowds).

Systemic Integration

Were we to presume that the involvement of any East European WTO member in hostilities is most likely to take place as a part of that Soviet-led alliance, systemic integration must then be recognized as a component of a states' mobilization potential. The "system" into which Soviet allies are expected to be integrated is the WTO alliance and its infrastructure. The Warsaw Pact does not, itself, have a military command structure or a mobilization system, but instead administers training exercise and "cooperation".[6] Alliance integration for the WTO, then, really means adherence to and linkage with, the Soviet command in wartime and prior Soviet mobilization plans. A measure of a WTO member's integration with that Soviet-led alliance is critical to an empirical understanding of mobilization potential and, thereby, reliability.

An alliance's integration refers to its members' attitudinal cohesion, unity of purpose, and coordination of action, principally with the USSR for WTO members. The USSR certainly desires such integration and has invested extraordinary amounts of its resources in subsidizing the militaries of Eastern Europe. When a threat to alliance integration has risen from political life within Eastern Europe (Hungary 1956, Czechoslovakia 1968, Poland 1980-81), the USSR has exhibited a readiness to intervene with military force and to inflict civilian casualties if resistance is offered. The Soviet leadership has demanded via its action and statements (e.g., the Brezhnev "Doctrine"), that no East European Party contemplate leaving the WTO, and that none of these regimes deny that the Pact's primary mission is to counter a NATO threat. Coordination of policy, while suffering setbacks as with Romanian refusals and Polish inabilities to increase military spending, has nevertheless been enforced by frequent joint exercises, numerous high-level visits of defense personnel, standardization of weapon systems, a wartime command structure subservient to the USSR, extensive training of East European officers in the USSR, and (of course) a Soviet military presence in all but Romania.

In the background, moreover, are other "levers" by which the USSR can apply pressure including the intra-CMEA trade dependencies of East European states. Several of these means by which systemic integration is sought by the Soviet Union can be measured with considerable precision.

1. The frequency of state's joint military maneuvers with the USSR;

2. The proportion of joint maneuvers in which a state's forces participated that were conducted elsewhere in the WTO;

3. The ratio of Soviet troops to indigenous forces on territory of each member state;

4. Intra-CMEA trade dependency of the member state.

Pact field exercises have been followed closely by American analysts.[7] Data from such observations, while not complete, are indicative of the degree to which various WTO members' forces train with Soviet units and their mobility within the alliance. The much greater frequency of maneuvers involving Northern Tier forces (East German, Czechoslovak and Polish units) cannot be disassociated from either Soviet estimates of current reliability or their perceived political and military need for reliable allies in the Northern Tier (see Table 1.3).

The pattern of WTO exercises, however, is more revealing than frequency of maneuvers alone. We find, for example, that Czechoslovak forces train very often with Soviet units but rarely go outside Czechoslovakia. The Bulgarian military, by contrast, is a relatively infrequent participant in exercises but Sofia's forces are often transported elsewhere for the maneuvers (see Tables 1.4a and 1.4b). A plausible conclusion is that Czechoslovak forces must, by their critical location, be conditioned to operations with the USSR; Prague's military is not, however, regarded by Soviet planners as sufficiently reliable to be mobile. Bulgarian units train rarely with the Soviets because the Southern Tier is probably regarded as less critical--but Bulgarian units apparently are regarded with enough assurance to be more mobile. The chapters by Condoleezza Rice and Ivan Volgyes (on Bulgaria) confirm these characterizations. Soviet troops are by far most numerous and combat ready (Category I) in the GDR's territory, and outnumber by several times the "host" country's indigenous forces. Elsewhere, they are a less dominant military presence--never without massive nearby reinforcements, of course (see Table 1.5). Soviet garrisons not only offer the tactical advantages of forward basing and some insurance that native forces would perform as commanded, but could also intervene quickly in the domestic politics of East Europe. Such forces again signal the Soviet need for reliable allies and exist as one means by which to "encourage" adherence to Soviet security

TABLE 1.3
Distribution of Involvement in Major WTO Maneuvers or Joint Exercises With Soviet Forces, 1961 Through Mid-1979

Soviet Forces With Units of*:	Number of Joint Exercises	As Proportion of All Maneuvers** Involving Soviet & East Europeans
East Germany	35	.50
Poland	35	.50
Czechoslovakia	31	.44
Hungary	23	.33
Bulgaria	19	.27
Romania	11	.16

*Ground, Air or Naval
**Based on 70 known major joint exercises

Sources: Tabulated by author from Christopher Jones, Soviet Influence in Eastern Europe (New York: Praeger, 1981), pp. 301-309. Additional references included. Graham H. Turbiville, Jr., "Soviet Bloc Maneuvers: Recent Exercise Patterns and Their Implications for European Security", Military Review 58 (August 1978), pp. 22-23 and Thomas W. Wolfe, Soviet Power and Europe 1945-1970 (Baltimore: Johns Hopkins University Press, 1970), pp. 478-480.

TABLE 1.4a
Location of Major WTO Exercises 1961-1979

	N	Proportion of Total**	Rank
East Germany	23	.33	3
Poland	24	.34	2
Czechoslovakia	27*	.39	1
Hungary	16	.23	4
Bulgaria	12	.17	5.5
Romania	9	.13	7
USSR	12	.17	5.5
Baltic/Norwegian Sea/Barents Sea	8	.11	8
Black Sea	2	.03	9

*One involved Soviet troops only
**Calculated on basis of 70 maneuvers; see Table 1.5

Source: See Table 1.5

TABLE 1.4b
Index of Force Mobility for WTO Maneuvers, 1961-1979

	Index*	Rank
East Germany	17	1
Poland	16	2
Czechoslovakia	5	5
Hungary	10	3.5
Bulgaria	10	3.5
Romania	3	6

*Difference between proportion of all maneuvers in which a state's forces participated and the proportion of joint WTO maneuvers held in that state.

Source: Author's calculations based on Jones, 1981.

TABLE 1.5
Approximate Ratio of Soviet Ground Forces to Native Ground Forces in East European States, 1982-83

	Soviet Ground Forces Stationed in Country	Ratio
Bulgaria	insignificant	advisors/technical only
Czechoslovakia	5 divisions	.4/1
German Democratic Republic	20+ divisions	2/1
Hungary	4 divisions	.7/1
Poland	2 divisions	.15/1
Romania	no Soviet troops	0

interests. The absolute number of Soviet troops in an East European country, of course, provides a misleading indicator of Soviet intentions; that the USSR has concentrated ground forces in the German Democratic Republic makes sense vis-a-vis principal stationing in relatively "out of the way" Bulgaria. But the proportionate size of the Soviet garrison suggests strongly the Soviet need for a reliable ally and its full commitment to insure that reliability.

Other considerations being equal, the higher the ratio of Soviet to native ground forces, the higher the reliability. One may assume that a dominant Soviet presence, denoted as close to or above a 1:1 ratio, would be required for "corseting" native forces for any offensive operation. A somewhat smaller presence, but still substantial (perhaps near .5:1) might be adequate to assume performance in lesser hostilities. A minimal Soviet presence, as in Poland, is certainly insufficient to "corset" Polish forces--but, then, huge numbers of Soviet reinforcements would stream through Poland from the Ukraine and Byelorussia. In the GDR, Czechoslovakia and Hungary, however, current Soviet deployments are at or above levels necessary for their armed forces potential roles, and the Polish case must be considered in light of dozens of nearby Soviet divisions. Were hostilities to occur in a scenario of a WTO conventional/TNF offensive, only Bulgaria appears to be either sufficiently reliable in Soviet eyes or to have a role deemed to be so secondary that the arrival of Soviet forces in strength to "bracket" the Bulgarians (perhaps on their way to Istanbul) can wait a few days after hostilities begin.

Finally, and critically, a member state's integration into the Pact is enhanced by its dependency on trade within the CMEA. The domain of energy resources has become increasingly important since the early 1970s, and might be considered as the most crucial component of trade dependency. Romania, alone among all of Eastern Europe, avoided Soviet oil imports during the 1960s and 1970s, and that distinction is often cited as a principal factor explaining Bucharest's ability to diverge from the USSR in international behavior (see Table 1.6). Intra-CMEA trade, generally, constituted a far lower proportion of Romania's imports and exports as compared with Bulgaria, Czechoslovakia and the GDR during the 1970s (see Table 1.7).

The four measures of integration can be grouped by ranking WTO members on each. A test of the strength of association among these rankings (Kendall's "W") allows us to infer (at p=.10) that these measures "agree" generally with each other, tapping a quality I have called systemic integration.[8] (See Table 1.8)

To these four indicators one would want to add

TABLE 1.6
East European Energy Imports From the USSR as Proportion of Domestic Consumption, 1977

	Bulgaria	Czechoslovakia	GDR	Hungary	Poland	Romania
Crude Oil	93	95	100	88	90	--
Natural Gas	100	89	30	16	27	--
Total Energy	70	35	28	44	15	2

Source: CIA, Energy Supplies in Eastern Europe (1979)

TABLE 1.7
Trade With USSR as Proportion of Total East European Trade

	Exports			Imports		
	1970	1976	1977	1970	1976	1977
Bulgaria	54	54	54	52	54	57
Czechoslovakia	32	34	34	33	32	34
GDR	38	32	35	40	32	35
Hungary	34	30	31	33	27	27
Poland	35	30	32	38	25	29
Romania	28	18	19	26	17	19

Source: U.N. Monthly Bulletin of Statistics (June 1978, June 1979).

TABLE 1.8
Rankings on Four Indicators of "Systemic Integration"

	Frequency of Maneuvers with Soviets	Force Mobility	Ratio Soviet to Indigenous Troops	CMEA Trade Dependency 1977
East Germany	1.5	1	1	2
Poland	1.5	2	4	4
Czechoslovakia	3	5	3	3
Hungary	4	3.5	2	5
Bulgaria	5	3.5	5	1
Romania	6	6	6	6

Kendalls "W" = .64 (significant at p=.10)

recent data about the international interactions of likely combatants. A data-set utilized in one study of East European foreign policies, for example, enabled the author to infer considerable variation in patterns of Warsaw Pact international interactions during the late 1960s.[9]

Creating such a composite index of "systemic integration" can, then, be employed as part of one's empirical assessment of mobilization potential. Refinements obtained by adding more indicators as data are available, or by including data without the margin of error now present concerning, for example, the frequency of military maneuvers, would produce an essentially judgment-free index of systemic integration. As it now stands, the rankings of Table 1.8 confirm not only the great differences between the degree of East German and Romanian WTO integration, but also suggest that the GDR's integration is much more complete than any of the other alliance members. Put another way, the level of WTO integration is uneven and perhaps uncertain in all cases other than the GDR. If additional data were to further substantiate this interpretation, the force availability of most East European Warsaw Pact members would be affected negatively by a lack of systemic integration.

Socioeconomic Conditions

Were East European forces to be committed to combat in any external scenario, the social and economic conditions within combatant states would become increasingly important as the duration of hostilities lengthened. A nation in the midst of social turmoil or economic crisis would be less able to apply maximally its available forces. Of course, there are numerous examples from history of leaders using aggressive behavior against traditional enemies as a means by which to deflect domestic crisis. But it is much more doubtful that, as a consequence of committing non-Soviet WTO forces to a Soviet-led offensive, the cohesion of East European societies would be enhanced or that the productivity or quiescence of workers would be stimulated.

For these suspicions, there is very little empirical evidence. But we can draw limited inferences from indirect opinion surveys conducted by polling organizations under contract to Radio Free Europe. Were a major conflict between the Soviet Union and the United States to erupt, according to one such survey of East Europeans traveling in the West, sympathies would range from decidedly anti-Soviet to neutral.[10] Popular sympathies say little about the initial behavior of non-Soviet Warsaw Pact forces, but were these data to approximate views of a broader public, then one might infer that such societies are disenchanted with Soviet domination to the extent that people exhibit ambivalent or positive attitudes regarding Soviet defeat in a conflict with the U.S. (see Table 1.9).

Unfortunately, we have no other cross-national opinion data with which to test these intriguing "hunches". One might expect, nevertheless, that a populace which has experienced a general decline in economic conditions under comminist party rule, particularly vis-a-vis the USSR, will be unlikely to support maximally the use of the nation's armed forces in hostilities initiated by the Soviets. Among the six East European WTO members, interestingly, only Romania, the GDR, and Bulgaria increased their per capita national income, industrial and agricultural output relative to the Soviet Union between 1950 and 1973. Under communist rule, Poland and Hungary "lost ground" relative to the USSR, while "Czechoslovakia came out as the remarkable loser..."[11]

One can, of course, imagine a scenario in which--particularly in combat of minimal duration for the military forces of a highly integrated WTO member--the sentiments of a population would play no role whatsoever. But the linkage among these components of mobilization potential will always be present; Marshal Kulikov and other WTO commanders no doubt prefer, and hope to create a scenario of combat in which the perception of "defensive" action vis-a-vis traditional enemies is maximized, while limiting duration of hostilities and placing the greatest responsibilities on the most integrated forces. Assuming, however, that the WTO will not be able to create such ideal conditions, socioeconomic conditions would loom as critical variable in Soviet efforts to extract manpower and material resources from Eastern Europe.

While it is an inferential leap to suggest that such economic trends might have consequences for military activity, it remains plausible that a society's perception of their hegemonic ally would be affected negatively by relative economic decline. That Soviet hegemony may be perceived in more critical terms by Czechoslovak, Polish and Hungarian citizens as a consequence of the relatively poor economic outcomes of state socialism is a factor linked to mobilization potential. And, while Hungarian economic fortunes took an upswing in the 1970s to early 1980s because of Kadar's policies away from rigid central planning, Poland's economic collapse and Czechoslovakia's stagnation still reflect poorly on what East Europeans view as the Soviet system. In the Polish case, because of the greater latitude for research by social scientists during the 1970s, one can document declining public confidence in regime performance. For example, periodic

TABLE 1.9
Sympathies in a "Serious Conflict"

	Czechoslovakia	Hungary	Poland	Overall
US	67	53	64	61
USSR	6	16	9	10
Neither	19	25	21	22
Undecided	8	6	6	7
	100	100	100	100

Adapted by the Author from Radio Free Europe, East European Area Audience and Opinion Research, "Czechoslovak, Hungarian and Polish Attitudes Toward a "Serious Conflict" Between the United States and the Soviet Union" (December, 1981).

surveys during a five year period using a random national sample found that the percentage of Poles assessing their material conditions as "deteriorating" rose from 3 percent in mid-1975 to 50 percent in September, 1980.[12] These national samples have not been, as one might expect, replicated in other Warsaw Pact states.

Our ability to assess empirically the effect of socioeconomic conditions on mobilization potential is, thus, limited in crucial respects. But the erosion of a regime's performance, particularly if the populace sees decline relative to the USSR, could engender a serious constraint on mobilization potential. At the very least, there is an intriguing association between those nation-states which benefitted least in economic terms from state socialism and those which exhibit least sympathy toward the USSR in a conflict with the US (Czechoslovakia and Poland being high on both variables). Military planners may not, in the first hours or days of battle, confront the recalcitrance of populations evident in such indicators. Socioeconomic conditions will be a more important consideration, however, as duration lengthens, integration weakens, or scenario shifts away from the optimal for WTO strategy.

Domestic Political Conditions

The relationships among political elites and between rulers and ruled together constitute another indicator of mobilization. As with socioeconomic conditions, the immediate hours or days of military conflict are not likely to place untenable demands on the political capacities of East European regimes, principally because of information control and coercive instruments available to the Party elites. But polities in which violent acts against the system have been recent and large-scale, and in which participatory involvement in sanctioned institutions is minimal, will be subjected to greater and earlier strains than where conditions are absent.

Disruptive events in Eastern Europe such as riots, strikes and protests are, of course, noted in Western media with some omissions and/or exaggeration. Nevertheless, past efforts to use a compilation of such events as part of an aggregate data-set have helped to document intuitive suspicions, e.g., that events one might label as "political turmoil" have been more a part of some communist party states than others. In general, findings over much of the post-war period suggest that the states with highest socioeconomic levels and lowest rates of socioeconomic change have been most plagued by violent or disruptive events.[13] One might expect, then, that the "Northern Tier" of Eastern Europe will continue to exhibit in decades to come a pattern of greater political turmoil. Poland bears out this expectation without question, while observers of Eastern Europe are aware of a significant peace movement in the GDR and intellectual dissent in Czechoslovakia (with a nucleus in "Charter 77").

As a balance against such tendencies, one might expect communist regimes to encourage an expansion of Party ranks to integrate elites and encourage political cohesion. But a growth of party membership is, in and of itself, no guarantee of stability. The Polish United Workers' Party, for example, gained members in proportion to the population from the late 60s to late 70s, only to suffer a drastic (one-third) loss in membership in 1980-82, principally through voluntary resignations. Great fluctuations also occurred in the Czechoslovak Party, suffering a net decline in the same decade. Only in the GDR and Romania did the Party reach and maintain high membership levels relative to the population (reaching almost 13 and 14 percent, respectively, by the early 1980s).[14]

Other forms of political involvement--mass organization membership, attendance at rallies, etc.--do not offer reasonable indication of underlying system stability. That the regime's mobilization efforts can demand nominal membership and attendance suggests nothing of the diffuse support which would be necessary for a national commitment to engage its military in lengthy or costly hostilities. Seen from the opposite perspective, however, disorderly or even violent outbursts against those in political power are symptomatic of the Party's lack of legitimacy. Other less overt kinds of non-sanctioned behavior are practiced as well in Eastern Europe and can reflect political conditions limiting mobilization potential.

Among workers, skilled and unskilled, there is a high level of "political and ideological disinterest," especially in Hungary, Romania and Bulgaria of WTO members in Eastern Europe.[16] The comparison between the more advanced "Northern Tier" of that region and the Balkans regarding workers' politicization has been made in other data-based studies, with the differences between Polish and Romanian labor being significant in the degree, if not kind, of alienation from political authorities.[17]

We cannot be precise about comparative indices of attitudinal disaffection among any stratum of the population in Eastern Europe or the causal link between such attitudes and non-sanctioned or anti-regime behavior. Yet, the higher incidence of protests, riots and strikes in Poland, the GDR and Czechoslovakia--with Hungarian events in 1956 being a violent but unique event in that nation's communist history--do not contradict public opinion data gathered in Poland and Czechoslovakia or indirect measures of such opinion by other organizations.[18] We can conclude tentatively that no regime of Eastern Europe can be sanguine about its popular support, but that the Polish, Czechoslovak, and East German regimes must confront the most volatile populations--with the Communist Party only the latter case (the S.E.D.) providing a kind of "balance" via its mass membership and consistent growth.

Political conditions which influence mobilization potential also encompass the extent to which the military is integrated into the regime and is, itself, cohesive. The stress placed on the political socialization of the military, officers and conscripts, and the pressure for Party membership among officers is intense throughout Warsaw Pact states. Surely it has been concluded by Soviet commanders that the value of their East European allies in less optimal scenarios--when the non-Soviet units operate outside their own territory in an offensive mode, for example--will be enhanced by thorough socialization and the integration of military leaders into the Party hierarchy.

Most observers of the Soviet and East European military establishments have noted the prominence given to Party membership as a technique of political control:

> "Party membership has long been seen as one of the basic characteristics of a Communist military officer. Not only does membership in the Communist Party imply at least passive acceptance of the 'leading role' of the Party in the armed forces, it also enables the Party to keep a close watch on the military officer."[19]

Consequently, very high proportions of officer corps are in party ranks. Although most reports of Party composition do not break down membership to identify the number in military service, at least 85 percent of Romanian officers were in the Communist Party by 1968 while comparable figures were reached in the Polish army by 1975 (and Navy in the late 1960s). By contrast, the Volksarmee of East Germany exhibited much earlier higher levels of SED membership--96 percent of all officers by 1964, and 99 percent by 1974.[20] The magnitude of difference in party membership among East European officer corps by the early 1980s, then, is not large. Nevertheless, the Polish military was less an integral party of the ruling communist regime for several decades than had been the Volksarmee in the GDR. Indeed (as discussed by Henry Krisch later in this volume), the identity of regime with military is very strong in East Germany--a linkage the Polish military minimized until its assumption of power in

December 1981.

These data, however, are cited here only to exemplify a broader point--namely, that the Soviet and East European rulers are sufficiently unsure of officers' political commitments to require the assurance of almost universal Party membership. From such an insistence, one can infer that the maximal performance of troops and their weapons is assumed to be more likely if officers' professional advancements have been linked to party membership; the chain of command, in other words, will be more secure to the degree that military officers have become integrated into the civilian political structure.

Political socialization of all ranks within East European militaries is an omnipresent concern as well. The presumption among Soviet commanders, from Kulikov down, is understandable; greater indoctrination will foster greater reliability. Chris Jones, in an earlier work, has done extensive research on such political socialization efforts. At the highest levels--for "generals, admirals and senior officers"--the Voroshilov General Staff Academy in the USSR has served as the Warsaw Pact's principal "collator and synthesizer of doctrine on operational art and strategy".[21] Although Jones estimates that only a few East European officers graduate from the Voroshilov Academy each year, being alumni has been a *sine qua non* for "top posts in East European defense ministries."[22] Although the numbers are too small to provide an indicator of differential emphasis on political socialization of East European high commands, the absence of Romanians from the Voroshilov Academy is noted by Jones. Bulgarian and East German officers appear to have been frequently the recipients of awards for their work at the Academy, but speeches to graduating classes and other indicators imply an effort to distribute attention evenly among officers and the states they "represent".

Political conditions are, then, objects of concern for WTO commanders as they assess the reliability of forces available to them. One focus of this concern is the degree of diffuse support for communist Party regimes in Eastern Europe. Concern is also evident, however, for the political conditions *within* the militaries of Warsaw Pact members, particularly among officers. Party penetration of the entire officer corps, and training in the USSR for the higher echelons, have been steps taken to add to the assurance with which Soviet commanders view their allies' mobilization potential. While the GDR's military evinces the highest levels of Party membership and likely exceeds other East European states in the degree to which military officers receive training in the USSR, its record on other political indicators (e.g., events of political turmoil, presence of organized dissent, etc.) suggest that mobilization potential would be hindered. Such politically-induced limits to mobilization potential are most evident in Poland--with belated Party penetration of the military, and a populace with a long record of opposition to the PUWP. From the perspective of political conditions, the "Northern Tier" is an uncertain reservoir of Warsaw Pact strength.

Military Preparedness

As discussed earlier, the military equipment of the Warsaw Pact says little about the reliability of East European forces. Indeed, the mere number of weapons or their firepower is tangential to the likelihood that extant forces would be employed to maximum effect. A large army, bristling with modern arms, of course, can be highly unreliable, and examples such as from South Vietnam in 1975 or Iran in 1979 are not difficult to recall. It is plausible that WTO commanders would rather have at their disposal East European forces the mobilization potential of which was unimpeded, even if those forces did not deploy the "hardware" equivalent to the enemy.

A nation-state's military preparation, however, can be suggested by broadly comparative data which tap the resource potential into which a regime could "dip" were hostilities to occur. Mobilization potential will be less constrained if manpower and material resources are less scarce. If one assumes that the closer a regime approaches demanding all of a nation's resources for military efforts, the more difficult it becomes to ensure obedience, then large reservoirs of "power" imply that mobilization efforts are less likely to encounter socioeconomic or political obstacles (at least in conflict of short duration in optimal scenarios). Ray Cline's interesting "world power assessment" provides a rough sense (based upon several empirical and judgmental indicators) of such a resource reservoir (See Table 1.10).

These data imply not only that Soviet allies are relatively weak when considered independently, but also that the USSR has a very uncertain "most powerful" ally--Poland.

That WTO Pact members have manpower and material resources more limited than principal European members of NATO, however, has not meant proportionately smaller defense budgets. Although the calculations of defense expenditures vary greatly among available sources, the U.S. Arms Control and Disarmament Agency (ACDA) has published comparative data through 1979. These data support the general impression of heavier defense

TABLE 1.10
Warsaw Pact States According to World Power Assessment, 1977

	Country Rank[a]	Total Power Capability[b]
Bulgaria	67	3
Czechoslovakia	60	10
GDR	49	22
Hungary	64	5
Poland	25	48
Romania	46	24
USSR	2	402
*USA	1	468

* Included for comparative purposes.

a Rank among 76 countries.
b Calculated by adding several "capability" factors, with no upper limit to the scale.

Source: George T. Kurian, The World Book of Rankings (New York: Facts on File, 1979), pp. 69-70, cited by Gary Bertsch, Power and Policy in Communist Systems (New York: John Wiley, 1982), p. 32.

burdens in the Warsaw Pact states vis-a-vis NATO, and also suggest considerable variation within the WTO. (See Table 1.11)

As with measures concerning systemic integration, Bulgaria and East Germany follow policies which devote larger proportions of their national product to military spending than other East European states and more than most NATO members as well (Greece and, by the early 1980s, the U.S. probably exceeded East German levels in proportion to GNP).[23] Certainly, there is greater investment by the Zhivkov and Honecker regimes to prepare more fully for hostilities and to use more completely the reservoir of power, gauged approximately in Table 1.10, available to each.

It is uncertain what that greater investment "buys", however. For Bulgaria, because of its much smaller economic base than states in the "Northern Tier" of Eastern Europe, a considerably larger defense burden still falls far short in terms of total resources. For that reason, and the USSR's concentration of its own strength in the Northern Tier, Bulgaria remains (aside from Romania) the least modern military in the Warsaw Pact. It, with Romania, was the only East European military to maintain T-34 tanks (from World War II) in its inventory as late as 1980-81 (about 10 percent of Bulgaria's tanks and 12 percent of Romania's, in 1980, were T-34s). The Warsaw Pact's emphasis on force modernization during the 1970s was targeted on the Northern Tier, as one can note by the delivery dates for principal weapons systems such as the T-72 tank and Mig-23 Flogger. Polish and East German ground forces were first to utilize the T-72 in the late 1970s, the highest concentration being in the GDR, while the Flogger (in limited quantities) appeared in the airforces of Czechoslovakia, the GDR and Hungary at about the same time.[24] The T-80 tanks and Mig-25s and Foxhound fighters now being deployed to Soviet forces might be expected to make their appearance in the militaries of the GDR, Czechoslovakia and Poland, as well in the mid to late 1980s. Romania has received none of the 1970s vintage systems (T-72s or Mig-23s).

The concentration of Warsaw Pact mobility and firepower in the Northern Tier, especially in the GDR, is suggested as well by the number of tanks per 10,000 men in ground forces. East German units, on average, deployed close to 300 tanks (of all vintages) per 10,000 in the early 1980s, while Romania and Bulgaria deployed little over 100 tanks per 10,000 troops.[25]

It is not necessarily true that a more modern force is a more reliable instrument in hostilities. However, one may speculate that the Soviets emphasize force modernization in the Norther Tier not only because they see greater NATO strength arrayed in the

TABLE 1.11
WTO Defense Spending

WTO Members	Defense Spending as Percentage of GNP, 1979	Rank in Proportionate Defense Spending
Soviet Union	14.40	1
Poland	5.44	4
East Germany	5.65	3
Romania	3.77	7
Czechoslovakia	4.92	5
Hungary	4.26	6
Bulgaria	7.53	2

Source: Adapted by the Author from U.S. Arms Control and Disarmament Agency, World Military Expenditures and Arms Transfers: 1970-1979 (Washington, D.C.: U.S. Arms Control and Disarmament Agency, 1982).

Fulda Gap/Northern German Plain vicinity, but also because they (the Soviets) believe force modernization may help to assure reliability in nation-states where socioeconomic and political conditions weaken the regimes' mobilization potential. The Soviets may, in that sense, be guilty of throwing rubles at the problem of reliability in the Northern Tier.

Despite such speculation, one must assume that troops in modern tanks or armored personnel carriers, firing more accurate and deadly weapons, will perform more effectively than if they were denied those kinds of equipment. At the very least, the Soviets are betting on such an equation.

One additional element concerning a nation's commitment to military preparedness affects mobilization potential. The capacity of the regime to promote voluntary enlistments in the military and the public's responsiveness to those appeals reflect on the potential to be mobilized and to perform maximally during hostilities. The susceptibility of enlisted personnel, especially ground forces, to the stress of modern warfare, and the concomitant reduction in their effectiveness, can be presumed to be greater among conscripts than among volunteer soldiers. Even in Eastern Europe, the professional soldier may now have some experience in hostile or potentially hostile environments (the Czechoslovak invasion within the alliance, or as part of advisory/training units sent to Ethiopia, Afghanistan, Yemen, Angola, etc.). The professional non-commissioned officer will also have better knowledge of the tasks expected of him if engaged in combat. Moreover, there is the suspicion that conscripts will be more likely to place other values ahead of a military objective and will be less pliant to the norms of military discipline. Perhaps, then, the lower proportion of conscripts in GDR ground forces (62 percent) contributes to the assurance with which Soviet planners would utilize such units vis-a-vis Polish or Czechoslovak divisions in the Northern Tier (with conscripts comprising 73 and 71 percent, respective, of ground forces). The Bulgarian army, interestingly, has the second lowest proportion of conscripts at 67 percent.[26]

CONCLUSION

Reliability was denoted here as the expectation of an unimpeded application of all available forces to combat when commanded. "All available forces", however, are not likely to enter combat without some impedence, i.e., the mobilization potential of a regime is never complete. Some of the manpower or material resources available to East European regimes and/or Soviet Warsaw Pact commanders, will not be utilized maximally or at all. This contribution has offered an assessment of six indicators or components of mobilization potential, each of which are themselves operationalized through several variables.

Scenario and duration, necessarily, remain imprecise elements of mobilization potential (mp). In this chapter, I have suggested ordinal scales by which one might estimate likely consequences of certain roles in which an East European military might be employed and by which the effect of time on mobilization potential could be gauged. These components of mp, notwithstanding my judgmental scales representing their effect on reliability, can be affected by Western policies and preparation. Were the duration of a Soviet-led offensive in Central Europe extended by NATO resistance, and quick, decisive victory by Warsaw Pact forces prevented, I (and other observers) would expect East European reliability to decline precipitously. By preventing Soviet-initiated hostilities in scenarios more optimal for East European reliability (e.g., by maintaining strength in NATO's flanks as well as in Central Europe), the West can, in a sense, limit the USSR's options were there an inclination in Moscow to test the military responsiveness of NATO.

Other components of a regime's mobilization potential, however, provide empirical reference points with which we can better guide our assessments. My comments about systemic integration, for example, cited a number of variables from which one could construct a composite index of integration. Domestic socioeconomic and political conditions, likewise, are likely to affect mp in a manner which can be tapped through available data. Finally, military preparedness was discussed through the use of empirical indicators. I do not wish to suggest that any measurements of the latter four components of mp are without judgmental qualities; defense expenditures, for example, involve an estimating procedure rather than a literal translation of Soviet and East European budgets. Neither should analysts rotely assume that all components are weighted equally. That the domestic political component of mobilization potential would expand enormously in importance given a scenario such as hostile action against one's own population is obvious. Even in the most ideal scenario from a Soviet perspective, lengthy duration would strain domestic socioeconomic conditions and the military preparedness of the USSR's WTO allies.

I take it as a given, then, that one must adjust the reliability model suggested earlier, stressing "indigenous" components as scenario and duration--"exogenous" components insofar as East European regimes or populations would have little effect on either--change.

For the sake of illustration, however, one might focus on the four components of mobilization potential which can be affected by, and within, East European systems. By excluding here both scenario and duration, one can also address the issue of reliability with fewer questions of a judgmental nature.

Based upon data included in earlier tables and/or cited in the text, I have tabulated "mean rankings" on four components of mobilization potential for the six WTO members in Eastern Europe. (See Table 1.12) It should be emphasized that the means convey an artificial precision, and are meant only to suggest ordinal distinctions among these cases, i.e., how a country tended to rank on variables discussed for each of the four components. Poland, for example, tended to rank about third on variables I cited for systemic integration. Each "mean rank" was based upon several variables discussed for each component (all of which are mentioned in subscripts below Table 1.12).

Through the vehicle of such a condensed portrait of the four components, some empirical bases for earlier "hunches" about reliability become evident. The GDR's thorough systemic integration and high degree of military preparedness, relative to the WTO members, are readily apparent, as are its relatively positive socioeconomic conditions. Poland's systemic integration and military potential, however, are countered by highly negative political and socioeconomic conditions. Romania's lack of military preparation (for WTO purposes) and clearly non-integrated stance are also evident, juxtaposed with tight political control. These examples are unlikely to startle most observers of East Europe, but suggest instead that conventional wisdoms are not contradicted by available data.

The reliability model I suggested, however, can be employed using such findings. If one were to set aside momentarily the judgmental, exogenous components of scenario and duration, what contraints on Soviet allies' mobilization potential would reduce force reliability? Which WTO members, in fact, are most reliable from the Soviet perspective?

The principal arenas of strength and weakness for the mobilization potential of each East European state on behalf of the WTO appear, from these data, to be as follows:

	+	-
GDR	systemic integration military preparedness socioeconomic conditions	some question about political control, countered by Party penetration of society and military

Poland	systemic integration military preparedness	very weak socioeconomic and political conditions
Czechoslovakia	systemic integration	very weak socioeconomic conditions and dubious political control or military preparedness
Hungary	socioeconomic conditions	very weak military preparedness and dubious political control; systemic integration variable
Bulgaria	socioeconomic and political conditions; large military effort, although weak overall	systemic integration variable
Romania	political conditions	not integrated military preparedness low socioeconomic conditions dubious

This aggregate portrait errs, no doubt, by its generality. Subsequent case studies in this volume provide much of the detail lacking here. Yet, if one begins from empirical references and moved toward general conclusions about the problems faced by East European regimes were their militaries ordered into combat as part of the WTO, the results appear not to contradict seasoned observers' intuitive assessments. The advantage here, however, is that we have the rudiments of a model which can be utilized by others at other times to consider the issue of reliability.

From these data, I infer that the GDR and Bulgaria represent the Soviet Union's only reliable allies, insofar as the mobilization potentials of their regimes are least constrained. Neither of these allies, however, presents Moscow with an ideal partner--East Germany having continued political uncertainties and Bulgaria remaining a small, weak country. Poland has significant military potential, but is far too volatile (especially in the 1980s). Czechoslovakia and Hungary have different "strengths" regarding mobilization potential, but both cases present major obstacles to unimpeded mobilization of available forces. Romania continues to be nothing less than a "non-member", nominally part of an alliance but shunning integration entirely. As scenario and duration vary, to be certain, the reliability of the GDR or Bulgaria might wither, and as hostilities took on a different

TABLE 1.12
Mean Ranks for East European WTO Members on Four Components of Mobilization Potential

	Systemic Integration[a]	Socioeconomic Conditions[b]	Political Conditions[c]	Military Preparedness[d]
German Democratic Republic	1.4	2	2.5	1.6
Poland	2.9	4.5	5.7	3.3
Czechoslovakia	3.5	5.5	3.8	3.8
Hungary	3.6	3.5	4.7	4.5
Bulgaria	3.6	1.5	2.2	3.5
Romania	6	4	2.2	4.4

a Calculated from ranks on frequency maneuvers with Soviets, Force mobility, Ratio of Soviet to Indigenous Troops and CMEA Trade Dependency
b Calculated from ranks on Public Sympathies in Serious Conflict and Net Economic Trends
c Calculated from ranks on Political Violence Events, Proportion of Population in Party, Proportion of Officer Corps in Party
d Calculated from ranks on Net Power Assessment, Defense Expenditures as Proportion of of GNP, Tanks per 10,000 Ground Troops, and Proportion Conscripts in Ground Forces

character, other nations' forces might appear relatively more reliable. The estimates with which I have concluded, however, offer an empirically-grounded starting point for discussions of Warsaw Pact reliability.

NOTES

1. There are exceptions to this statement such as efforts by Ivan Volgyes and Dale Herspring, "Political Reliability in the Eastern European Warsaw Pact Armies," Armed Forces and Society (Winter 1980), pp. 270-296.

2. A popularized version of one scenario was on the New York Times bestseller list for many months, entitled The Third World War by General Sir John Hackett, et.al. (New York: MacMillan, 1979). In it, domestic unrest in Eastern Europe is a significant factor in the NATO "victory" after a WTO-initiated "invasion" of Central Europe.

3. Ross Johnson, Robert Dean and Alex Alexiev, East European Military Establishments: The Warsaw Pact Northern Tier (Santa Monica: RAND, 1980), R-2417/1-AF/FF p. vii.

4. R. F. Staar writes that "Bulgaria, Hungary and Romania are not powerful and not particularly reliable..." Communist Regimes in Eastern Europe, 3rd ed. (Stanford: Hoover Institution Press, 1977), p. 238. Ross Johnson refers to Eastern Europe as a "military asset" on which Soviet "reliance" has been further increased. See his "Soviet-East European Military Relations" in Dale Herspring and Ivan Volgyes, eds., Civil-Military Relations in Communist Systems, p. 262. Another assessment refers to the "often questionable reliability of individual Pact members..." and the "uneasy" domination of Moscow in the WTO. See Richard E. Darilek, "Organization Versus Alliance: The Warsaw Pact in Retrospect and Prospect," Parameters VIII, no. 2 (June 1978), p. 78.

5. John Erickson, "The Ground Forces in Soviet Military Policy," Strategic Review VI (Winter 1978), p. 76.

6. Erickson, Ibid.

7. A few examples of such studies available to the public over the past decade are John F. Meehan, "Soviet Maneuvers: Summer 1971," Military Review (April 1972), pp. 14-21, Thomas Salisbury, "Kavkaz-76", Military Review (June 1977), pp. 47-55 and several by Graham Turbiville such as his "Warsaw Pact Exercise Shield-72", Military Review (July 1973), pp. 17-24, "Warsaw Pact Amphib Ops in Northern Europe", Marine Corps Gazette (October 1976), pp. 20-27 and "Soviet Bloc Maneuvers", Military Review (August 1978), pp. 19-35. Such standard reference works as John Erickson, Soviet Military Power (London: Royal United Services Institute, 1970) also

discuss WTO and Soviet exercises of the 1960s. Christopher D. Jones, Soviet Influence in Eastern Europe (New York: Praeger, 1981) provides the most up-to-date summary of WTO joint maneuvers. See pp. 301-309.

8. See Sidney Siegel, Nonparametric Statistics (New York: McGraw-Hill, 1956), pp. 229-232 for a discussion of Kendall's W and its calculation.

9. Ronald Linden, Bears and Foxes (Boulder: East European Monographs, 1979).

10. Radio Free Europe, East European Area Audience and Opinion Research, "Czechoslovak, Hungarian and Polish Attitudes Toward a 'Serious Conflict' Between the United States and the Soviet Union" (December 1981). Question: "If a serious conflict should develop between the U.S. and the Soviet Union, would your sympathies lie with the United States, with the Soviet Union or with neither". Data collected in 1979 and 1980 via interviews with 4,878 travelers from these three states.

11. George R. Feiwel, "Industrialization", in Stephen Fischer-Galati, Eastern Europe in the 1980s (Boulder: Westview Press, 1982), p. 61.

12. Osrodek Badania Opinii Publicznej, "Summary of Results" (Poll Number 16, p. 3).

13. Daniel N. Nelson, "Socioeconomic and Political Change in Communist Europe," International Studies Quarterly, vol. 21, no. 2 (June 1977), p. 359-388.

14. Trond Gilberg, "The Political Order," in Stephen Fischer-Galati, ed., Eastern Europe in the 1980s (Boulder: Westview Press, 1981), p. 125.

15. Ibid.

16. William Welsh, "Summary and Conclusions" in William Welsh, ed., Survey Research and Public Attitudes (New York: Pergamon, 1981), p. 492.

17. Kenneth M. Coleman and Daniel N. Nelson, "State Socialism, State Capitalism and the Politicization of Workers," The Carl Beck Papers (University of Pittsburgh Press, forthcoming 1984).

18. Daniel N. Nelson, "Public Opinion and Public Policy in Communist Systems", paper presented at the APSA Annual Meeting (August 1981), New York, New York.

19. Dale Herspring, "Technology and Civil-Military Relations: The Polish and East German Cases," in Dale R. Herspring and Ivan Volgyes, eds., Civil-Military Relations in Communist Systems (Boulder: Westview, 1978), p. 124.

20. Herspring, p. 132 and p. 133.

21. Christopher D. Jones, Soviet Influence in Eastern Europe (New York: Praeger, 1981), p. 219.

22. Ibid.

23. Data regarding NATO members' defense expenditures and other comparisons are found in ACDA, World Military Expenditures and Arms Transfers: 1970-1979

(Washington, D.C.: U.S. Arms Control and Disarmament Agency, 1982), pp. 48-84.

24. The Military Balance (London: IISS, 1980-81), pp. 15-17.

25. Author's calculations based on data reported by Thomas O. Cason, "The Warsaw Pact Today: The East European Military Forces," in Robert W. Clawson and Lawrence S. Kaplan, eds., The Warsaw Pact (Wilmington, Del.: Scholarly Resources, 1982), pp. 137-162.

26. Author's calculation from data reported by Thomas O. Cason, op.cit.

2
The Warsaw Treaty Organization's Third Decade: Systemic Transformations

Robin Alison Remington

INTRODUCTION

> "This is just the kind of relationship that ordinary language--at least any Western language is least well equipped to describe. Ordinary language with its subjects and predicates, is geared to handling only one independent factor at a time. Someone is always doing something to somebody. Cause and effect thinking rather than mutual dependence thinking is built into speech."
>
> George Homans, The Human Group, New York: Harcourt Brace and World, Inc., 1950, p. 98.

In May 1983 the Warsaw Treaty Organization was twenty-eight years old, well into its third decade of institutional existence. This is the only multilateral political/military alliance among European communist states, and like NATO, a key component in the organizational infrastructure dividing Europe.

As an academic exercise, the WTO itself could be considered a system in the process of transformation. Such an exercise, however, would be artificial. For the Warsaw Pact[1] is at best a residual system, an institutional reflection of the state of Soviet-East European relations. Although it is correct to consider the alliance as an institutional actor, its actions are not independent of the restraints and options inherent in the larger political dynamic. It follows that the reliability of the WTO and/or its member states cannot be understood from an intra-alliance perspective alone.

Robin Alison Remington is a Professor of Political Science at the University of Missouri-Columbia and a research affiliate of the MIT Center for International Studies.

Therefore, this analysis is an attempt to move away from the analytical problem so aptly raised by Homan's reflection on the limitations of cause and effect thinking by placing communist coalition politics and the issue of reliability within the context of multiple "systemic transformations" that have occurred since World War II.

First, the WTO functions within an international system in which nation states are the primary but certainly not the only political actors. Second, the alliance is also a factor in what may be considered a world communist sub-system within the international community composed of both communist states and non-ruling parties. Third, the Warsaw Pact provides part of the institutional infrastructure of an interstate system among European communist regimes (excluding Yugoslavia and since 1968 Albania) with identifiable norms and behavioral expectations. Each of these political frameworks within which the WTO operates has undergone significant transformation during the past twenty-eight years. Moreover, so have the domestic political systems of its member states, and most importantly that of the Soviet Union itself. In the following account, attention will be devoted to each of these frameworks--international, intra-communist, and East European systems--assessing at each level the changing milieu for WTO actions.

SYSTEMIC TRANSFORMATIONS: THE FIRST DECADE

At the end of World War II, U.S. production had increased four times and the U.S. was the only nation in the world to have developed nuclear weapons. There was one superpower, and the U.S. was it. Yet at the same time, the U.S.S.R. had emerged as the strongest power in Europe, and with the acquisition of Soviet nuclear capability, Moscow was able to seriously challenge Washington's dominance. This is not the place to recapitulate the origins of the Cold War. Its consequence, however, was to freeze in place a bipolar international system that simultaneously reinforced and, in the communist view, justified a dominant-subordinate relationship between the Soviet Union and the postwar communist regimes emerging in Eastern Europe. As the first and most powerful socialist state, the U.S.S.R. was recognized as leader of the communist sub-system not only by virtue of history and experience but due to a felt need for the Soviet nuclear umbrella.

During this period, the Stalinist interstate system characterized by an almost feudal relationship between Eastern Europe and the Soviet Union was political reality. East European states were satellites. It was quite accurate to speak of a Soviet "Empire" in Eastern

Europe. This system involved a substantial level of military integration. Local communists controlled the defense ministries, but many East European officers were sent to the Soviet Union for political as well as technical training. At the same time, Russian officers penetrated East European command structures, while uniforms, drill, and marching were coordinated with Soviet usage.[2] It is not an exaggeration to say that by 1950 East European armies had been remolded in the Soviet image. That process involved rapid physical build up, education, and modernization on all levels. Thus, well before the Warsaw Pact, East European armed forces amounted to tokenly separate components of the Soviet military establishment.

By the time the Warsaw Treaty Organization was established in 1955, Moscow's East European empire had begun to crack. The death of Stalin in March 1953 had begun the transformation of Soviet domestic politics that for a quarter of a century had withered in the ever-lengthening shadow of Stalin's personality cult. East European communism, no less than the Soviet system, had been legitimized by the myth of Stalin's infallibility. The reliance on charismatic authority symbolized by the Stalin cult gave way to a collective leadership that papered over a bitter power struggle among the Soviet dictator's would be successors. These contenders for power in the Kremlin had risen during the purges of the 1930s, strengthened their positions in World War II, survived the postwar crackdown on incipient ideological diversity, and had few illusions about the Hobbesian world at top echelons of the Soviet political hierarchy.

Emphasizing collective leadership, concessions to economic consumerism, and "socialist legality", the Malenkov New Course was designed to win popular support and to protect Soviet leaders from each other. De-Stalinization was a consequence of factional struggle. Khrushchev's attempt to woo Tito back into the Socialist Camp was intended as a foreign policy coup to strengthen his domestic position and to dovetail with his increasingly conciliatory East-West diplomacy.

Through this intense, complicated maneuvering, the Soviets expected that, as a matter of course, the East Europeans would follow the zig-zags of the current Moscow line. Of necessity, the New course had to be legitimized by collective leadership, economic emphasis on light industry, and finally, rehabilitation of purge victims in Eastern Europe. Stalin was gone but the feudal relationship of East European communists to their Soviet counterparts was assumed to remain the same.

The Warsaw Pact was formed on one level as a reaction to bringing West Germany into NATO via the West

European Union. On another, it was to provide justification for keeping Soviet troops in Romania and Hungary after the Austrian State Treaty (signed the day after the signing of the Warsaw Treaty creating the WTO) neutralized Austria. That East Germany was not initially included in the joint command indicates that Moscow had not as yet given up hope for a united, neutralized Germany as well. Then, from Khrushchev's perspective, there was a hoped for payoff in terms of his coming meeting with Eisenhower, while from the start Molotov stressed a control function vis-a-vis East Europe.[3]

The institutional structure was only a skeleton Political Consultative Committee (PCC) empowered to appoint auxiliary bodies, and the Joint Command. At the January 1956 PCC meeting in Prague, a few other organizational details were elaborated.[4] The Political Consultative Committee was to meet at least twice a year with chairmenship of these meetings to rotate among member states. A standing commission to consider recommendations for foreign policy coordination and a joint secretariat to be staffed by representatives of all treaty members were set up. Both auxiliary bodies were to be located in Moscow. On the military side, Soviet Marshal I.S. Konev was appointed commander-in-chief of the Joint Command with the defense ministers of the East European member states to serve as his deputy commanders. The East Europeans were to retain explicit control over the armed forces they contributed to the Joint Command, while disposition of the joint forces on the territories of member states was left to presumably separate agreements among the states involved.[5] A staff of the joint armed forces with permanent representatives from East European general staffs was to be located in Moscow.

Despite the political reality of East European subordination, the formal principles upheld in the Warsaw Treaty were egalitarian, pledging equality, sovereignty, territorial integrity and noninterference in internal affairs. Although its form may have been partially dictated by East-West objectives, there is substantial reason to believe that Moscow saw the WTO as a future channel for Soviet influence that could no longer rely on love or fear of Comrade Stalin to achieve its objectives.

Whatever was intended, before the East bloc alliance had taken on more than token organizational life, the Soviets were faced with the unintended consequence of their insensitivity to the needs of East European leaders during the power struggle in Moscow. First the Polish October (1956) dramatically demonstrated the political cost of insisting on Soviet control of the

Polish domestic political process. The virtual collapse of the Hungarian Communist party then led to an agonizing reappraisal and eventual use of Soviet troops to keep Hungary from rolling off the road to socialism all together. These were sobering events. They led the Soviets both to attempt to justify their action under the auspices of the Warsaw Pact and to an expressed preference for multilateralization of alliance decision making in the Declaration of October 30, 1956. This trend was reinforced by presentation of the decision to withdraw Soviet troops from Romania in May 1958 as a Pact decision rather than the result of bilateral agreement between Bucharest and Moscow.[6]

By the late 1950s, the domestic transformation of Soviet politics had destabilized East European communist regimes and, in a ripple effect, transformed the domestic East European systems. Soviet policy choices essentially had made the continuation of the Stalinist interstate system impossible, resulting in what Ross Johnson calls the renationalization of East European armed forces.[7] Without intending to do so, Moscow had begun the process of transforming its East European satellites into client states. This modification of the pattern of Soviet-East European relations strongly affected the value of the Warsaw Pact both for the Soviet Union and its East European members.

In terms of the concept of mobilization potential (discussed in Chapter 1 by Dan Nelson), however,the events of the late 1950s could hardly have been encouraging to Soviet strategic planners. Political unrest in East Germany, Czechoslovakia, Poland, and Hungary revealed that communist takeover had been followed by only the most superficial political consolidation. Deep popular resentment remained, while in Poland and Hungary anti-Sovietism had been openly expressed. Moreover, both Polish and Hungarian troops had proved themselves fundamentally unreliable as instruments of internal control along the lines desired in Moscow. Despite Soviet penetration of Polish armed forces, there was a real danger that, had the Soviets attempted to forcefully prevent the return of Gomulka, Polish troops would have fought against rather than with the Red Army.[8] In Hungary, the military had not joined Soviet-defined "counter-revolutionaries" to resist Moscow's intervention, although individual Hungarian soldiers had gone over to the side of the uprising. On the other hand, neither had the Hungarian army supported Soviet troops "saving" Hungarian socialism.

Equally important, Soviet in-fighting and the manipulation of foreign policy slogans had begun the process of transforming the world communist sub-system as well. Admission of Soviet mistakes vis-a-vis the

1948 break with Yugoslavia, and recognition of national roads to socialism by Khrushchev in his effort to benefit from a rapprochement with Tito legitimized multiple interpretations of the rules of the game in intra-communist politics. Meanwhile, the imperatives of de-Stalinization within the USSR ignited smoldering differences with the Chinese. Thus Beijing, paradoxically, became a political actor in Moscow's most traditional sphere of influence. When Zhou Enlai preached patience with Soviet domestic imperatives in East Europe during the winter of discontent following use of Soviet troops in Hungary, the handwriting was on the wall. Despite the supportive nature of the message, China was demanding voice in the direction of Soviet leadership of the communist world.

SYSTEMIC TRANSFORMATION: THE EROSION OF BIPOLARITY IN THE 1960s

By the WTO's second decade in the 1960s, both superpowers were faced with adjusting to the erosion of the postwar bipolar international system. In Asia and Africa East-West ideological differences were often considered irrelevant to the urgent problems of modernization, economic, and political development facing many of the newly independent third world nations. Nonalignment became popular not only as an alternative to taking sides that allowed for freedom of economic/political maneuver vis-a-vis superpower pressures but as an alternative set of priorities and principles for international relations, what its supporters consider a significant democratization of international decision making. Thus, the nonaligned movement made East-West struggle for the hearts and minds of the developing countries difficult. Both Moscow and Washington had to respond to a growing number of countries insisting on the right to function as independent actors within an increasingly polycentric international system.

Nor was Europe, East or West immune. Soviet attempts to substitute joint institutions for Stalin's charismatic authority; socialist legality for terror as an instrument of control had inadvertantly supported substantial political diversity among East European roads to socialism. Romanian resistance to Bucharest's assigned role in Khrushchev's socialist division of labor within the Council for Mutual Economic Assistance (CMEA) soon spilled over into alliance politics within the Warsaw Pact. Albania challenged Soviet German policy,[9] and Hoxha effectively utilized Chinese support to block Khrushchev's irrate efforts to force him back in line. For all practical purposes, Albania had been excluded from WTO councils by 1962. France withdrew from the military aspects of NATO, while West Germany developed Ostpolitik to counter declining U.S. interest in German reunification.

The changing international system was in itself a response to the escalating destructiveness of weapons technology and Soviet ideological reaction to the demands of living in a nuclear age. A fundamental tenet of Leninism had been the inevitability of war not only between capitalist countries fighting for colonial territory and markets but between those countries building socialism and capitalist states determined to prevent indigenous socialist development. Leninist peaceful coexistence postulated a position of weakness; much like his New Economic Policy (NEP) it was considered a transitional tactic--in this case to ward off a war the Soviet Union was too weak to win. Stalin's only elaboration had been to insist that, should war occur, it would somehow destroy capitalism while socialism would survive in an unexplained fashion.

Once the Soviet Union became a nuclear power, the sobering reality of what nuclear war would mean for all sides became ever harder to ignore. Khrushchev openly accepted that nuclear war would mean the destruction of communism as well as capitalism.[10] Soviet policy turned toward a new type of peaceful coexistence as essential to survival in a nuclear world, a long-term stalemate in which confrontation must be limited to non-nuclear means. These changes in Soviet ideology and policy substantially contributed to Moscow's problems with a Chinese leadership dedicated to the proposition that Soviet power should be devoted to bringing about the victory of the "East Wind". That the West was a "paper tiger" with nuclear teeth regardless of what the Chinese might say,[11] strengthened Moscow's commitment to a restructuring of East-West relations to avoid direct military confrontation. The result was to accelerate the polycentric tendencies in both alliance systems.[12]

The possibility of complete destruction meant, ironically, that the superpowers' influence declined within their respective coalition. Notwithstanding their overwhelming power as compared with alliance partners, the horrible risk of using that power diminished its utility. That process was reinforced by the suspicion, in both halves of Europe, that the nuclear umbrella would not open because their respective patrons might not have the will to use it except in the case of a direct attack on their own homelands. In any case, talk of a limited nuclear war in Europe implied a willingness to turn Europe into a nuclear wasteland that many Europeans found incompatible with their national interest.

With respect to the Warsaw Treaty Organization,

this process is perhaps best demonstrated in relation to the changes in Soviet military doctrine dating from the early 1960s which had transformed the WTO from an essentially political instrument in the Soviet foreign policy arsenal into a military coalition intended to play a serious role in the event of war in Europe.[13] Whether one sees this shift as a component of deterrence Soviet style or as an offensive military strategy, its organizational consequences for the alliance are the same.

Khrushchev's preference for relying more heavily on Soviet nuclear capability at the expense of conventional forces brought an expanded role for East European militaries in Soviet strategic planning. To whatever extent East European members of the WTO could substitute for Soviet ground forces by 1961, it was considered desirable that they do so. Consequently, a program of modernization of East European military establishments, standardization of armaments within the Pact, joint military exercises and increasingly regular consultation of national defense ministers pushed ahead. This was the logical consequence of the doctrine of "coalition warfare" under which East European forces were expected to participate in a mobile offensive operation against NATO. At least in principle, East European militaries had become a significant component of Soviet military power directed against West Europe. The Warsaw Treaty Organization that had appeared to wither politically despite the formal multilateralization of alliance decision making (or perhaps in reality partly because of it) had acquired a solid military identity. The reliability of East European militaries had become an issue of significance to Moscow.

This partial transformation of communist coalition politics in Europe had resulted from a Soviet military strategy that made certain assumptions about East European regimes. It was undoubtedly assumed that the stability of allied governments continued to depend on Soviet troops stationed in East Europe. Notwithstanding mounting evidence to the contrary,[14] it also seems to have been assumed that even if Moscow lost control over the political guideposts along East European roads to socialism, the Soviets could continue to dictate joint military doctrine. Further, that the Warsaw Pact would serve as an effective instrument for achieving the desired military objectives[15] and at least contain political differences.

These Soviet assumptions failed, however, to consider the other side of the coin with respect to a reasonable level of political consolidation within Eastern Europe that was apparent by the mid-1960s. East European regimes had survived the time of troubles in 1956. The same increasing stability that made them viable military partners, meant that the East European leaders themselves were more vulnerable to domestic pressures. They governed societies tied to ancient nationalisms, with non-communist political cultures insistent on reasserting societal norms within ideological superstructures.[16] Moreover, these were no longer the same prewar foreign communists that came to power at the end of World War II. Even when the same individuals were involved, they no longer lived in Moscow on a Soviet subsidy, psychologically surviving on Soviet myth. Rather, East European communist leaders had been transformed subtly by the responsibility of having real estate and the apparatus of power that comes with running a country. Although many links remained, East European armies were no longer simple extensions of the Soviet military establishment. The penetration level characteristic of the Stalinist period had ended. Soviet officers had gone home and renationalization of the East European militaries had taken place.

It is not surprising that, as the imperatives of Soviet military doctrine professionalized East European military establishments, demands appeared for a more equal relationship precisely within the military councils of the Warsaw Pact. Romanian deviation has been well-documented.[17] There is little evidence in terms of to what degree Bucharest's views reflected a more widespread resentment of excessive Soviet domination of the military aspects of the WTO. Yet it is likely that, had there been substantial agreement on the permanent coordinating mechanism for which Brezhnev kept pushing in the context of the Soviet leader's call for "further perfecting the Warsaw Treaty Organization", Ceausescu's blocking tactics would not have been so successful.

We do know that the Czechoslovaks realized with consternation that their southwestern front was expected to suffer losses amounting to 60-70% in the first few days of a projected limited nuclear war, and that this understanding contributed to considerable dissatisfaction.[18] Indeed, as the Prague spring merged into the long, hot summer of 1968, Dubcek's pledges of solidarity with the Warsaw Pact were undercut substantially by his own military supporters. The most visible evidence was at General Prchlik's press conference where there was a public call for a more nationally-oriented Czechoslovak military doctrine within the context of criticizing the lack of East European input into the WTO Joint Command. In retrospect, the Czechoslovak reform movement stalled in part due to the KSC's inability to control increasingly politicized key sectors of its own officer corp. This crisis of communist civil-military relations interacted disastrously with the crisis of confidence between the Dubcek regime and dogmatists in the CPSU and more orthodox East European parties.

Soviet propaganda notwithstanding, the allied socialist invasion of Czechoslovakia in August 1968, was in no sense a Warsaw Pact operation. The military operation was under the direction of the commander of Soviet ground forces, General Pavlovskii, while those East European units that took part were mobilized by the Soviet command. The token nature of this multilateral effort is underlined by the speed with which East European troops were withdrawn. Its demoralizing impact on East European participants nonetheless has substantial implications for the mobilization potential of these forces for more prolonged occupations by Moscow.

The invasion of Czechoslovakia affected the WTO from both political and military perspectives. First, by precipitating a crisis of legitimacy within the communist world, Soviet military action to enforce an orthodox road to socialism accelerated polycentrism in intra-communist politics. Although this military solution aborted Dubcek's "socialism with a human face", the ghost of the Prague spring reappeared in the socialist pluralism of the Spanish and Italian Communist parties. More seriously, the invasion united the autonomist parties of Western Europe with the Yugoslavs and Romanians in what Kevin Devlin has identified as the southern axis in opposition to Soviet priorities vis-a-vis the world communist movement.[21] This Eurocommunist grouping further undermined Soviet control of inter-party relations during the maneuvering centered on the 1976 Berlin Pan-European Communist Conference.

Second, military activity of the Warsaw Pact increased in the context of reorganization of the WTO military institutions.[22] This process involved formal acceptance of the Committee of Defense Ministers as the primary body for military consultation within the alliance. A WTO Military Council was created presumably to facilitate consultation among senior Soviet and East European officers along with a Technical Committee to coordinate military research and development, the production of weapons. The Joint Command was reconstituted so that deputy defense ministers of the East European members now served as the deputy commanders under a Soviet Commander-in-Chief, while a permanent Joint Staff composed of the Soviet Chief-of-Staff, East European deputies, and other officials apparently in relation to manpower and budget contributions. These institutional reforms, and those specifically for political administration (as Chris Jones details in this volume) were incorporated in an as yet unpublished new Statute of the Joint Armed Forces.

Western speculation to the contrary,[23] these changes did not appear to add up to a quantum jump in alliance military integration or some kind of supranational planning body directing communist coalition politics. These misinterpretations of comments by the then WTO Chief-of-Staff General Shtemenko come from a less than careful reading of what he actually said and ignored the useful barometer of Bucharest's reaction.[24] In my view, Mackintosh correctly evaluated these changes as a Soviet response to East European pressure dating back to at least 1965 for improved access to more genuinely consultative organs in the handling of Warsaw Pact military affairs.[25] Whether the reorganization went as far as Prchlik's demand for an allied command that would enable East Europeans to "cocreate and participate in the whole process of learning and deciding" is doubtful. Yet it is likely that the degree to which Czechoslovak military dissatisfactions exacerbated intra-alliance crisis during 1968 did increase Soviet awareness of the cost of postponing reforms that must have been under discussion long before the Budapest PCC meeting in March 1969.

SYSTEMIC TRANSFORMATIONS: AN ERA OF NEGOTIATIONS

By the actual beginning of the Warsaw Treaty Organization's third decade in 1975, the enemy of the Cold War had become a "limited adversary" in an Era of Negotiations. This restyled language of foreign policy transformed perceptions in Moscow and Washington only superficially, if at all. Rather the detente process was a substantially reluctant response to the de facto polycentrism that was eroding the influence of both superpowers. The Soviets perceived detente as stabilizing nuclear risk and the victory of their version of peaceful coexistence.[26] Unwilling to be upstaged by German and French initiatives, Henry Kissinger engaged in what he viewed as behavior modification of Soviet aggression via his own version of containment and linkage politics.[27] In reality, both Moscow and Washington believed in ideological struggle although they differed on the means that could be employed. Neither assumed, as had some advocates of detente, that mutual advantage meant equal advantage.

For our purposes, however, the much maligned Helsinki Agreements of August 1975 made four important contributions. First, Helsinki symbolized the reassertion of the small and medium-sized states of Europe via their insistence on a piece of the action when it came to deciding matters relating to European security. Second, Helsinki recognized postwar European borders, thereby collectively ratifying the nonaggression pacts that Bonn had signed with Moscow and Warsaw in 1970. This further reduced a sense of threat in Europe, making a defensive war less likely from the Polish and East

German perspective. To the degree that such fears lessened, the mobilization potential of East European militaries for a preventive attack on Western Europe must be considered diminished. Third, the insistence that the principles of Helsinki applied equally to all signatories implicitly rejected the Brezhnev Doctrine on the part of the East European states to which the Soviets at least tokenly acquiesced by their own signing. This flat rejection of the use of force as a legitimate instrument for resolving differences also potentially weakens mobilization potential of East European forces for intra-alliance crackdowns, at a minimum providing those reluctant to use troops with delaying tactics. Fourth, Helsinki sanctioned economic contacts between East European regimes and the West that have contributed substantially to the current economic woes of East European economies, in Poland's case precipitating major political crisis while generally operating as a restraint on the prospects for military mobilization.

Moreover, the impetus given the detente process by the signing of the Helsinki agreements interacted with and reinforced centrifugal forces within the communist sub-system. This was most evident at the June 1976 Berlin conference of twenty-nine European Communist parties. No longer was the Soviet definition of proletarian internationalism an acceptable criterion for interparty relations. Instead, the final document directed the world communist movement to rely on "voluntary cooperation".[28] It reaffirmed the oft-repeated Romanian/Yugoslav principles of equality, sovereignty, non-interference in internal affairs and national roads to socialism. In short, changes in the rules of the game in intra-communist politics were providing substance to the formally egalitarian provisions of the Warsaw Pact.

In these circumstances, the policy coordination functions of the alliance took on added urgency in Moscow just as they were becoming more and more difficult to achieve.[29] This matter was complicated by a new level of Romanian political gymnastics in which Bucharest assiduously developed its ties to the non-aligned political movement and its identity as a developing rather than as a socialist country.[30] Although Ceausescu has yet to gain general acceptance of his efforts simultaneously to be and not to be a member of the Warsaw Pact, the Romanian leader has succeeded in further distancing himself from coalition obligations. The visibility of Romanian refusal to agree to increased defense budgets at the November 1978 Warsaw Pact meeting notwithstanding, Polish response must be considered at least equally damaging to Soviet objectives. Warsaw faithfully agreed in principle but plead inability to implement on the grounds that to do so might precipitate economic collapse. Verbal acquiescence without implementation is perhaps the most difficult response to deal with for any alliance irrespective of ideological/ political orientation.

THE POLISH DILEMMA AND THE WTO'S THIRD DECADE

At the heart of the concentric circles of international and domestic transformations that will determine the nature of the Warsaw Treaty Organization and the limit of alliance options in the 1980s is Poland. No serious scholar of communist systems would deny that Poland underwent dramatic domestic transformations in 1980-1983. There are, however, a wide number of interpretations as to just what these changes add up to and still more as to the role of the Soviet Union in directing the Polish drama.[31] The assumptions one makes about Polish domestic transformation are crucial to evaluating the impact of these events on communist coalition politics. Therefore, although this is not the place to retrace the rise of a mobilized Polish working class and its demands for Party and economic reforms, several points must be kept in mind. (In Jan de Weydenthal's chapter in this volume, additional detail is available about domestic events in Poland and their effect on reliability.)

This analysis assumes that events in Poland from the signing of the Gdansk charter in August 1980 until the collapse into martial law on December 13, 1981 are best understood in terms of the failure of institutions to adjust to what had become a genuinely revolutionary situation. The Polish Communist Party, PUWP, had lost credibility and was rapidly losing members as well; according to Western estimates the party had dropped from three and a half million to just over two million. Conversely, the independent trade union, Solidarity, had grown from 190,000 in August 1980 to an estimated ten million members by November of that year. Neither the Party nor the trade union could cope with the resulting organizational pressures.

The Party divided on what to do about Solidarity and how to reform itself so as to stop what amounted to political hemorrhaging of Communist power. To speak of a "leading role" of Polish communists was a joke. Yet no serious steps could be taken toward desperately needed economic reforms without the Party. Solidarity was neither willing nor able to spearhead such reforms.

Indeed, as power flowed away from the Communist Party, Solidarity staggered under too much power too fast. The trade union could not absorb radicalized students, the demands of Rural Solidarity, the heavy responsibility of becoming the symbol of the Polish nation virtually overnight. To make the analogy, the charismatic leader of the Gdansk interfactory strike committee, Lech Walesa, increasingly occupied the leading role within Solidarity in name only; that his position had been weakened greatly was obvious from the open factionalism displayed at the two-stage Solidarity Congress in September/October 1981.

When Stanislaw Kania was replaced as head of the PUWP by General Jaruzelski on October 18, it was evident that the efforts to mend the political fabric of party life at its July 1981 Congress had failed. The miracle was not that the Polish Communist Party had been unable to work with Solidarity to establish a genuine national front with the workers and the Catholic Church. It was, instead, a miracle that, under circumstances of escalating Soviet pressure and economic scarcity, these institutional actors managed to conduct almost sixteen months of negotiations before Jaruzelski declared a stalemate and set up his Military Council of National Salvation.

The volume of Soviet insistence that the General take a strong stand went up during the fall of 1981. Ever more strident attacks were made by Moscow on Solidarity as having fallen into the hands of counter-revolutionaries, anti-socialist and anti-Soviet forces. There may have been an ultimatum delivered by WTO Commander-in-Chief Viktor Kulikov while he was in Warsaw the week before martial law was declared. Moscow may have threatened that if Polish troops did not restore an acceptable level of order, Soviet troops would. We do not know.

We do know that General Jaruzelski moved without public high-level consultations with any member of the Soviet Politburo and that the first meeting of the Polish general with the Soviet leadership did not occur until the end of February 1982. We know that for all practical purposes two major institutional actors stopped normal functioning with the declaration of martial law: Solidarity and the Polish United Workers' Party. For although Jaruzelski did supplement his Military Council for National Salvation with what would appear to be handpicked committees of former high ranking party members, the former organizational structure of the Party went out of business. Whether or not two members of the Politburo elected in July 1981 were among those arrested, reports from Warsaw that Jaruzelski did not consult that body before declaring martial law may not be verified but are certainly plausible considering how it was subsequently pushed aside.[32] The PUWP Central Committee met for the first time towards the end of February to rubberstamp the General's decision to continue martial law.

In these circumstances, analyses that put forward martial law in Poland as a victory of Polish Communism over the independent trade union movement are blind to fact and are no more than a knee-jerk analytical response to stereotypes of Lenin's prescriptions for communist civil-military relations. The situation in Poland was one in which the party had lost control by December 1981. Conversely, lack of capacity to deal with burgeoning pressures and its swollen constituency had reduced Solidarity to virtually suicidal demands such as the December 12 call for a national referendum on whether the Polish Communist Party should be replaced.[33] Both party and trade union effectively were paralyzed by organizational overload. This left the Polish military as the only cohesive political actor. Martial law in Poland as around the world was a response to the demise of civilian legitimacy, economic chaos, and social disorder. No amount of rhetoric can obscure that reality.

This is not to say that Moscow did not have a hand in the process. Soviet pressure was undeniably one of a package of precipitants that Jaruzelski could no longer ignore. Nor have the consequences for Solidarity and the Polish United Workers' Party been the same. Solidarity is banned yet remains a symbol of national resistance. The PUWP has resumed, at least officially, its "leading role." Whether the Party can reestablish anything resembling real political authority is still an open question.

From the perspective of the Warsaw Treaty Organization, the relationship of the alliance to events in Poland operates on two dimensions. First, there were ways in which the WTO related to the euphoric rise of Solidarity as a symbol of workers demanding to speak for themselves in a communist society and of Polish nationalism. Second, there are the potential consequences of martial law in Poland for the alliance itself.

For the WTO, Poland must be seen as a case of major domestic instability within the second largest contributor to Warsaw Pact forces. Leaving aside the ideological dangers posed by declining control of the Polish Communist Party, the situation influenced WTO military capabilities. Hence, a high level of concern was to be expected. It was intensified by the ideological homogeneity of the member-states, compounded by the dependence of any communist system on the working class as a fundamental source of legitimacy.

That such concern was expressed by a meeting of top ranking Warsaw Pact leaders, including Romania, in December 1980 indicates a level of multilateral political activity that had not existed during the crises that led to Soviet intervention in Hungary in 1956 or the "allied socialist" move into Czechoslovakia in 1968.

This meeting both expressed confidence that the Poles could solve their own problems and pledged "fraternal solidarity and support to socialist Poland, the Polish United Workers' Party, and the Polish people." Although the final statement left open the question of a resort to military means to "save Polish socialism", it underlined the responsibility of the Poles to reestablish order.[34]

In sum, this document was a masterpiece of ambiguity. It waffled and could easily be all things to all people. It could justify Soviet inaction, rationalize the application of the military component of the Brezhnev Doctrine in the Polish case, or set the stage for a move into Poland by the WTO Joint Command. Academically, one could argue that it made mobilization of Pact forces to interfere in Polish internal affairs easier or harder depending on the individual analyst. The only indisputable fact is that, whether Soviet troops did or did not move into Poland, the WTO had institutional input in the decision making process. Given the nature of the ambiguous statement, it is also quite likely that the member states did not agree on what was to be done.

The extent of bilateral and multilateral Warsaw Pact consultation in the six weeks prior to declaration of martial law in Poland makes it appear that some form of policy coordination was underway.[35] The key contact person with Jaruzelski was Kulikov himself. Kulikov also met with party leaders in East Germany, Bulgaria, and Romania. Soviet Politburo member Andrei Kirilenko and CPSU Central Committee Secretary Ivan Kapitonov met with both Czechoslovak and Hungarian delegations, while General Aleksei Epishev (head of the Soviet MPA) conferred with Hungarian party leader Janos Kadar in Budapest. Soviet foreign minister Andrei Gromyko met the Polish foreign minister in Moscow, November 4, and headed an official delegation to Romania, December 2 and 3. At the multilateral level, the Warsaw Pact Military Council met in Hungary October 27-30. Pact foreign ministers held a session in Bucharest December 1-3, while alliance defense ministers caucused in Moscow, December 1-4.

It remains to be answered whether these meetings were gearing up for a joint military move into Poland, were primarily to mobilize collective support to push Jaruzelski to activate the contingency plan for martial law, or were reassessing the cost/benefit calculation in terms of a proposed Soviet intervention. It is equally possible that East European members of the alliance urged Moscow to go in as that they recommended that the Kremlin stay out. For our purposes, these meetings must be seen as alliance generated pressure on

Jaruzelski. In this sense, they fall into the same category as the joint military maneuvers in and around Poland during the summer and fall of 1981.

In terms of the consequences, some will undoubtedly see martial law in Poland as the achievement of Moscow's mobilization of the Polish army to restore internal order, thereby substituting for a Soviet occupation force. In this view, perhaps one could say that the mobilization potential of the Warsaw Pact when turned inward had increased. The fact remains, however, that while Polish soldiers ran the government and managed the Polish economy, Polish potential contribution to WTO military effectiveness diminished, and the long-run impact of that experience, indeed its reoccurance, should not be dismissed.

When added to fact that Hungarian armed forces remain at less than half their 1956 size,[36] while the Czechoslovak military is still involved in a long (at best partial) recovery from the demoralization of 1968,[37] this means that the feasibility of the Soviet doctrine of "coalition warfare" is questionable. (The Volgyes and Rice chapters provide full consideration of the Hungarian and Czechoslovak cases, respectively.) One need not predict that Moscow will be required to develop a new strategic doctrine vis-a-vis the Warsaw Pact to conclude that the official lifting of martial law in July 1983 notwithstanding, Soviet faith in a substantial East European military contribution to the alliance must have been shaken.

Moreover, although the East European members of the WTO joined the Soviet campaign to force the Polish military to crack down on Solidarity, the political implications of the outcome must be disquieting even for its most vocal supporters. If the good news was that Solidarity no longer threatened to replace the Polish United Workers' Party as the vanguard of the working class, the bad news is that for nineteen months the Polish army performed the Party's "leading role." Although martial law has ended, many of the officers who took over Party jobs do not appear to have returned to the barracks. Even if they eventually do so, it will not be forgotten that the army restored order when the Party failed.

In or out of uniform General Jaruzelski retains control. In fact, if one takes the view that a cult of the personality is intrinsically incompatible with genuine political institutionalization, then the Polish Party was weakened in the wake of the July 1982 9th CC Plenum. For that leadership reshuffle did more to consolidate the General's personal position than strengthen the Party institutionally. Subsequently, the call to parliament to lift martial law came not in the name of the Party but of Jaruzelski's own attempt at a popular front, the Patriotic Movement for National Revival (PRON). It was a slight not calculated to revive Party credibility. Moreover, given the tendency to rely on government rather than Party bodies to stabilize the country during martial law, the prospects for PUWP organizational "renewal" appear more symbolic than real.[38]

Ideological differences aside, politically Poland resembles Egypt under Nasser. The Military Council of National Salvation has disappeared, as did Egypt's Revolutionary Command Council. Yet Like Nasser, Jaruzelski continues to accumulate power. Even with the lifting of martial law, he remained head of Party and Premier and only relinquished his post as Defense Minister in November 1983. At that time, he added two more jobs, chairman of a new National Defense Committee with power to oversee the economy and government as well as to reimpose martial law in the event of unrest and that of supreme commander of the armed forces, meaning that in case of war he would outrank the new Defense Minister Florian Siwicki.

In my view, to see the Polish military as "the Party in Uniform" is to miss the point.[39] Jaruzelski comes considerably closer to the military leaders playing the role of iron surgeons in developing countries than he does to the other heads of Communist parties in East Europe. One should not forget the General's own reminder to those drawing him into the political morass when he became Premier in February 1981: "I am first of all a soldier."[40]

The implications for Party-army relations are decidedly unLeninist. The example of the military rescuing the Party can hardly be reassuring to Party leaders in the other East European member-states of the Warsaw Pact, or for that matter to the new leadership in Moscow. Despite Andropov's death and Chernenko's assumption of the office of General Secretary, Ustinov remains prominent, and the Soviet military may continue to serve as a power broker in the next round of the transition process. In these circumstances, it is not unthinkable that those most relieved to see the end of martial law in Poland make policy in Moscow not Washington.

That Jaruzelski presided over the January 1983 session of the Warsaw Pact in civilian clothes rather than his customary military uniform showed the General's sensitivity to such concerns abroad. Nonetheless by May there was visible Soviet dissatisfaction with his domestic pluralism, fears that PRON might rival the Party.[41]

From this perspective, evaluation of mobilization potential of the Pact must be less optimistic.[42] If we count alliance pressure on Jaruzelski to crackdown as a success, that must be balanced against the fate of a restyled Polish Party. The fact remains that even if Jaruzelski eventually retreats backstage, the Polish military is likely to stay on as what the literature on civil-military relations characterizes as a "moderator" regime with unforseeable consequences for Poland and the Warsaw Treaty Organization alike.[43]

CONCLUSION

Within this complex political/military equation, there are many unknowns. Among the most important of these will be the impact of the political pressures generated by the current serious economic difficulties within East European economies and the USSR itself.[44] This is a two-edged sword. In times of economic hardship, communist and non-communist societies alike have a desire to cut defense expenditures. In Eastern Europe, there may be a need to choose between contributions to the Warsaw Pact and precipitating economic crisis, which in turn sets off political destabilization. Poland provides a graphic example of potential consequences for the level of political consolidation essentially taken for granted during the WTO's second decade.

However, perversely, this could also make East European forces easier to mobilize as they become more dependent upon the Soviets for resources that local communist leaders have convinced Moscow their own societies are too fragile to part with for the collective good. This result would be contingent on still another unknown, i.e., whether in light of its own economic problems and expanding global commitments, the Soviet Union will be willing to pick up the tab or will instead insist that its coalition partners make do with less. If this were to be Moscow's response, we might expect to see even deeper disillusionment on the part of East European military elites than the dissatisfaction of the mid-1960s.

Concerning the fundamental question of the systemic transformation, three decades have seen the frameworks within which the Warsaw Treaty Organization functions to have increased the salience of the alliance for the Soviet Union and its East European members alike. The coalition has been transformed from a throw-away card in Khrushchev's foreign policy deck into a multipurpose alliance reflecting East European organizational maneuvering as well as Soviet preferences. The Pact undeniably serves a range of Soviet purposes even as it provides an arena for East European delaying tactics so aptly exploited by the Romanians since the mid-1960s and even the East Germans in 1969-70.[45] Although, the Soviet Union will continue to dominate WTO military planning, it will no longer be certain that East European allies will permit Moscow to commit them to courses of action perceived as contradictory to the national interest of the state involved.

This uncertainty is likely to intensify to the extent that the dangerous possibility of yet another transformation of the international system maintains. If those military planners in Moscow and Washington whose worse case scenarios have come to include the illusion that either side could win a nuclear war[46] manage to convince themselves or their populations, then both superpowers can expect high levels of alliance dissatisfaction. The current international system depends on the belief that nuclear deterrence can avoid mutual destruction. A serious belief on either side that nuclear war can be won would be fundamentally destabilizing. In such circumstances, East European military establishments are likely to be decidedly unenthusiastic at the prospect that their forces and societies might be transformed into nuclear rubble. The real danger is that in the event of accident or a disastrous miscalculation, the East European members of the Warsaw Pact might not have time to be unreliable.

NOTES

1. The expressions Warsaw Pact and Warsaw Treaty Organization are used interchangeably and in both cases refer to institutional identity rather than the larger arena of Soviet-East European relations.

2. Ithiel de Sola Pool, et.al., _Satellite Generals: A Study of Military Elites in the Soviet Sphere_ (Stanford, Calif.: Hoover Institution Studies, Stanford University Press, 1955). For Hungarian reaction, Ferenc A. Vali, _Rift and Revolt in Hungary_ (Cambridge, Mass.: Harvard University Press, 1961), p. 73.

3. Statement to the 1954 Moscow Conference, _New Times_, 49 (December 4, 1954): 15, a viewpoint spelled out still more explicitly by the correspondent for the military newspaper in his coverage of the PCC meeting in Prague, _Krasnaia zvezda_, January 29, 1956.

4. _Pravda_, January 29, 1956; English text of Declaration in a supplement to _New Times_, 6 (February 2, 1956).

5. "Establishment of a Joint Command of the Armed Forces of the Signatories to the Treaty of Friendship, Cooperation, and Mutual Assistance," _New Times_ 21 (May 21, 1955). By the January 1956 session of the Political Consultative Committee hoped for Western concessions had not materialized, and East German participation in the Joint Command was accepted on an equal footing with that

of the other East European members.

6. Pravda, May 27, 1958.

7. A. Ross Johnson, "Soviet-East European Military Relations: An Overview," in Dale R. Herspring and Ivan Volgyes, eds., Civil-Military Relations in Communist Systems (Boulder, Colorado: Westview Press, 1978), p. 246 ff.

8. Proceedings of the Polish Eighth Plenum revealing the depth of the conflict between the Polish Party and the Soviets were published in Nowe Drogi, no. 10 (October 1956). English excerpts available in Paul E. Zinner, ed., National Communism and Popular Revolt in Eastern Europe (New York: Columbia University Press, 1957). See also Konrad Syrop, Spring in October, The Polish Revolution of 1956 (London: Weidenfeld and Nicolson, 1957) and Raymond L. Garthoff, Soviet Military Policy: A Historical Analysis (London: Faber and Faber, 1966), p. 155 ff.

9. Zeri popullit, August 8, 1961. For analysis, Robin Alison Remington, The Warsaw Pact: Case Studies in Communist Conflict Resolution (Cambridge, Mass.: The M.I.T. Press, 1971), pp. 50-51.

10. Khrushchev speeches in Pravda, January 15 and June 22, 1960. Also Garthoff, Soviet Military Policy...., pp. 193-194.

11. Report of M.A. Suslov on February 14, 1964 at the Plenum of the CPSU Central Committee gives a vivid account of the Soviet side of this question, Document 10 in William E. Griffith, ed., Sino-Soviet Relations, 1964-1965 (Cambridge, Mass.: The M.I.T. Press, 1967), pp. 216-220.

12. Herbert S. Dinerstein, "The Transformation of Alliance Systems," American Political Science Review, 59, no. 3 (September 1965): 589-602. Specifically re WTO, Lawrence T. Caldwell, "The Warsaw Pact: Directions of Change," Problems of Communism, XXIV, no. 5 (September-October 1975): 1-19.

13. V.D. Sokolovskii, ed., Soviet Military Strategy (Englewood Cliffs, N.J.: Prentice-Hall, 1963). For recent analyses of the impact on the Warsaw Pact, Dale R. Herspring, "The Warsaw Pact at 25," Problems of Communism, XXIX, no. 5 (September-October 1980): 1-15; John Erickson, "The Warsaw Pact--The Shape of Things to Come?" in Karen Dawisha and Philip Hanson, eds., Soviet-East European Dilemmas: Coercion, Competition, and Consent (London: Heinemann, 1981) and A. Ross Johnson, The Warsaw Pact: Soviet Military Policy in Eastern Europe (Santa Monica: RAND P6583, July 1981).

14. The removal of Soviet troops from Romania in 1958 substantially contributed to Romanian maneuvering within both the Council for Mutual Economic Assistance (CMEA) and the Warsaw Treaty Organization. See Alexander Alexiev, Romania and the Warsaw Pact: The

Defense Policy of a Reluctant Ally (Santa Monica: RAND P-6270, January 1979).

15. Sokolovskii, for example, assumed that some units of the Joint Command "can be assigned to the Supreme High Command of the Soviet armed forces," while others would be under their own commands. Sokolovskii, Military Strategy, p. 475. See also John Erickson, "The European Military Balance," in Grayson Kirk and Nils Wessell, eds., The Soviet Threat (New York: The Academy of Political Science, 1978), p. 115.

16. Alfred G. Meyer, "The Comparative Study of Communist Political Systems," in Frederic J. Fleron, Jr. ed., Communist States and the Social Sciences (Chicago: Rand McNally, 1969), p. 194.

17. Alexiev, Romania and the Warsaw Pact.... is the most comprehensive treatment to date.

18. Interview with Czechoslovak officers cited in A. Ross Johnson, Robert W. Dean, Alexander Alexiev, East European Military Establishments: The Warsaw Pact Northern Tier (Santa Monica: RAND, December 1980), p. 137.

19. English text of Prchlik's press conference in Robin Alison Remington, ed., Winter in Prague: Documents on Czechoslovak Communism in Crisis (Cambridge, Mass.: The M.I.T. Press, 1969), pp. 214-219.

20. A. Ross Johnson, The Warsaw Pact: Soviet Policy in Eastern Europe, p. 17.

21. Kevin Devlin, "The Interparty Drama," Problems of Communism, XXVI, no. 4 (July-August 1975): 28.

22. For Soviet descriptions of these changes, A.S. Bakhov, Organizatsiia Varshavskogo dogovora (Organization of the Warsaw Pact) (Moscow: Nauka, 1971), p. 90, and N.N. Rodionov, et.al., eds., Organizatsiia Vashavskogo dogovora, 1955-1979: documenty i materialy (Organization of the Warsaw Pact 1955-1975: documents and materials) (Moscow: Politizdat, 1975), p. 114.

23. Neue Zucher Zeitung, January 29, 1970 and The Economist, February 21, 1970.

24. Krasnaia zvezda, January 24, 1970. For Ceausescu's blunt statement that the point of these decisions was to strengthen the combat capacity of each national army within the alliance, Scinteia, February 6, 1970.

25. Malcolm Mackintosh, "The Evolution of the Warsaw Pact," Adelphi Papers, no. 58 (June 1969) and "The Warsaw Pact Today," Survival, 16, no. 3 (May-June 1974): pp. 122-126.

26. Brezhnev's Report to the 25th CPSU Congress is quite explicit concerning Soviet expectations, Pravda, February 25, 1976; Current Digest of the Soviet Press (CDSP) XXVIII, no. 8 (March 24, 1976), p. 10.

27. Henry Kissinger, White House Years (Boston: Toronto: Little, Brown and Company, 1979), pp. 1143 and

1254-1255.

28. New Times, 28 (July 1976), p. 27.

29. The value of foreign policy coordination via the alliance had been stressed by Brezhnev at the 23rd CPSU Congress in March 1971 and was strongly reiterated in the Soviet leaders remarks at the 11th Hungarian party congress, Pravda, March 19, 1975. Simultaneously, Soviet military leaders emphasize the security advantage of combined military/political guarantees of the member countries "socialist gains". See I.I. Iakubovskii, ed., Boevoe sodruzhestvo bratskikh narodov i armii (The Combat Confederation of the Fraternal Peoples and Armies) (Moscow: Voenizdat, 1975), p. 107. In actual fact meetings of WTO political bodies declined sharply in 1975, while alliance military organs returned to the 1970 high. See Figure 1, Herspring, "The Warsaw Pact at 25," p. 2, based on V.G. Kulikov, ed., Vashavski Dogovor--soiuz vo imia mira i sotsializma (The Warsaw Pact--An Alliance in the Name of Peace and Socialism) (Moscow: Voenizdat, 1980).

30. These efforts date back to April 1975 when the Romanians sought observer status at the nonaligned summit scheduled to meet in Colombo, Sri Lanka the following year. They amount to what Ceausescu has called "dejure recognition of existing reality...Romania's relations with nonaligned countries," press conference, Le Monde, July 25, 1975. For analysis see Robert R. King, "Romania and the Third World," Orbis (Winter 1978) pp. 882-885.

31. U.S. statements and sanctions assume direct Soviet responsibility. Western sources in Bonn stress that despite the almost continuous presence of Warsaw Pact Commander Kulikov in Warsaw from December 7, there is no evidence that he ordered the crackdown. Indeed, West German diplomats credit "knowledgeable sources" to the effect that Jaruzelski's December 13 declaration of martial law may have preempted an alleged coup plot by the pro-Moscow wing of the Polish party set for December 15. Elizabeth Pond, reporting from Bonn, Christian Science Monitor, December 22, 1981.

32. Roger Boyes of The Times (London) and Brian Mooney of Reuters, "Inside Poland: A Diary of the First Four Days," The Times, December 17, 1981.

33. Boyes report from Warsaw, The Times, December 14, 1981.

34. Pravda, December 6, 1980; English translation, CDSP, XXXII, no. 19 (January 8, 1981), p. 7.

35. "Chronology of Soviet-Polish and Selected East European Bilateral and Multilateral Contacts, October 18-December 13, 1981," Radio Liberty Research (January 4, 1981).

36. A. Ross Johnson, The Warsaw Pact: Soviet Military Policy in Eastern Europe, p. 27.

37. A. Ross Johnson, Robert W. Dean, Alexander Alexiev, East European Military Establishments...., pp., 163-164. Note the concern of the new chief of Czechoslovak Main Political Administration, Lt. General Vaclav Horachek for ideas that "had resulted in deformation of the concept of the probable enemy," Tribuna, November 15, 1972, quoted from Christopher D. Jones, Soviet Influence in Eastern Europe: Political Autonomy and the Warsaw Pact (New York: Praeger, 1981), p. 200-201.

38. See RFE-RL Background Report (Poland), Roman Stefanowski, "A Partial List of Martial Law Institutions," September 7, 1982.

39. Amos Perlmutter and William M. LeoGrande, "The Party in Uniform: Toward a Theory of Civil-Military Relations in Communist Political Systems," The American Political Science Review, Vol. 76, no. 4 (December 1982): 778-789.

40. The Statesman (Delhi) February 12, 1981. The political environment that he had to function in during the months leading up to the Extraordinary Nineth Congress in July 1981 was one of visibly declining civilian control, aptly characterized by George Sanford's excellent analysis, "...office holder's were being rotated around according to what became colloquially known as the leadership 'carousel'. The participants in that process, however, felt that it was more like riding an unsafe and heady rollercoaster without a definite stopping point." George Sanford, "The Response of the Polish Communist Leadership and the Continuing Crisis (Summer 1980 to the Nineth Congress, July 1981): Personnel and Policy Change," in Jean Wodall, ed., Policy and Politics in Contemporary Poland: Reform, Failure, and Crisis (London: Frances Pinter, 1982), p. 44.

41. New Times, May 6, 1983 in a critique that can only be considered an attack on the Deputy Prime Minister Mieczyslaw Rakowski. For the Polish response, Polytika, May 12, 1983. There is a certain irony in the Soviet's awarding Jaruzelski the Order of Lenin on the General's 60th birthday shortly before martial law was lifted in July 1983. One might almost say wishful thinking.

42. For example, communication is a two-way street, and it is quite possible that the Soviets might be less than enthusiastic about what would be communicated during future meetings of Soviet and Polish officers such as those that Christopher Jones details in his chapter on the political administration of the Warsaw Pact in this volume.

43. As of this writing, the situation within Poland remains tense, note the official anxiety implied by creation of a new Committee for the Observance of Law,

Public Order and Social Discipline shortly before the December 13, 1983 anniversary of martial law. Nor are Poles unaware that the consequence of military rule is frequently more military rule, Trybuna ludu (Warsaw) December 3, 1982. For a persuasive Western assessment, see A. Ross Johnson, Barbara Kliszewski, "The Polish Military After Martial Law: Report of a RAND Conference, October 14, 1982." (A RAND NOTE: N-2001-AF, June 1983). It would be difficult to disagree with this conference's key research thesis that "the Polish military is likely to dominate the Polish Communist system for some time."

44. Pravda, February 3, 1982 called for a crackdown on villagers feeding bread and cereals to livestock, presumeably due to shortage of grain. Not too surprisingly, there have been no official acknowledgements of the reports that thousands of tons of Soviet food went to Poland in the first few months following the declaration of martial law. It is unlikely that the substantially improved harvest of 1983 will decrease the sensitivity of this issue.

45. N. Edwina Moreton, East Germany and the Warsaw Alliance: The Politics of Detente (Boulder, Colorado: Westview Press, 1978). See also Robert W. Clawson and Lawrence S. Kaplan, eds., The Warsaw Pact: Political Purposes & Military Means (Wilmington, Del.: Scholarly Resources, Inc. 1982).

46. Richard Pipes, "Why the Soviet Union Thinks it Could Fight and Win a Nuclear War," Commentary 64, no. 1 (July 1977), pp. 21-35, reprinted in the author's U.S. Soviet Relations in the Era of Detente (Boulder, Col.: Westview Press, 1981). For a chilling account of the appeal of the "Star Wars" plan to President Reagan personally if not his advisers, see The Los Angeles Times supplement, Robert Scheer, "Teller's Obsession Becomes Reality in 'Star Wars' Plan," July 10, 1983, p. 6. The consequences of a damage limitation strategic doctrine are discussed by Adam Yarmolinsky and Gregory D. Foster, Paradoxes of Power: The Military Establishment in the 1980s (Bloomington, Ind.: Indiana University Press, 1983), p. 17.

3
The Political Administrations of the Warsaw Pact and the Reliability of the East-Bloc Armed Forces

Christopher Jones

INTRODUCTION

Most Western analyses of the reliability among the Warsaw Pact's East European personnel have not examined the joint activities of the Main Political Administrations of the armed forces of the Warsaw Treaty Organization (WTO). The WTO political administrations are the agencies officially designated by the WTO states to secure the political reliability (i.e., an attitudinal loyalty) of the allied armies, and thereby to promote reliable performance in hostile circumstances.

In the discussion below, I will examine: the interlocking structures of the WTO political administrations; the joint activities of the WTO political administrations in ideological indoctrination, including joint programs of political work during WTO military exercises; the primarily bi-lateral (Soviet-East European) nature of the joint programs in political indoctrination; and the doctrinal writings of Soviet political officers on the question of the political reliability of socialist soldiers. This essay will argue that the WTO programs of political indoctrination reflect, at least in part, Moscow's experience with the non-Russian troop formations of the Soviet army during World War II. I will suggest that the integration of Soviet and East European personnel into the joint armed forces of the Warsaw Pact accounts, at least in part, for the reorganization of the devices for integrating non-Russian soldiers into the Soviet Army and for conducting political work among Soviet personnel. In my conclusion, two primary objectives of the joint

---

Christopher Jones received his Ph.D. from Harvard University. After teaching at Marquette University, he returned to Harvard where he is now a Research Fellow at the Russian Research Center.

political programs of the WTO political administrations will be considered. One is to minimize the possibility that anti-Russian sentiments or outright defections will spread from East European units to the non-Russian soldiers of the Soviet army. The other, related objective, is to acculturate as much as possible the non-Russian soldiers of the Soviet army to the military ethos of the Russian contingent of the Soviet Armed Forces and in turn to acculturate as much as possible the East European soldiers of the Warsaw Pact to the military ethos of the Soviet army.

THE PACT'S INSTITUTIONS FOR POLITICAL ACTIVITIES

The Political Administrations of the Six Loyal Members of the WTO

The structure of the political administrations of the Bulgarian, Hungarian, East German, Polish and Czechoslovak armed forces is virtually identical to the structure of the Soviet Main Political Administration (MPA). Romania, which refuses to participate in the joint political activities of the WTO political administrations, has a system of party committees in the military very similar to the system of party committees in the Yugoslav Armed Forces. The Romanians established this system in 1964.

In the MPA structures of the six loyal members of the Warsaw Pact, the Chief of the MPA serves as a deputy of the Minister of Defense and has the "rights" but not the title of a secretary of the party's Central Committee. Below the Chief is a "Bureau" made up of his principal deputies. Below the Bureau are "Administrations": one for each national service branch, one for each national military district, and one for each Soviet Force Group in East Europe. There are also at least three central Administrations: one for agitation and propaganda, which supervises all military publications; one for organization and party work within the military, and administration concerned with the party organizations of officers; a third for cadres, that is, evaluation and promotion of political officers.

The next bureaucratic tier consists of "Departments", responsible either to the MPA Chief or to the head of an Administration. There are two central Departments--one for the party youth organizations in the military and one for military research. Departments also exist in national General Staff, the staff of each national service branch, in each mid-career national military academy and in each national military research institute. Departments also exist in "Formations"--groupings the size of a brigade, division or corps.

Below each department are the primary MPA and party organizations directly responsible for the conduct of work among military personnel. These agencies correspond to the types of "units" and "sub-units" found in the national service branches.

In 1967, the Hungarians created a separate system of party committees alongside the existing MPA organs, but this system does not replace the Hungarian MPA agencies or even compete with them. The purpose of the Hungarian party committees in the military is to involve Hungarian officers in the corresponding party committees of civilian agencies and vice versa. In the event of mobilization, the party committees organized at the regimental level and above dissolve and those below the regimental level become subordinate to the MPA bodies.[1]

Multi-Lateral Activities of the WTO Political Administrations

Parallel administrative hierarchies in MPA structures of loyal WTO armed forces facilitates the conduct of joint meetings of bureaucratic agencies to plan coordinated programs of political indoctrination. The Romanian military, which lacks political agencies corresponding to those of the other WTO members, does not participate in joint political indoctrination. Aside from the Romanians, chiefs of the WTO main political administrations have frequently met to discuss ideological work in the Warsaw Pact. These meetings have often taken place in the company of other high-ranking WTO political officers.[2]

The Chief of the Soviet MPA, General Epishev, notes that in addition to the meetings of his fellow chiefs, there is a plethora of meetings among lower-level WTO political agencies:

> The political organs do a great deal for the strengthening of contacts among the fraternal armed forces and the development of their all-round cooperation.
>
> There are meetings of the representatives of the Main Political Administrations; the political administrations of (national) service branches; meetings of the political administrations of force groups with political administrations of (national) military districts.
>
> There are meetings of the political workers of formations and units and there are conferences and seminars.
>
> Such meetings make possible the organization of a broad exchange of experience on various

> problems of the guaranteeing of the high quality of combat training of troops, of Marxist-Leninist training of officers, of the political studies of soldiers and non-commisioned officers, of the organization of socialist competition and other forms of the teaching and training of the soldiers of the socialist confederation.[3]

In his study of the cooperation of the WTO armed forces, Colonel General P. I. Efimov of the Soviet MPA called attention to the "participation of responsible workers of the party-political apparatus of the fraternal armed forces in various conferences, symposia, colloquia and seminars on military-theoretical problems and on practical questions of party-political work."[4] In addition, there is an annual exchange program of Soviet and East European military journalists which helps to coordinate the publication programs of the allied military and journals.[5] The WTO political administrations also send annual delegations of touring political lecturers to speak to the fraternal armed forces.[6]

These programs of multi-lateral exchanges involve not just the Soviet Force Groups stationed in East Europe but also at least three of the four western military districts of the USSR. A Soviet study of the Belorussian Military District noted that during a two-year period "generals and officers" from the fraternal armed forces delivered "about 200" speeches to the soldiers of the district,[7] i.e., about two speeches a week. The speakers included unidentified military attaches posted to Moscow, lecturers from the Polish MPA and military historians from East Germany.[8] A Soviet history of the Transcarpathian Military District declares that this district participates in the "systematic exchange of military delegations with other socialist states", including Poland, Czechoslovakia, Hungary and Bulgaria. The exchange includes delegations of commanders, technical specialists, political officers and military journalists. According to this study, political work in the Transcarpathian Military District focuses on the Warsaw Pact countries, the armed forces of these states and "the internationalist duty" of Soviet soldiers to defend socialism in East Europe.[9] A Soviet volume on the Odessa Military District took note of a similar program of regular exchanges of delegations with Warsaw Pact armies. According to this study, the district had conducted "about 40 recent exchanges of delegations of commanders, political organs, party and party-youth organizations."[10]

Political Activities in WTO Military Exercises

The conduct of joint political activities during WTO exercises goes back at least as far as 1962, the first full year of WTO multi-lateral troop maneuvers.[11] In an examination of the conduct of political activities during joint WTO exercises, Colonel Semin of the Soviet army notes that "usually" the political administration of the commander of the exercise organizes the program of joint political activities.[12] This suggests that, if an East European officer is commanding a joint WTO exercise, his national political administration organizes the political activities. But it also implies that if one of the Soviet officers serving as an exercise commander is also a WTO official, such as the Commander-in-Chief or Chief of Staff, a separate WTO political agency, rather than the Soviet MPA, may organize the political activities of the exercise.

Regardless of the agency with ultimate responsibility for the conduct of political activities in a given exercise, field responsibilities are assigned to what Colonel Semin calls "a united operational group" consisting of representatives of the political administrations whose soldiers are participating in the exercise. According to the Iakubovskii study of the Warsaw Pact, the united operational group has its representatives in the political Departments of the national forces assigned to the exercises and also in the staff which plans and directs the exercise.[13] The united operational group organizes meetings of the fraternal troops, meetings of the soldiers with the local population and programs of "agitation-propaganda" and "cultural enlightenment." This group also supervises a joint press center, a joint multilingual newspaper published during the larger exercises, joint multilingual radio broadcasts, and a joint cinematography group.[14]

Colonel Semin writes that "as a rule" political activities take place during pauses in military action. "When the situation permits" the joint operational group organizes joint discussions of "military-political and theoretical themes", speeches by propagandists and the exchange of films and stage performances. The meetings of soldiers and civilians sometimes include performances by choral groups, dance troupes and orchestras.[15]

WTO sources report that during the Brotherhood in Arms exercises of 1970 in East Germany there were more than 40 meetings of allied military units, more than 200 political rallies involving soldiers and civilians and about 300 cultural programs.[16] Such joint political activities are not confined to the large multilateral exercises. According to a WTO study, during an unidentified routine training exercise of Central Force Group and the Czechoslovak People's Army, there were five meetings of commanders and political officers, six meetings of outstanding enlisted military personnel, four large political rallies and 50 joint excursions.[17] Political activities appear to take place even during low-level joint tactical exercises. Krasnaia Zvezda reported in 1971 that, after jointly laying a pontoon bridge across the Danube, Soviet and Hungarian soldiers advanced to a concert given by the orchestra of the staff of the Southern Force Group.[18]

Bilateral Ties of Soviet and East European Political Agencies

The available evidence indicates that the multilateral activities of the WTO political administrations are less extensive than the bilateral activities of the Soviet MPA with each of the main political administrations of the loyal East European members of the WTO. These bilateral ties involve Soviet officers serving in the central agencies of the Soviet MPA, Soviet officers serving in military districts within the Soviet Union, and the political officers of Soviet force groups in Europe.

A joint Polish-Soviet study gives a typical example of the ties between Polish political officers and their opposites stationed in the USSR. This work reports "systematic meetings of political workers at all levels.. ...every year there are visits to Poland and to the USSR of dozens of delegations of Soviet and Polish political workers at the most diverse levels.[19] Among these exchanges are an unspecified number of Soviet military delegations to Poland led by General Epishev. Epishev's delegations have included Colonel General P. I. Efimov, a deputy chief of the Soviet MPA and the editor of a Soviet study of the WTO; Major General G. V. Sredin, a deputy chief of the Soviet MPA; General M. I. Moroz, Chief of the Political Administration of the Soviet Air Force; and General I. F. Khalipov, Chief of the Political Administration of the Soviet Anti-Aircraft Troops. In addition, the political administrations of other Soviet service branches and of Soviet military districts conduct exchanges with their Polish opposites. A Soviet study of the Belorussian Military District noted that the political officers of this district engage in frequent exchanges and joint activities with unspecified Polish units.[20] There are also what such studies refer to as "traditional ties" between the Moscow and Warsaw Military Districts, the Baltic Military District of the USSR and the Maritime Military District of Poland.[21]

The political administrations of Poland and the USSR regularly send officers on lecture tours among the units of each other's armed forces. The officer clubs of the two armies participate in a regular exchange of lecturers, films, "oral newspapers", thematic evenings and cultural exhibits. Many of these exchanges are prepared by the staffs of the military museums of each country, in particular by the staff of the Museum of Polish-Soviet Military Friendship in the Belorussian city of Lenino. The political administrations of the Polish and Soviet armed forces also assist each other in the conduct of joint sports competitions, song and dance festivals and exchanges of military journalists and cinematographers.[22] There are Soviet and East European materials which suggest that a comparable system of joint activities exists between the central agencies of Soviet MPA and the political administrations of Bulgaria, Hungary, East Germany and Czechoslovakia.[23]

Bi-Lateral Ties for Soviet Force Groups with East European Armies

The available evidence suggests that each of the Soviet force groups in East Europe maintains its own network of extensive political ties with some or all of the corresponding military forces of the host East European army. According to Efimov's study of the WTO, the Group of Soviet Forces in Germany (GSFG) engages in "regular meetings and exchanges of experience" between representatives of the corresponding central administrative agencies of the Political Administration of the GSFG and the MPA of the National People's Army, corresponding Departments of Soviet and East German troop formations, and corresponding political organs among the youth groups and military journalists of the two fraternal armies.[24] A Soviet study of the GSFG reports that East German and Soviet units frequently engage in joint friendship evenings, and joint visits to industrial enterprises, military museums and cultural institutions.[25] These exercises annually culminate in the traditional "Week of Combat Friendship".[26] The Efimov text claims that "it is hard to find an (East German) military unit which does not maintain multi-faceted ties with a neighboring unit of the Group of Soviet Forces in Germany."[27] A Krasnaia Zvezda correspondent discovered such ties even at the levels of the sub-units he visited.[28]

According to Soviet sources, the Political Administration of the Central Group of Forces and the Czechoslovak MPA conduct an extensive series of joint political activities. An article by a Czechoslovak major in Krasnaia Zvezda declared, "We devote great attention to the political and internationalist training of army youth....such work proceeds with the aid and participation of our Soviet comrades, Communists and Komsomol members."[29] This officer noted that joint Soviet-Czechoslovak political exercises take place not only during joint training exercises but even during purely national Czechoslovak training exercises.[30] In 1974, Colonel Jan Khmelik, editor of the Czechoslovak army journal, reported in the Soviet newspaper, Pravda:

> Our Army has the possibility to draw directly upon the rich experience of the Soviet armed forces through direct cooperation with the commanders, political organs, party and Komsomol organizations of the Central Force Group.
>
> We make good use of such possibilities on the basis of a joint plan of the Main Political Administration of the Czechoslovak People's Army and the Political Administration of the Central Force Group.[31]

In its discussion of the ties between the Southern Force Group and the Hungarian People's Army, the Soviet Military Encyclopedia notes that the soldiers of the two fraternal armies participate frequently in joint political meetings, joint observations of historical anniversaries, joint wreath-laying ceremonies, joint excursions to industrial and cultural facilities, joint cultural programs, Soviet-Hungarian sports competitions, "weeks" and even whole "months" set aside to celebrate Soviet-Hungarian military friendship. The Encyclopedia also calls attention to the joint conduct of party-political work in the two socialist armies.[32]

The Northern Force Group maintains an extensive series of political contacts with Polish units in the Silesian Military District and with local governments and economic enterprises in this region.[33] In a 1975 article in Krasnaia Zvezda, a Polish officer reported that units of the Northern Group and units of the Silesian Military District had recently introduced a two-week summer program of joint military-political study by Polish and Soviet military personnel.[34] According to a 1974 Krasnaia Zvezda article, "There is not a single unit of the Northern Force Group which does not maintain friendly contacts with the troop collectives of the Polish Armed Forces." This article explained how the Polish and Soviet forces in the Silesian military district maintained such ties;

> "Each year they (Soviet and Polish forces in Silesia) draw up joint plans for the conduct

> of measures for the strengthening of friendly ties, for the exchange of experience of combat training, of party-political work and of ideological and cultural work.
>
> And these plans are put into effect without deviation."[35]

WTO RELIABILITY

Themes of Political Education

The political administrations of the WTO conduct their synchronized work on three main themes: 1) socialist patriotism, defined as loyalty to the party and state hierarchies of the respective socialist fatherlands of the WTO members; 2) proletarian internationalism, defined as joint defense of the gains of socialism in each fraternal country against not only external threats but internal threats as well; 3) class hatred for the imperialists, who are defined in the case of each WTO member according to its historical experience with the West in general and Germany in particular.

Each of the WTO political administrations conducts indoctrination in socialist patriotism through lectures and readings on the nation's history and through a program of extensive civil-military activities, including excursions to civilian installations of various types and visits of political leaders, military veterans and national celebrities to military installations.[36] Political indoctrination on the theme of socialist patriotism addresses the problem of the political loyalty of national armed forces to the national party and state leadership. This problem of reliability arises not only in the possibility of a war with NATO but also in the possibility of a domestic crisis pitting civilians against the native Communist regime, a scenerio discussed further by Dan Nelson in this volume.

Each of the loyal WTO political administrations engages in indoctrination in proletarian internationalism.[37] Some of this indoctrination is addressed to the conduct of multi-lateral political activities within the WTO. Such activities are facilitated by such practices as naming some units of one East European army after the military heroes of another East European army.[38] But the overwhelming emphasis in the programs of indoctrination in proletarian internationalism is on developing a bilateral relationship between each East European army and Soviet Armed Forces.[39] A Krasnaia Zvezda editorial published during a joint WTO exercise called attention to the special role of the Soviet army in the alliance:

> Yes, the soldiers of the fraternal armies

> speak in different languages, but they think in the same way. In this regard, they are like brothers in one big family.
> Yes, and they understand and recognize that the elder brother in this family is the Soviet soldier who defended his Fatherland, who brought freedom to the people of Europe and who in his military victory, was always true to the international proletariat and struggled for the happiness of mankind.[40]

In turn, the programs of the WTO political administrations emphasize to Soviet soldiers their special role of providing inspiring examples to other national armies of the WTO. On his return from invading Czechoslovakia, Lieutenant Kristo Radulov of the Bulgarian People's Army and his unit stopped by in the Odessa Military District to hold a joint political meeting. In his address to his Soviet comrades, Lieutenant Radulov declared,

> It was difficult for us in the first days. The counterrevolutionaries ranted and raved. It was necessary to have iron nerves in order not to succumb to the provocations.
> But for us, the example was always the Soviet soldier, who demonstrated obvious self-control and self-mastery.[41]

Indoctrination in proletarian internationalism does not address only the question of reliability in a NATO-WTO conflict. Indoctrination in proletarian internationalism also addresses the issue of reliability in WTO interventions against the member states of the fraternal alliance.

In published writings, Soviet officers have identified the relationship between the use of a socialist army to put down a domestic rebellion and the use of foreign socialist military forces to assist in "defense of the gains of socialism" against an internal threat. Soviet Army Colonel Timorin has identified three aspects of the internal function of a socialist army: 1) as a psychological deterrent against anti-socialist forces; 2) as a back-up for internal security forces; 3) as a combat force "in those cases when the opposition of the enemies of socialism within a country acquire significant scale, intensity, duration and sharpness (a counterrevolutionary uprising, mutiny, banditry, the unleashing of civil war)."[42] In his volume on the Warsaw Treaty Organization, Marshal Iakubovskii, former commander of the WTO, specifically declared that each socialist army could count on fraternal assistance from other socialist armies in fulfilling its internal function. Iakubovskii's text declares that a socialist army must be prepared to assist another in "joint defense of the gains of socialism when these gains are threatened by internal or external reaction."[43]

The WTO programs of political indoctrination in class hatred for the imperialists appears to focus mainly on past instances of foreign non-Communist armies attacking East European states--in other words, the Nazi Wehrmacht. It also focuses on the actions of "imperialist" armies against national liberation movements outside Europe.[44] The available evidence suggests that the main thrust of political indoctrination in class hatred for the imperialists is making patriotic appeals to past instances--if any--of the defense of national territory against an invader from outside the Soviet bloc.

Judging by these themes of indoctrination, WTO political officers have set their sights no higher than securing their troops' loyalty during internal turmoil, an intra-bloc intervention or the invasion of East Europe by NATO Armies. Rather modest goals of WTO indoctrination reflect a practical application of conclusions in Soviet writings regarding the reliability of socialist soldiers.

Soviet Texts on the Political Reliability of Socialist Soldiers

Western analysts generally have ignored the factors which, in Soviet writing, are thought to affect the political reliability of socialist soldiers. This body of Soviet literature, "The Marxist-Leninist Teaching on War and the Armed Forces," claims to address the question of the political reliability not just of Soviet soldiers but of the soldiers of all socialist armies.[45] Although this literature discusses a large number of factors affecting military morale, these Soviet texts seem to identify two main factors determining the political reliability of soldiers during the course of a protracted war: 1) popular attitudes toward the prevailing socio-political systems; 2) popular perception of a given war as a "just war" in defense of the homeland.

The technical term used by the Soviet literature on political reliability is "the moral-political factor." N. P. Prokop'ev defines the moral-political factor as "readiness by the people to endure the extremely heavy trials of modern warfare and not to lose the will to fight and defeat the enemy." But according to Prokop'ev, specifying the components of the moral-political factor is "a very complicated matter." He writes that these components include "the confidence of the population in its civilian and military leadership," the "real unity" of the country's citizens, and the "depth of patriotic feeling." According to Prokop'ev, the moral-political factor also depends on "the character of the social and state order" and "the national and historical peculiarities of a people."[46] All of these factors, of course, are related to the concept of mobilization potential introduced by Nelson earlier in this volume; that the Soviets emphasize so much the "moral-political factor" suggests their recognition that reliability is lessened by negative attitudes as much as by faulty or obsolete equipment.

Colonel Belyi distinguishes between two sets of components of the moral-political factor: the first set includes popular attitudes toward the socio-political system of a state and toward the specific military policy being pursued by the state. A second set of factors includes the soldier's confidence in his commander, his weapons and his logistical support.[47] Marshal Sokolovskii's Military Strategy also divides the moral-political component into two sets of factors: one concerns attitudes of soldiers toward the domestic and foreign policies of the regime and the other set includes purely military considerations which affect the soldier's confidence in his commander and his unit.[48] Other Soviet discussions note additional elements in the moral-political factor: socio-psychological and individual psychological characteristics which affect a soldier's view of himself.[49]

Soviet writers on military affairs warn that it is impossible to specify beforehand just how great a role the moral-political factor will play in a particular hostile scenerio. They caution that the importance of this factor varies enormously from situation to situation and exists in an elusive dependence on the whole complex of elements which they have identified as components of the moral-political factor. Perhaps the reason that they are so vague on the relative importance of the components of moral-political factor is that they hesitate to say directly what all their definitions imply: in the last analysis, the moral-political factor combines popular attitudes toward the regime and popular attitudes toward the hostilities in which the regime has chosen to engage. As Colonel General Lomov explains, "The moral-political potential of a country....is expressed in the relation of a people to a war and in the degree of their unity around the ruling party and its government."[50]

Just Wars and Socialist Armies

When a socialist government is faced with prospect of going to war, it is not in a position to bring about abrupt changes in the degree of its popular legitimacy. But it is in a position to make a deliberate choice of the war aims. Soviet texts emphasize that the choice of war aims is a conscious political act by a government.

In Soviet military treatises, a positive moral-political attitude on the part of soldiers and civilians depends in large part on whether or not they view the war as a "just war" in defense of the nation. They emphasize that the distinction between "just" and "unjust" wars has nothing to do with the technical aspects of a particular conflict. Prokop'ev states that it does not matter "who began the military action and on whose territory the war is being fought. The character of a war is defined by the question of why it is being fought..."[51] N. V. Pukovskii argues that the size or scale of a war does not determine its political character. He declares that the war's political objectives determine whether or not the war takes on a just or unjust character in the eyes of a nation.[52] What these theorists mean by a "just war" is a war that socialist soldiers and civilians view as a conflict to insure the survival of the nation as a distinct socio-cultural entity. Soviet military theoreticians declare that the most just of all possible wars is a "just war in defense of the socialist fatherland." Colonel Dziuba declares that a war in defense of the socialist fatherland has "an unconditionally just character": He adds,

> Because of the just aims and tasks of such a war, which fully corresponds to the working people's interest, the masses take an active part in it, support and implement the policy of the Marxist-Leninist party and government and rally even more closely around them.[53]

Soviet theorists acknowledge that capitalist armies are capable of fighting "just" wars if such wars appear to soldiers and civilians as patriotic defenses of the nation. After noting that military morale is of course highest in a society with no class antagonisms, the Sokolovskii text cautions that "high steadfastness of army morale can be achieved even without such (class) unity." This text explains that "such a situation arises when a belligerent country is united by a feeling of national solidarity and when class antagonisms are temporarily less pronounced than the ideas of national independence and sovereignty."[54]

The Soviet texts on political reliability imply that in a multi-national military force the moral-political factor can vary from one national contingent to another. Such varying levels of commitment to the war effort in turn implies a high degree of uncertainty about the cohesion and reliability of the multi-national force as a whole. In a 1975 volume on the Soviet armed forces edited by Marshal Grechko, former commander of the Warsaw Pact, the text notes previous historical instances in which nationality tensions have undermined the cohesion of multi-national military forces, whether organized into one imperial army or an allied coalition. This text specifically says that the cohesion of a multi-national military force is dependent on whether or not the various nationalities under arms see themselves fighting "just wars" in defense of their respective homelands or "unjust" wars of imperial expansion. Marshal Grechko's study declares,

> History has seen examples of the creation of armed forces of multi-national states... The troops of subjugated countries are forcibly included in these armed forces... Such were the armies of the Persian King Cyrus II and of Alexander of Macedon, the armies of Rome, Byzantium and the Arab caliphate, the armies of the vast empires of the Franks, the Tatar-Mongols and Ottoman Turks, and the armies of Napoleonic France and Austro-Hungary. While constituting a rather impressive force, they quickly fell apart, either on encountering a serious enemy or as a result of the decay of the empires themselves... The most important causes for the short-lived nature of these armies were the unjust goals for which they were formed and fought, class antagonisms, and the lack of a cementing force such as the unity of social interests of all ethnic groups, nationalities and nations which were a part of the state.[55]

In sending Soviet and East European forces into joint combat the Warsaw Pact command inevitably will link the moral-political factors affecting the cohesion of the multi-national components of the WTO as a whole to the moral-political factors affecting the cohesion of the multi-national components of the Soviet Armed Forces. According to the criteria used in Soviet texts, the political reliability of each national component of the WTO and of each national component of the Soviet army depends mainly on two considerations: the attitude of each national contingent toward its prevailing socio-economic system and the attitude of each national group toward the war aims of the coalition.

The National-Territorial Formations of the Soviet Army During the Great Fatherland War

Soviet emphasis on nationality when discussing the moral-political factor may have origins in their experience with the political reliability of the "national-territorial" divisions of non-Russians which were formed in the Caucasus, Kazakhstan and Central Asia during the first two years of the Great Fatherland War, the official Soviet designation of the struggle of nationalities of the Soviet Union against the armies of Nazi Germany.

In his discussion of the political factors affecting the cohesion of multi-national armed forces, Marshal Grechko did not have to confine himself to historical discourses on Napoleon's multi-lingual army. He could just as well have referred to his own experiences in leading three different Soviet armies in the battles of 1941-43 for the Caucasus. To defend the Caucasus, and its oil supplies, the Soviets mobilized non-Russian soldiers from the national republics and autonomous regions of the area.

According to a Soviet historian, V. A. Muradian, "more than 600,000 Azerbaidjanis, Armenians and Georgians" were called up in the first ten months of the war.[56] Most, if not all, of the native military personnel recruited in the Caucasus appear to have served during 1941 and 1942 in "national-territorial" divisions made up mainly of one particular nationality or in multi-national divisions made up mainly of non-Russian soldiers from the regions of the Caucasus. The Soviets appear to have mobilized such detachments out of necessity rather than preference, for the Soviet army had officially disbanded its national-territorial formations in 1938.

According to another Soviet historian, A. P. Artem'ev, during 1941 and 1942, the Soviets formed 15 national-territorial rifle divisions composed principally of one particular Caucasus nationality and 14 multi-national rifle divisions made up primarily of two or more Caucasus nationalities.[57] A contingent of Russian personnel appears to have served in each of the 29 rifle divisions raised in the Caucasus, probably at the upper levels of the officer corps. These divisions appear to have been assigned to the Caucasus front.

The Soviets also mobilized about 600,000 soldiers of non-Slavic origin from the republics of Kazakhstan and Central Asia.[58] Soviet sources indicate that these forces were assigned mainly to the Stalingrad front, thought it is not clear how many of these non-Slavic soldiers saw actual combat. Soviet sources indicate that the divisions raised in Kazakhstan and Central Asia were mixed-nationality divisions which included at least two or three non-Slavic nationalities plus a contingent of Russians and Ukrainians.[59]

After the victories at Stalingrad and in the Caucasus in 1943, the Soviet army dismantled its national-territorial divisions of non-Slavic military personnel. According to Soviet historians, beginning with the counteroffensive of 1943, the proportion of native peoples in the ranks of the national-territorial divisions formed in the Caucasus, Kazakhstan and Central Asia dropped so precipitously that these divisions became indistinguishable from other Soviet divisions in the national composition of their personnel. This change could have been due to the complexities of reinforcing divisions now operating in the Ukraine, Central Russia and regions further west. It could also have been due to an influx of Slavic manpower from the liberated zones of the Soviet Union. But it also could have been due to a lack of confidence in the <u>reliability</u> of the non-Russian military personnel of the Caucasus, Kazakhstan and Central Asia. The Soviet command may have anticipated problems of reliability if these divisions were sent to battles distant from the borders of their national fatherlands where they had first fought the Nazis.

Artem'ev does not offer any explanation for the decline in the proportion of the nationalities of Kazakhstan and Central Asia in the national-territorial divisions formed in these republics. He simply notes that this decline took place, beginning in the spring and summer of 1943. He writes,

> In the rifle divisions which were established in the Central Asian republics and Kazakhstan, the proportion of the representatives of the Kazakh, Uzbek, Turkmen, Kirghiz and Tadzhik peoples was comparatively great...
> In many divisions, they made up from 40 to 50 percent of all personnel...
> But in the course of military actions, the personnel of these divisions departed and dispersed into other military units...
> These divisions received new reinforcements and in this manner were transformed into ordinary divisions of the Red Army which had in their composition only an insignificant portion of soldiers from the national republics for which the divisions were named.[60]

In the case of the Caucasus nationalities, Artem'ev does offer an explanation for the decline in the proportion of these nationalities in the national-territorial divisions formed in the republics of the Caucasus:

> To the degree that these divisions went further from their republics, it became more difficult to reinforce their personnel in the required time with representatives of the corresponding

> nationalities...
> And furthermore, there was not the same kind of necessity, as in the initial period of the war, since the soldiers of non-Russian nationality had by 1943 received good military tempering and experience, and many of them had mastered the Russian language and had received a good internationalistic training...
> This in no small degree facilitated their blending with the soldiers of all other nationalities.[61]

The experience of the Soviet Defense Ministry in integrating non-Russian soldiers from the Caucasus, Kazakhstan and Central Asia into combat units is probably so complex that even officials with access to military archives may not be entirely sure what conclusions to draw concerning the mobilization of soldiers from these republics for future combat. It may be that in examining the historical record of non-Russian nationalities Soviet military analysts have had to limit themselves to the conclusion that there is a "moral-political factor" which varies from one socialist nationality to another. To such analysts, the two most important components of the moral-political factor may be the attitudes of each nationality toward native socialist regimes and the attitudes of members of each nationality to the question of whether they are fighting a "just" war in defense of the national homeland.

The Soviet MPA and the Non-Russian Divisions of the Caucasus, Kazakhstan and Central Asia

Evidence from Soviet sources concerning the work of the Soviet MPA during the Great Fatherland War, suggests that political work with the national-territorial divisions of the Caucasus, Kazakhstan and Central Asia attempted to persuade each of these non-Russian nationalities that they were defending their respective fatherlands from a Nazi threat. The MPA appears also to have argued that the only possible means of defending non-Russian fatherlands was close cooperation with other Soviet nationalities and in particular with the Great Russians.

The pattern of political work by the Soviet MPA with the non-Russian divisions during 1941 and 1942 appears to be very similar to the current pattern of political work in the Warsaw Pact. Political work by the Soviet MPA during 1941-42 stressed: 1) ties of the non-Russians to their native fatherlands, their cultures, histories, local governments and economic enterprises; 2) the proletarian unity of the multi-national Red Army, with particular emphasis on the fraternal relationship of each Soviet nationality to the Great Russian people; 3) the immediate threat posed by the imperialist armies just beyond the borders of the fatherlands of the non-Russian personnel.

Soviet historians trace the development of political education work among non-Russian personnel during 1941 and 1942. According to Artem'ev, the difficulties of integrating these soldiers into combat divisions arose because most of them did not know the Russian language, few of them were familiar with industrial technology and many had no previous military training.[62] Muradian adds that many soldiers "adjusted with difficulty" to combat because of "religious prejudices," "harmful customs," and the lack of familiarity with climates much colder than those of the southern regions of the USSR.[63]

Fragmentary information available suggests that, during the first year of the war, the problems noted by Artem'ev and Muradian adversely affected the military reliability of the soldiers drawn from the Caucasus, Kazakhstan and Central Asia. The Soviet historian K. Tskitishvili writes that during one of the early battles of the Caucasus, the 223rd Azerbaidjani Rifle Division suffered a collapse of morale and discipline. According to his analysis, the disintegration of this division was due to poor training in the use of weaponry, lack of knowledge of Russian military commands, and poor political work.[64]

According to Artem'ev's study, the prerequisite for teaching both the use of weaponry and the use of elementary Russian military terminology was the conduct of political indoctrination in the native languages of the non-Russian soldiers.[65] Muradian writes that on May 22, 1942, the Main Political Administration of the Soviet Armed Forces issued a decree to the political administrations of military districts on improving political work among non-Russian soldiers. Muradian quotes the following passage from the decree:

> Conduct mass-political work with Red Army personnel who do not know Russian in their native languages. Do this by making use of the national cadres in the units of your districts --commanders, political workers, rank-and-file Communists and Komsomol members--people who know the national languages.[66]

According to Muradian, the decree also required that political workers take action to instill in soldiers awareness of the friendship of the peoples of the USSR. The decree placed a special responsibility on

Russian personnel to cultivate such awareness by helping non-Russian soldiers to learn Russian military terminology.[67] The decree apparently did not produce the desired results. Muradian writes that on June 12, 1942, the Central Committee of the CPSU issues a resolution calling for an immediate improvement in political work among the non-Russian personnel of the Red Army. The Central Committee removed L. Z. Mekhlis from his post of the Chief of the Main Political Administration and replaced him with A. S. Shcherbakov, whose previous post had been that of a Central Committee Secretary in charge of cultural matters.[68]

On September 17, 1942, Shcherbakov issued a decree entitled "On Educational Work with Non-Russian Red Army Soldiers and Junior Officers." Muradian writes that this document declared that "a significant stratum of the personnel of a majority of divisions consists of non-Russian soldiers and junior officers, a part of whom know Russian poorly or not at all."[69] Muradian then quotes directly from the decree:

> ...political organs and military commissars of formations and units have not taken the necessary measures to organize educational work among this stratum of personnel...
> Commissars and political organs have underestimated the entire importance of the political education of non-Russian soldiers and have forgotten that each of them has a native language, native customs, and a well-defined form of national life...
> They have treated every one of these nationalities alike, not taking into account their national characteristics...
> Moreover, many political workers do not know how to organize explanatory work on the question of the friendship of the peoples of the USSR and the role of the Great Russian people as the elder brother of the peoples of the Soviet Union.[70]

According to Muradian, and Artem'ev as well, the decree of September 17, 1942 required the conduct of political work in the native tongues of the non-Russian soldiers on topics such as:

- What the Hitlerites Are Intending for the Peoples of the Soviet Union
- On the Fronts of the Fatherland War Defends the Independence of All the National Republics
- The Red Army is the Army of Brotherhood Among the Peoples of Our Country.

-The Role of the Great Russian People in the Fatherland War of the Peoples of the USSR Against Hitler's Germany.[71]

The decree of September 17, 1942 also resulted in the publication of millions of leaflets in the non-Russian languages of the USSR; the use of appropriate texts from national literatures in political indoctrination sessions; the organization of regular correspondence between non-Russian soldiers and the agricultural and industrial enterprises of their native republics; and many other steps designed to bring Central Asian troops into contact with their culture and language.[72] By the beginning of 1943, the Main Political Administration began publishing 49 non-Russian military newspapers, all of them in the languages of the Caucasus, Kazakhstan and Central Asia.[73]

The National Composition of the Political Workers of the Panfilov Eighth Guards Divisions, October 1942

To conduct political work in the native languages of the non-Russian soldiers during 1941 and 1942, the Soviet MPA appears to have tried to staff the political apparatus of the national-territorial divisions with political workers of a particular nationality in approximate proportion to the share of that nationality among enlisted personnel. This appears to be the case particularly for agitators, the lowest-level political workers. The statistics assembled by Artem'ev on the national composition of the Panfilov Eighth Guards Rifle Division, an elite formation drawn from Kazakhstan and Central Asia, suggest these patterns. Artem'ev's data, which come from the Soviet Ministry of Defense, produce Table 3-1. In assessing Table 3-1 data, Artem'ev concludes:

> Such composition of the agitation collective corresponded to the composition of the soldiers of the division and permitted the organization of agitation-political work with soldiers of various nationalities in their native languages.[75]

The statistics compiled by Artem'ev from the archives of the Ministry of Defense on the Eighth Guards Division suggest that Russians enjoyed a near-monopoly on the higher-level positions in the party-political apparatus of this division; that the Uzbeks were very much under-represented in the party-political apparatus at every level except that of the agitators; and that

Kazakhs in the division, who were greatly over-represented among the deputies of political officers in charge of political work in sub-units, among the party membership, and among the party-political apparatus as a whole, may have carried out much of the political work with the Central Asian nationalities.

Although he does not provide specific information on other multi-national divisions or the national divisions of the Great Fatherland War, Artem'ev does note, "The agitation collectives of the other formations of the Soviet army were filled through a similar process of taking into account the national composition of the troops."[76] Artem'ev's discussion of the Eighth Guards Rifle Division suggests that the principle of proportional representation also obtained in the assignment of command personnel:

> The assignment of command and political cadres in the (Eighth Guards Rifle) Division was carried out in such a manner that in each sub-unit there were representatives of several nationalities...
> For example, the commander of the 7th Company of the 19th Regiment was a Tartar who knew Russian well. The political officer was a Russian. The head of the party organization was a Kirghiz.
> The Deputy of the political officer was a Kazakh...
> When the commanders of platoons and squadrons were Russians or representatives of other nationalities who did not know the languages of the peoples of Central Asia, the most well-prepared Red Army men of Kazakh, Kirghiz, Uzbek or other nationalities were designated as their deputies...
> Such assignment of leading military cadres provided the opportunity to conduct work in the combat training and ideological-political upbringing of multi-national personnel more correctly and in a more differentiated manner...
> It promoted the integration of soldiers into a united military collective.[77]

The Warsaw Pact and the Abolition of the National-Territorial Units and Formations of the Soviet Armed Forces

Some evidence suggests that after the creation of the WTO in 1955 the Soviets abolished the national-territorial detachments of the Soviet army in order to eliminate potential conduits for the spread of political unreliability from East European personnel in the Warsaw Pact to non-Russian personnel in the Soviet armed forces in the event that Soviet and WTO troops should ever go into battle together.

A decree of the Supreme Soviet of February 1, 1944, made three changes in the 1936 Constitution concerning the organization of national-territorial "units" and "formations." In Soviet usage, a military "unit" is a regiment, ship or similar self-contained detachment; a "formation" is either a brigade, division or corps or equivalent detachment. The constitutional changes of February 1, 1944 gave each union republic of the USSR the right to muster its own "units" and "formations." The decree provided that the Supreme Soviet of each republic should decide on the particular formations and units to be raised in the republic. The decree also changed the Ministry of Defense from an all-union ministry to a union-republic ministry.[78] I have been unable to find any information on the implementations of this decree.

However, the Soviet Military Encyclopedia indicates that some unspecified national-territorial units and formations survived until the mid-1950s, probably because of their utility in training soldiers who did not know Russian and because of the utility of such units and formations for integrating non-Slavic personnel into a predominantly Slavic military force. The Encyclopedia declares that "in the mid-1950s, the national formations and units were disbanded and their personnel assigned to multi-national troop formations."[79]

The 1967 Law on Universal Military service specifically required military service without regard to race or nationality.[80] According to a Soviet officer, the implementation of this law results in mixed-nationality "sub-units" as well as units and formations.[81] The 1977 Constitution retained none of the provisions of the 1944 decree on the establishment of national formations and units. It contained only a series of articles on the obligation of all Soviet citizens to defend the Socialist Fatherland.[82]

Placing all Soviet military personnel in integrated sub-units, units and formations could not have removed the problems of the military and political training of the non-Slavic nationalities who had previously been able to train in national-territorial units for soldiers who did not know Russian. This policy simply removed a battle-tested device for integrating non-Slavs into the Soviet army. In a 1975 volume on the Soviet armed forces edited by Marshal Grechko, a discussion of "the internationalist education of servicemen" obliquely acknowledged the recurring problems of integrating different nationalities into multi-national sub-units, units and formations: "Particular attention is given to the fight against vestiges of nationalism. One cannot ignore the fact that a certain part of service personnel, albeit a very small part, sometimes displays elements of national conceit and aloofness. There have been attempts to make a nationality issue out of various disagreements or personal affronts."[83]

The Soviet Military Encyclopedia offers two reasons why the Soviet Defense Ministry prefers the disadvantages of integrating Soviet nationalities into multi-national sub-units, units and formations to the disadvantages of integrating national units and formations into the armed forces as a whole. The Encyclopedia says that the necessity for national units and formations "fell away" because of the further drawing together of all Soviet nationalities and because of the formation of the world socialist system.[84]

Perhaps by the mid-1950s, the Soviet education system taught enough Russian to non-Slavic youths to make it possible for non-Russians to train in multi-national units using Russian as the language of military life. By the late 1970s, pre-induction military training of non-Russian youth took place only in Russian--including education on military-political topics.[85]

The single most important development in the military affairs of the world socialist system in the mid-1950s was the creation of the Warsaw Pact. If the Soviets had retained national units and formations of the non-Russian nationalities they would have had to deal with the complexities of integrating these units and formations not only into the Soviet armed forces but into the forces of the Warsaw Pact as well. This problem would have arisen sooner or later in the staffing of the Soviet Force Groups in Europe and of the western military districts of the USSR.

During the late 1950s, Soviet forces stationed in East Europe began conducting joint tactical exercises with the forces of the East European members of the Warsaw Pact.[86] If the Soviets had retained national sub-units, units and formations in the Soviet army, it would have been possible that at some point in multi-lateral WTO exercises, Soviet units of predominantly Russian-Ukrainian-Belorussian composition would find themselves surrounded by non-Russian speaking units of East European armies and of the non-Slavic republics of the USSR.

East European soldiers would probably have had an even greater exposure to the ethnic differences among Soviet soldiers in the course of joint WTO political exercises. Such activities often take place in small groups and require personal interaction between Soviet and East European personnel. A Soviet volume on the work of the Soviet MPA notes that the Soviet Main Political Administration undertook a major reorganization of political work in the late 1950s. This study specifically declares that one of the reasons for the organizational and programmatic changes in MPA work--especially from 1958-1961--was to prepare Soviet soldiers for participation in joint political activities with East European soldiers.[87]

In an article published just prior to the "Buria" exercise of 1961, the first major WTO multi-lateral exercise, Marshal Grechko, then Commander of the Warsaw Pact, noted that Soviet Force Groups in Germany, Poland, and Hungary already participated in a wide variety of joint political activities with East European soldiers. Such activities included evening programs of combat friendship, meetings of allied soldiers who had won national training competitions, joint visits of WTO personnel to local industries and collective farms, and other meetings. The WTO Commander-in-Chief added that the Military Councils of the Soviet Force Groups in Europe regularly discussed "questions of internationalist training."[88]

A Soviet officer responsible for the internationalist training of the Group of Soviet Forces in Germany (GSFG) published a 1972 article in which he called attention to the close relationship between conducting political work among the multi-national components of Soviet personnel in the GSFG and conducting joint political activities between the GSFG and the East German army. In the course of this discussion, Lt. General I. S. Mednikov, Chief of the Political Administration of the GSFG, also suggested that the Soviet army still observes the principles of personnel staffing by nationality which Soviet historians have described in the Panfilov Guards Rifle Division during 1942. Lt. General Medinkov wrote:

> One has to consider very carefully the specific manifestation of the multi-nationality of units and sub-units...
> It is extremely significant that in any of our troop collectives, the sons of various peoples have approximately equal proportionate representation in the leadership nucleus, in the party organization, and in the ranks of the soldiers officially recognized as outstanding in combat and political training...
> Work in internationalist education in units and sub-units begins with the first day a young soldier puts on a military uniform...
> Right next to our garrison are deployed the garrisons of the National People's Army of the German Democratic Republic. We are class brothers and comrades in arms...
> Literally all events of life and service testify to the close ties of combat brothers--from joint

> evening meetings conducted in one sub-unit or another to major troop exercises...[89]

Lt. General Mednikov might also have called attention to the military oath required of each East German soldier: "I swear as a soldier of the National People's Army always to be ready to defend socialism on the side of the Soviet Army...."[90]

The abolition of national sub-units, units and formations within the Soviet army probably increased the difficulties of the military and political training of the non-Russian recruits who enter the Soviet Armed Forces without a good working knowledge of the Russian language. But the abolition of national sub-units, units and formations within the Soviet army probably avoided even more difficult problems of integrating Soviet and East European soldiers into the joint activities of the Warsaw Pact. The abolition of national sub-units, units and formations also minimized the possibility that anti-Russian nationalism in the East European armies could contaminate the non-Russian personnel of the Soviet army.

CONCLUSION

The organization and conduct of political indoctrination by the WTO political administration is directed primarily at securing the political reliability of East European armies in the event of either a domestic political upheaval or an intra-alliance military intervention. In the event of a conflict with NATO on the territories of either East or West Europe, the WTO political administrations have sought to maximize the reliability of the East European armies by enmeshing each of them in a network of bilateral military-political ties with the Soviet army.

In the event of war with NATO, the principal concern of the WTO political administrations appears to be preempting the spread of East European defections to the non-Russian soldiers of the Soviet Armed Forces. The Soviets have used the same military-political mechanisms to maximize the political reliability of non-Russian WTO soldiers in either a war with NATO or a Soviet military intervention in East Europe. Within the Soviet army, these military-political mechanisms seek to acculturate non-Russian personnel as much as possible to the military ethos of the Russian component of the Soviet Armed Forces. Within the Warsaw Pact, these military-political mechanisms seek to acculturate East European personnel as much as possible to the military ethos of Soviet personnel.

TABLE 3.1
Eighth Guards Rifle Division During October, 1942

(Percentages)

Nationality	All Personnel	Soldiers & Junior Officers	Agitators	Membership: Party & Komsomol	Deputies of Political Officers in Sub-Units	All Political Workers of Division
Russians	48.0	44.3	44.5	39.0	43.0	56.0
Kirghiz	16.3	18.5	19.4	10.0	10.7	7.0
Kazakhs	14.7	16.3	19.7	28.5	27.5	20.0
Uzbeks	8.0	9.1	4.9	4.8	not given	0.7
Ukrainians	7.2	6.4	6.5	14.2	9.5	10.3
Tatars	2.1	not given	not given	not given	not given	not given
Others	3.7	5.4	5.0	3.5	8.1	6.0
Total Percantage	100.0	100.0	100.0	100.0	98.8	100.0

Total Number of agitators: 712. Rough estimate of size of division: 10,000 personnel.

Total Number of Party and Komsomol members among agitators: 675.

NOTES

1. The information on the structure of the WTO political administrations comes from the author's study, Soviet Influence in Eastern Europe: Political Autonomy and the Warsaw Pact (New York: Praeger, 1981).

2. See Col. D. Diev, Lt. Col. K. Spirov, "Combat Collaboration of the Armies of the Warsaw Pact States," Voennaia Mysl no. 2 (1968) in Central Intelligence Agency/Foreign Broadcast Information Service: Foreign Press Digest 0049/69 Selected Translations from Voennaia Mysl, April 25, 1969, p. 25. See also I. I. Iakubovskii, ed., Boevoe sodruzhestvo bratskikh narodov i armii (The Combat Brotherhood of the Fraternal Peoples and Armed Forces (Moscow: Voenizdat, 1975), p. 289 for mention of meetings of the MPA Chiefs in September 1970 and October 1973. See M. S. Kirichenko Nadezhnyi strazh mira (Reliable Guard of the Peace) (Minsk: Belarus, 1975), pp. 112-113 for mention of a meeting of the MPA Chiefs in April 1972. See Col. A. Verbitskii, "V dukhe protarskogo sotsialisticheskogo internatsionalizma" ("In the spirit of Proletarian and Socialist Internationalism:) Kommunist vooruzhennykh sil (Communist of the Armed Forces) no. 17, 1977 p. 80 for documentation of a meeting of June 1976.

3. A. A. Epishev, Ideologicheskaia bor'ba po voennym voprosam (Ideological Struggle in Military Questions (Moscow: Voenizdat, 1974), p. 110.

4. P. I. Efimov ed., Boevoi soiuz bratskikh armii (The Combat Alliance of the Fraternal Armed Forces) (Moscow: Voenizdat, 1974), p. 28.

5. Ibid., pp. 20; Iakubovskii, Boevoe sodruzhestvo, p. 165 and A. I. Prokvatilov, V. I. Lenin i sovetskaia voennaia pechat' (V. I. Lenin and the Soviet Military Press) (Leningrad: Izdatel'stvo leningradskogo universiteta, 1976), p. 83.

6. Efimov, Boevoi soiuz, p. 29.

7. A. G. Ovchinnikov, et.al., eds., Krasnoznamennyi Belorusskii voennyi okrug (The Red-Banner Belorussian Military District) (Minsk: Belarus: 1973), p. 505.

8. Ibid.

9. V. I. Varennikov et.al., eds., Krasnoznamennyi pricarpatskii (The Red Banner Transcarpathian Military District) (L'vov Izdatel'stvo 'Kameniar', 1976), pp. 188 and ff.

10. N. T. Panferov, et.al., eds., Odesskii krasnoznamennyi (The Red Banner Odessa Military District) (Kishinev: Kartiia Moldoveniaske, 1975), p. 238.

11. See Krasnaia Zvezda October 10, 1962 and October 20, 1962.

12. Col. V. Semin, "Partinnai politicheskaia rabota v armiakh stran Varshavskogo dogovora" ("Party-Political

Work in the Armed Forces of the Warsaw Pact Countries" in S. K. Il'in et.al., eds., Partiino-politicheskaia rabota v sovetskikh vooruzhennyk silakh (Party Political Work in the Soviet Armed Forces) (Moscow: Voenzidat, 1974), p. 599.

13. Iakubovskii Boevoe sodruzhestvo, p. 253.

14. Semin, "Politicheskaia rabota," p. 599.

15. Ibid.

16. P. A. Zhilin (USSR); E. Jadziac (Poland), Bratstvo po oruzhiiu (Brotherhood in Arms) (Moscow: Voenizdat, 1975), p. 355.

17. P. A. Zhilin (USSR) and E. Gefurt (Czechoslovakia), Na vechnye vremena (For Eternity) (Moscow: Voenizdat, 1975), p. 309.

18. Krasnaia Zvezda, July 14, 1971, p. 1.

19. Zhilin and Jadziac, Bratstvo, p. 359.

20. Ovchinnikov et.al., Krasnoznamennyi Belorusskii, pp. 501-504.

21. Zhilin and Jadziac, Bratstvo, p. 259.

22. Ibid., pp. 263-365.

23. For this evidence, see Jones, Soviet Influence in Eastern Europe, Chp. 7.

24. Efimov, Boevoi soiuz, pp. 124-125.

25. E. F. Ivanovskii et.al., eds. Na boevom postu: kniga o voinakh Gruppy sovetskikh voisk v Germanii (At the Battle Station: A Book About the Group of Soviet Forces in Germany) (Moscow: Voenizdat, 1975), pp. 276-283.

26. Ibid., pp. 288-289.

27. Efimov, Boivoi soiuz, p. 126.

28. Col. A. Khorev, "Iz putevogo bloknota: Krepnut novye traditsii" ("From a Travel Notebook: New Traditions are Strengthening"), Krasnaia Zvezda, November 15, 1977, p. 3.

29. Maj. Josef Dobosh, "Gotovnost' k podvigu" (Readiness for Victory"), Krasnaia Zvezda, October 10, 1970, p. 1.

30. Ibid.

31. Col. Jan Khmelik, "Predannost' delu sotsializma" ("Devotion to the Cause of Socialism"), Pravda, October 6, 1973, p. 5.

32. See N. V. Ogarkov, ed., Sovetskaia voennaia entsiklopediia (The Soviet Military Encyclopedia), vol. 8 (Moscow: Voenizdat, 1980), p. 628.

33. Zhilin and Jadziac, Bratstvo, p. 367.

34. Colonel L. Klievskii, "Dostiono vypolnaia zavety Kostiushkovetsev" ("Fulfilling in a Worthy Manner the Behest of the Followers of Koscziusko") Krasnaia Zvezda, October 12, 1975, p. 2.

35. Lt. Col. A. Pimenov, "Semi'ia splochennaia i krepkaia" ("A United and Strong Family"), Krasnaia

Zvezda, May 31, 1974, p. 3.

36. See Efimov, Boevoi soiuz, chapter on Bulgaria, pp. 51-53; chapter on Hungary, pp. 80-88; chapter on East Germany, pp. 115-123; chapter on Poland, pp. 150-158; chapter on Czechoslovakia, pp. 254-262.

37. Ibid.

38. See an article on this practice by Col. V. Nagornyk, Lt. Col. A. Pimenov, "Polki-pobratimy" ("Brother Regiments"), Krasnaia Zvezda, September 24, 1977, p. 3.

39. See the accounts of political work in Efimov, Boevoi soiuz, for Bulgaria, pp. 53-64; for Hungary, pp. 88-96; for East Germany, pp. 132-138; for Poland, pp. 156-160; for Czechoslovakia, pp. 259-263.

40. Krasnaia Zvezda, October 8, 1970, p. 1.

41. Panferov et.al., eds., Odesskii krasnoznamennyi, p. 280.

42. Col. A. A. Timorin, "Sotsialno-politicheskaia priroda i naznachenie sotsialisticheskhikh armii" ("The Socio-Political Nature and Function of Socialist Armed Forces") in S. A. Tiushkevich et.al., eds., Voina i Armiia (War and Armed Forces) (Moscow: Voenizdat, 1977), pp. 352-353.

43. Iakubovskii, Boevoe sudruzhestvo, p. 30.

44. See the texts cited in footnotes 36 and 39.

45. See the article on "The Marxist-Leninist Teaching on War and Armed Forces" in Sovetskaia voennaia entsiklopediia, vol. 5, p. 154: "This teaching instills in soldiers the belief in the invincibility of the armed forces of the countries of socialism and in their capacity to carry out their historical missions to the end...the teaching on war and the armed forces....is the reliable instrument of the Communist and workers' parties and the governments of the socialist countries of the socialist confederation..." See also Christopher D. Jones, "Just Wars and Limited Wars", World Politics, October 1975.

46. N. P. Prokop'ev, O voine i armii (On War and the Armed Forces) (Moscow: Voenizdat, 1968), pp. 91, 230-231.

47. Colonel B. Belyi in S. A. Tiushkevich et.al., eds., Marksizm-Leninizm o voine i armii (Marxism-Leninism on War and Armed Forces) (Moscow: Voenizdat, 1968), p. 257.

48. V. D. Sokolovskii, ed., Soviet Military Strategy (Santa Monica: Rand Corp., 1963), p. 125.

49. V. V. Sheliag, et.al., Military Psychology: A Soviet View (Moscow: Voenizdat, 1972) (USAF translation published by US Government Printing Office, no date).

50. N. A. Lomov, Problemy revoliutsii v voennom dele (Problems of the Revolution in Military Affairs), (Moscow: Voenizdat, 1965), p. 47.

51. Prokop'ev, *O voine i armii*, p. 64.
52. N. V. Pukhovskii, *O mire i voine (On Peace and War)* (Moscow: Mysl', 1965), p. 72.
53. Col. Ia. S. Dziuba in Tiushkevich, ed., *Marksizm-Leninizm* (1968), p. 139.
54. Sokolovskii, *Soviet Military Strategy*, p. 127.
55. A. A. Grechko, ed., *The Armed Forces of the Soviet State* (Moscow: Voenizdat, 1975) (US Air Force Translation, US Government Printing Office), pp. 110-112.
56. V. A. Muradian, *Boevoe bratstvo (Combat Brotherhood)* (Moscow: Voenizdat, 1978), pp. 74-74.
57. A. P. Artem'ev, *Bratskii boevoi soiuz narodov SSSR v Velikoi otechestvennoi voine (The Fraternal Combat Union of the Peoples of the USSR in the Great Fatherland War)* (Moscow: Mysl', 1975), pp. 44-46.
58. Muradian, *Boevoe bratstvo*, pp. 74-74.
59. Artem'ev, *Boevoi bratskii soiuz*, pp. 40-54; see also M. K. Kozybaev, "Narody Kazakhstan i Srednoi Azii" ("The Peoples of Kazakhstan and Central Asia") in A. A. Grechko et.al., eds., *Velikaia probeda sovetskogo naroda, 1941-1945 (The Great Victory of the Soviet People, 1941-1945)* (Moscow: Nauka, 1975).
60. Artem'ev, *Boevoi bratskii soiuz*, p. 54.
61. Ibid., p. 52.
62. Ibid., p. 68.
63. Muradian, *Boevoe bratstvo*, p. 74.
64. K. Tskitishvili, *Na frontakh Velikoi otechstvennoi (On the Fronts of the Great Fatherland War)* (Tibilisi: Izdatel'stvo Sabchota Sakartvelo, 1975), p. 283.
65. Artem'ev, *Boevoi bratskii soiuz*, pp. 71-74.
66. Muradian, *Boevoe bratstvo*, p. 75.
67. Ibid.
68. Ibid.
69. Ibid., p. 78.
70. Ibid.
71. Ibid., p. 79; see also Artem'ev, *Boevoi bratskii soiuz*, pp. 72-73.
72. Muradian, *Boevoe bratstvo*, pp. 79-80; 83-86 and Artem'ev, *Boevoi bratskii soiuz*, pp. 73, 85-87.
73. P. R. Sheverdalkin et.al., eds., *Vo glave zashchity sovetskoi rodiny (At the Head of the Defense of the Soviet Homeland)* (Moscow: Politizdat, 1975), p. 123. There were 11 Uzbek newspapers; 10 Kazakh; 8 Tatar; 6 Azerbaidjani; 5 Georgian; 4 Armenian; 2 Tadzhik; 1 Kirghiz; 1 Bashkir; 1 Turkmen.
74. Artem'ev, *Boevoi bratskii soiuz*, pp. 55-74, 75, 76.
75. Ibid., p. 76.
76. Ibid.,
77. Ibid., p. 54.

78, See Sbornik zakonov SSSR i ukazov Presidiuma Verhovnogo Soveta SSSR, 1938-68 (Collection of the Laws of the USSR and Decrees of the Presidium of the Supreme Soviet of the USSR, 1938-68) (Moscow: Izdatel'stvo sovetov trudiashchikhsia SSSR, 1968), vol. 1, p. 139.

79. Sovetskaia voennaia entsiklopediia, vol. 5, p. 553.

80. R. Rtishchev, "Leninskaia national'naia politika i stroitel'stvo Sovetskykh vooruzhennykh sil" (Leninist Nationality Policy and the Organization and Development of the Soviet Armed Forces") Voenno-istoricheskii zhurnal (The Military-Historical Journal) no. 6, 1974, p. 8.

81. Ibid.

82. See Robert L. Sharlet, The New Soviet-Constitution of 1977 (Brunswick, Ohio: King's Court Communications, 1978).

83. Grechko, Armed Forces of the Soviet Union, pp. 122-123.

84. Sovetskaia voennaia entsiklopediia, vol. 5, p. 553.

85. K. Pol'shin, "Tol'ko v russkom," ("Only in Russian") (Military Knowledge) Voennyie znaniia, no. 23, December 1980, p. 26.

86. See Iakubobskii, Boevoe sodruzhestvo, p. 151: "In the first years (of the WTO) joint exercises were conducted primarily on a tactical level, then beginning in 1961 they began to take place on the operational and strategic scale...." For accounts of two Soviet-East European exercises of the late 1950s see A. A. Epishev and Velko Panin, eds., Naveki vmeste (Forever Together) (Moscow: Voenizdat, 1969), p. 287 and M. I. Semiriaga et.al., eds., Zarozhdenie narodnykh armii stran-uchastnits Varshshavskogo dogovora (The Birth of the People's Armies of the Member States of the Warsaw Pact) (Moscow: Nauka, 1975), pp. 363-365.

87. S. A. Tiushkevich, et.al., eds., Sovetskia voouzhennye sily: istoriia stroitel'stva (The Soviet Armed Forces: A History of Their Organization and Development) (Moscow: Voenizdat, 1978), p. 438.

88. A. A. Grechko, "Patrioticheskii i internasional'nyi dolg Vooruzhennykh sil SSR" ("The Patriotic and Internationalist Duty of the Armed Forces of the USSR"), Krasnaia Zvezda, October 6, 1961, p. 3.

89. Lt. General I. S. Mednikov, "Druzhboi narodov sil'nyi" ("Strong Because of the Friendship of Peoples") in S. M. Isachenki, comp., Armiia bratstva narodov (Army of the Brotherhood of Peoples) (Moscow: Voenizdat, 1972, pp. 159-161).

90. Cited in Ivanovskii, Na boevom postu, p. 274.

Section II

Country Studies

4
Bulgaria

Ivan Volgyes

INTRODUCTION

At the outset of this volume, Daniel N. Nelson offered a view of reliability gauged in terms of mobilization potential. This chapter and my later contribution on Hungary are based upon a somewhat different understanding of the concept "reliability" and how it ought to be assessed. A short recapitulation of my perspective is, therefore, warranted before substantive analyses of Bulgaria or Hungary are begun.

I am in substantial agreement with Nelson that reliability connotes an expectation that certain behavior will be performed by another actor. But perhaps more than he, I place emphasis on the values upon which such expectations are based among elites and the values predominant in the armed forces which would form the bases for behavioral choices. It follows that I devote more attention to the socialization of professional military forces.

Because I see reliability of the armed forces as the behavioral consequence of values, I prefer the term "political reliability" to "military reliability." This is an important nuance in my two chapters which the reader should bear in mind.

Four categories of reliability, similar to the variable of scenario suggested by Nelson, guide my analysis. Internal-offensive reliability refers to the probability that significant segments of the professional officer corps will act against the party leadership by attempting a coup d'etat in the furtherance of military interests or try to oppose it by forcing such

---

Ivan Volgyes is Professor of Political Science, University of Nebraska, Lincoln. The introduction is from "The Concept of Reliability," Ivan Volgyes, The Political Reliability of the Warsaw Pact Armies: The Southern Tier Copyright 1982, Duke University Press, Durham, N.C., pp. 1-13. The remainder is reprinted from the same volume, pp. 24-40.

interests on an unwilling party leadership. As such, it is a sine qua non for other types of reliability, insofar as a military which is likely to overthrow its own government cannot be relied upon to support it during a crisis.

Internal-defensive reliability suggests the willingness of the armed forces to support the regime against an internal threat. Because the military is likely to be called upon only when the situation has deteriorated badly, only a large show of force by a highly-disciplined, well-armed military unit will disperse large angry crowds; in this context, the loyalty of a few officers will not suffice and the role of conscripts becomes paramount. Most instances of military action in post World War II Eastern Europe fall into this category.

External-defensive reliability refers to the probability that the armed forces will defend the state against external threats--from other East European Warsaw Pact members, from the USSR, or from NATO. In each case, the military's performance will depend on the attitudes of society towards the particular threat.

Finally, external-offensive reliability implies the willingness of the military to support the regime or offensive campaigns against other countries. Especially for the conscript, the perception that they are in battle on behalf of a repressive government or for Soviet interests rather than their own nation's destiny may lessen the intensity or initiative with which they fight. Again, one can imagine different scenarios for such offensive operations including an attack on another Warsaw Pact member, an attack on a neutral country, an attack on NATO or even an attack on the USSR.

Although these four different types of reliability require situational and country-specific analyses, I nevertheless believe (as does Nelson in his introductory chapter) that elements of reliability are common across nation-states. That is, regardless of circumstance, a number of main components of reliability should be considered. While the components considered in this chapter and in my contribution on Hungary overlap considerably with Nelson's analytical themes, I think both the Bulgarian and Hungarian cases necessitates consideration of the following elements of reliability:

1. The national environment; the evolution of the army and its officer corps
2. Size of the armed forces; percent of concripts
3. Equipment and training
4. Military doctrine regarding the mission of the forces
5. Mission as derived from nature of armed forces, equipment, and exercise participation

6. Soviet control, training, integration in Pact, nature of Soviet military forces, and mission in the country
7. The amount of party control, party secretary-political officer role, youth organization role, KGB liaison
8. The good life (both for army and security officers)
9. Fear of reprisals
10. The educational process and value socialization; values held; the gap between the values of officers and conscripts
11. Traditional enemy and nationalist claims where applicable
12. Situational elements; long and short range; conviction or doubt in victory; extreme force or compulsion for compliance to be used by the USSR

THE ARMY: ITS SIZE AND WEIGHT

The Bulgarian army would be, most likely, the only main front-line force with which NATO members have to contend in the southern flank as a unified national front and, consequently, the data regarding the Bulgarian People's Army should be carefully examined. The armed forces number 149,000, a number that has been relatively stable during the last decade (1975, 152,000).[1] The government has consistently tried to maintain its defense spending at 6 percent of the budget throughout the last five years; the other two states of the southern flank spend 3.8 percent (Hungary) and 4 percent (Romania) respectively on defense expenditures,[2] although Bulgaria's estimated GNP is the smallest of the three states ($34.8 billion in 1980).[3]

Moreover, the Bulgarian state has a population of only 8.9 million individuals compared with 10.7 million for Hungary and 22.2 million for Romania, and yet the Bulgarian army contains 1.67 percent of the total population of the country, while Hungary posts only 0.87 and Romania only 0.83 of the total population. These figures indicate the importance of the Bulgarian armed forces in the life of the state and tables 4.1 and 4.2 indicate the breakdown, organization, and equipment of the armed forces of the state.

The Bulgarian army utilizes universal military service with men being called up for service at age eighteen and serving for two years in the army and three in the navy. The percentage of conscripts for the armed forces is 63 percent of total strength, ranging from a low of 53 percent in the air force to 60 percent in the navy and 66 percent in the army.[4] Comparative data concerning conscription and length of service are indicated in Tables 4.1 and 4.2. These figures indicate the heavy reliance of the Bulgarian state on conscription and to some extent an unwillingness on the part of the population to pursue professional military careers; they also suggest the acceptance by the government of the need to rely largely on the smaller professional cadre.

We have no available information as to the exact nature of alert status of the Bulgarian army, with the exception that of the eight motorized rifle divisions within the three armies headquartered at Sofia, Plovdiv and Sliven, fully three divisions exist only in little more than cadre form.[5] Indirect evidence indicates that only two to three of the motorized rifle divisions normally are kept at category one strength (75 percent of established manning levels) and the rest exist with strength levels of roughly 50 percent.[6]

The Bulgarian army's equipment inventory is most up-to-date for the motorized rifle divisions, the five tank brigades, its one mountain battalion, and its two reconnaissance battalions, although only during 1980 have they been supplied with the new T-72s. Its air force, similarly, has received its first MiG-23s only during 1980 and there seems to be no great rush to improve these capabilities.

The training of the armed forces can be divided into two categories, that of the officer corps and that of the conscripts. The purpose of the leadership seems to be to offer primary training for the officers at home and the professional staff follows it up by training in the USSR. Consequently, it is not surprising that 33 percent of the cadres--in this context referring only to officers--"have studied in the USSR and another 14 percent had worked closely with Soviet army units."[7] Moreover, especially for young officers, friendly visits in the USSR for shorter or longer stays seem to be de rigeur.[8]

Aside from the various staff academies where training for professional cadres takes place, domestic training consistently includes a large dose of political education (with roughly 25 percent of the total training time being devoted to political socialization), and there is no indication that this percentage is considered excessive.[9] Needless to say, technical training for both enlisted men and young officers seems to be deficient in comparison to Soviet armed forces.

MILITARY DOCTRINE REGARDING MISSION

While there is no doubt that the Bulgarian army is capable of fulfilling a defensive role in any conflict that is regional in nature, the only statements regarding its external offensive role are those that echo Pact aims.[10] Although in all public statements it is stated

TABLE 4.1
Selected Data on Military Capabilities

Population & Forces	Bulgaria 1970	1980
Population	8,555,000	8,900,000
Military Service:		
Ground	2 years	2 years
Air Force	2 years	2 years
Navy	3 years	3 years
Total Regular Forces	148,000	149,000
Ground Forces:		
Motorized Divisions	8 divisions	8 divisions
Tank	5 brigades	5 brigades
Airborne	1 regiment	1 regiment
Air Force:	22,000	34,000
Combat Aircraft	252	210
Navy	9,000	10,000
Internal Security and Border Troops	15,000	27,000

Source: *Military Balance*, 1971-1981.

TABLE 4.2
Estimated Number of Reservists and Para-Military Forces

	Reservist (000)		Para-Military (000)	
	1970	1980	1970	1980
Bulgaria	n.a.	240.0	165.0	189.0
Hungary	n.a.	143.0	277.0[a]	75.0
Romania	n.a.	502.0	540.0	737.0

a. Includes 250,000 workers' guards, whose numbers had dropped to 60,000 by 1980.

Source: Military Balance, 1971-1981.

that an "offensive thrust would only take place as a response to imperialist aggression," the mission of the Bulgarian armed forces is characterized as both offensive and defensive[11] and according to Colonel Khachile Ambarian, the duty of the Bulgarian army is to unconditionally "support the Warsaw Pact in all its endeavors."[12] Looking at the mission some inferences can be derived from the following scraps of evidence: (a) previous participation where external offensive reliability was involved (e.g., Czechoslovakia); (b) participation in Warsaw Pact maneuvers; (c) nature of equipment and battle order.

The nature of the participation of the Bulgarian army in the occupation of Czechoslovakia leaves more questions unanswered than one cares to examine. It is clear that Bulgarian participation was minimal; a token force of probably one battalion is accepted by most analysts. But a battalion of what? No general mobilization order was in effect during August 1968 and given the fact that three of then nine motorized rifle divisions were in cadre form (category three), the likelihood is that the token force was not taken from them. The battalion landed at Ruzyne Airport on the night of 20 August 1968 and it was reported that a Bulgarian AN-12 type aircraft transported them there,[13] yet Bulgaria did not have AN-12s in 1968. One answer could possibly be that either the air force's one airborne paratroop regiment or portions thereof or the mountain battalion--normally kept at a fairly high state of readiness--may have been utilized. Yet there seems to be another explanation with a greater degree of credibility and certainty; it is most likely that the Bulgarian units utilized were state security units, either in their own or in Bulgarian army uniforms. Indirect confirmation of this theory also comes from Littel who quotes this heavy involvement from an eyewitness report within the Czechoslovak state security apparatus; the general evidence of those events tends to back his conclusions.[14] Although it was a token force--and presumably an elite fighting unit--it still seemed to have managed to blunder into shooting at Soviet forces on the night of August 20-21 in the incident on the Vltava.

Bulgarian participation in Warsaw Pact maneuvers also presents us with a less than coherent picture. The Bulgarian army participated in the least number of exercises of the Pact between 1961-79 (fourteen) as against the high of the German Democratic Republic (twenty-seven) and the next lowest, Hungary (with eighteen). What is even more significant, however, is that of these fourteen exercises, only one can be classified as a joint exercise with the full participation of the Bulgarian army; Bulgarian units had participated--presumably with Soviet, Czechoslovak, Polish, Hungarian, and East German troops--at the most in nine instances.[15]

In addition to the army exercises of 1962, 1964, 1967, and 1969,[16] Bulgaria participated in the naval exercises of 1972, in the rear services exercises of 1974, and in the antiaircraft exercises of 1970, 1973, and 1974.[17] Moreover, the most extensive report on the Bulgarian army participation occurs in the discussion concerning the 1967 Rhodope exercise involving the USSR, Romania, and Bulgaria. Here the emphasis was placed on the occupation of seashore areas for preparation of seaborne landings as well as for the "conduct of action in mountains and forest-regions."[18]

In summary, Bulgarian participation in joint exercises tended to involve mobile capabilities rather than the moving of large units; the semiannual army exercises of the Bulgarian units, however, tended to be more of the traditional army-oriented type.

In looking at the nature of the army as a whole and its special equipment one must note the enormous amount of defense expenditure Bulgaria has been undertaking compared to the more developed states discussed in other chapters. Its defense expenditures as a percent of all government spending are listed in Table 4.3.[19] It should be noted that the armed forces of Bulgaria are 50 percent larger than those of Hungary which has 20 percent more inhabitants than Bulgaria and only about 20 percent less than Romania with a population nearly three times the size of Bulgaria's population.

The size of the Bulgarian air force is the same as that of Romania, while Bulgaria possesses 33,000 more soldiers, mostly serving in the eight motorized rifle divisions. One must also note, however, that there are some 15,000 more professional soldiers than conscripts serving in the Bulgarian than in the Hungarian army.[20]

In assessing the Bulgarian army, it seems clear that the state follows the WTO policy of high mobility with emphasis on the operation of the motorized rifle divisions, relatively equally allocated among its three armies headquartered at Sofia, Plovdiv, and Sliven. They do not possess foot soldiers, that is infantry similar to the U.S. Ninth Division located at Ft. Lewis, Washington. And while the NATO forces in general are also mechanized units, any major thrust to the south or toward the east (e.g., Turkey and the Bosporus) must involve holding cities and here foot soldiers could conceivably be better used, especially if counteroffensive/defensive maneuvers are expected.

What is more interesting, however, are the five tank brigades; the ratio of motorized rifle divisions to tank brigades is higher than comparable ratios within NATO. With more than 1900 tanks and motorized armored carriers of various sorts, these units exceed in number and firepower both Hungary and even Romania as far as

TABLE 4.3
Defense Expenditures as Percent of Government Spending, 1975-80

	1975	1979	1980
Bulgaria	6.0	6.0	6.0
Hungary	3.5	3.6	3.8
Romania	3.7	3.5	4.0

Source: *Military Balance*, respective years.

the comparable units are concerned, and these five brigades possess more armor than comparable NATO divisions.

Precisely because of the aforesaid considerations, Bulgarian armies are likely to be used most effectively in armor-compatible theaters (e.g., the rolling hills and fields of northern Europe and the Middle East); they certainly would be bogged down in a long-range strike aimed at the south (e.g., Greece in a drive toward Athens). Because of the enormous diesel fuel needs of these heavily armored units, their deployment would cause major logistical problems and there are no indications that the Bulgarians are up to these tasks.

Short range targets of opportunity, however, are easily within the reach of equipment for these units and easily within the range of a mission that is compatible with this type of armed force. Such tasks, for example, as the thrust toward and the capturing of Thessalonika--not a very likely or worthwhile option--or even the thrust toward and capturing of Istanbul in a general scenario of all-out combat between the Warsaw Pact and NATO are conceivable and possibly could be accomplished. In fact, the Rhodope exercise and Bulgarian participation in the 1972 Black Sea exercise tended to concentrate on the establishment of bridgeheads and the seizure of seacoasts as a preparation for further deployment.[21] While this scenario could be suggested as farfetched if one views the forces of Bulgaria in its comparative size vis-a-vis Turkey alone, one should note that only under a general conflagration with Soviet troops heavily involved would such a scenario be plausible. As far as the size of the Turkish armed forces are concerned, one is also reminded of the relatively untested nature of and rather obsolete equipment possessed by the Turkish army contingent in European Turkey and the potential success of an all-out assault by the USSR on the lines of Turkish military communications and reinforcement to the region.

SOVIET CONTROL, TRAINING, INTEGRATION IN PACT, AND THE NATURE OF THE SOVIET MILITARY MISSION

On 5 September 1944, the USSR declared war on a Bulgaria that had already managed to extricate itself from its Axis alliance; by its very act of declaring war, the USSR very early attempted to force Communist domination of Bulgaria. Due as much to the "historic friendship" between Bulgaria and Russia as to the perceived loss of the war at the hand of the invading Soviet troops, when the Red Army crossed the Danube on 8 September 1944, it could accomplish its task with a certain degree of assurance that a Communist coup was already in the making. By 9 September 1944, the coup succeeded and the Soviet troops were suddenly transmogrified from invaders to liberators.[22] But the presence of Red Army troops in Bulgaria did not last long; they stayed there as an occupation contingent only three years and left Bulgaria on 14 December 1947.[23]

And yet, since the late 1960s persistent reports of a Soviet presence in Bulgaria have been published in the Western media as well as in Albanian sources. Thus, for example, in November 1968, Albanian radio repeatedly claimed "incontestible proof" of the presence of Soviet forces, which was quickly denied by Western correspondents.[24] These reports have continued to persist to date,[25] and have continued to be routinely denied by Bulgarian news agencies.[26] Moreover, the Soviet Union has not done all it could to dispel the rumors that tend to speak of anywhere from six thousand "military experts"[27] to two divisions of Russian soldiers stationed under the code name of Polarka on the Yugoslav-Bulgarian frontier.[28] In fact, in 1969 the New York Daily reported that Brezhnev himself had hinted that Soviet troops would be shifted to Bulgaria as a part of a new forward strategy employed by the USSR following the WTO operation to occupy Czechoslovakia.[29]

Consequently, the presence of Soviet troops, either in conjunction with various exercises or as part of the continuous joint training in new weapons' use, should not be totally disregarded. At the same time, the presence of large numbers of Soviet contingents above brigade size cannot be confirmed and the likelihood of such a presence is below 50 percent. That does not mean, however, that there are no Soviet advisers in various capacities on the operational and command levels of the army.

The Soviet presence is structured operationally by the Soviet military mission and by the local headquarters of the Warsaw Pact mission, directly subordinated to the staff of the Joint Command of the Warsaw Treaty Organization.[30] Working with Bulgarian military commanders are Soviet liaison officers at the staff level, and weapons and maintenance experts at major headquarters. Moreover, the presence of GRU and KGB agents at all levels can be confirmed from various indications, including the fact that the 1965 coup attempt by General Ivan Todorov-Gorunya, was first discovered by GRU/KGB personnel and then relayed for action to the security forces by the Soviet agents inside the country.[31]

In addition to these contact, regular interaction also takes place at the time of exercises held jointly with other Warsaw Pact forces, specifically with those of the USSR. Such exercises are viewed as assisting in "the raising of administration of the effectiveness of the troops... (and are undertaken for the purposes of) mutual exchanges of groups and representatives among units of the formations of various countries."[32] Epishev and Palin also mention specifically the importance of Soviet and Bulgarian officers jointly drafting documents and plans.[33]

Such contacts are, of course, facilitated by the similarity in the Bulgarian and Russian languages, and by the fact that a strikingly large percentage of the officers in field grade and above regularly spend time in the USSR. As far as one could identify it from the various sources located in the archives of Radio Free Europe, the sources located in the Schweizerische Osteuropa Institute and in the other documentation available to this author, officers promoted to field grade and above have to spend some time studying in the USSR. According to Bulgarian sources, fully 33 percent of the cadre--most of them officers, of course--of the army studied in the USSR and 14 percent of the officers had worked closely with Soviet units, either through training assignment or through major exercises.[34] Moreover, Bulgarian sources acknowledge that higher ranking officers and other cadres must spend two years in the military academies of the USSR.[35]

Mention, of course, must also be made that traditionally--at least as far as the pre-World War II traditions of the Bulgarian army were concerned--the army officer corps had been largely German trained, and consequently strongly pro-German. Such influences were dispatched easily in the army purge of the spring of 1946 as well as by the earlier restructuring of the new People's Army or People's Militia.[36] In a sense, therefore, pro-German influences in the officer corps did not survive as a result of having younger officers either promoted from the ranks or from within the party and its cadres. And as far as the relatively few survivors of the prewar army who could conceivably have been socialized into other than pro-Russian molds, these individuals by 1980 must have reached their sixties and have long lost any aspirations for or concentrations of power in their hands. It is thus safe to assume that the cadre of higher officers in Bulgaria are the products of socialist Bulgaria; more than thirty-five years of pro-Russian ethos and close Soviet ties have done a major job in establishing values that are directly opposed to those officers from whom they have taken away the mantle of defending the nation.

AMOUNT OF PARTY CONTROL

From its very inception, the Bulgarian People's Army has been under the party's Main Administrative Apparat: the Chief of the Defense Ministry's Main Political Directorate reports not only to the Minister of Defense, but also, simultaneously, to the central committee (CC) secretariat's administrative department head. This extremely close tie between the party and the army, of course, is not unusual for Communist politics; in the case of Bulgaria, however, the ties are probably the strongest among the party and army leadership and, aside from the 1965 coup, no tension has been manifest in their relationship.[37]

The political direction of party work among the army is carried out through several sets of overlapping functions. Based upon the general lines of party policy given through the CC secretariat's administrative department, political work is planned through the Main Political Directorate, which is responsible for the staffing and operational control over the "ideological-party-army cadres in charge of the daily work."[38] The function of the political officer at the division and subdivision levels is a complex function: he integrates the work of the low-ranking political officers, the local party, and Komsomol officers in accordance with the directives handed down from army headquarters and from the sources of power in Sofia.[39]

Although at the military academy one can specialize in becoming a political officer, political officers, depending on their ranks, are generally selected for full-time and permanent political work after receiving their first major promotion usually to the rank of First Lieutenant or Captain (four to seven years of line service).[40] This researcher's thorough examination of the ranks of political officers, which were reported in the Bulgarian press, revealed only fourteen people identified as political officers below the rank of First Lieutenant, out of some 270 people in the research universe. Promotions in this line of work are decided not upon military performance but on political success, although military consideration undoubtedly also must play a part. Political officers can rise, probably, somewhat more rapidly in rank than regular officers; on the other hand, failure to attain a politically successful career within the political part of the army apparat, inevitably brings with it a failure to reach higher ranks within the military because technical competence of the political officers must suffer as a result of one's concentration on political work.

The functions of the political officers are complex and wide ranging: the overseeing of political educational work within the party cells of the local units, the overseeing of the general educational, political socialization function for the units as a whole, the integration of the work of the Komsomol secretaries, and of course full cooperation with the Security Police and its representatives, as well as with the army's own military and intelligence department.[41] Regarding the political content of the socialization process within the army education process, depending on the nature of the units, between 10-25 percent of conscript training and 25-50 percent of the follow-up training for professional soldiers are spent dealing with political subjects. Naturally, the amount of time spent on political subjects has varied over time and the intensity of the message-relay function has also been very uneven. Nor has the amount of time been merely related to the external policy considerations, e.g., the Czechoslovakian intervention; in fact, quite understandably, the 1965 coup attempt has prompted an excessive concern with political education.[42]

The functions of the political officers are somewhat alleviated by the fact that approximately 80-83 percent of the officers are members of the party.[43] In fact, these figures are not distributed evenly because one of the requirements for working as an officer with the security apparat and the border troops is party membership, while the same requirement does not exist for line officers, especially of lower rank, within the regular army.[44] Nonetheless, there are no figures available to indicate the exact percentage of party-member officers for each branch of the armed services, although it seems highly unlikely that some branches--aside from the security police units--deliberately require less party-control or less loyalty to the party than others.

The party secretary's and the political officer's role and work is made more complex by the fact that 98 percent of the conscripts belong to the Komsomol (Dimitrovskii Kommunisticheski Mladezhskii Soiuz).[45] Mobilizing these young people through the Komsomol has more complex than originally imagined by the authorities; even though they seem to respond well to such movements as "Becoming an Excellent Unit!" and "Let Us Destroy the Target with the First Shot!", political activity qua political activity seems to leave the vast majority cold.[46] Nonetheless, there can be no doubt that the control over the Komsomol by the party--and hence the political control over the vast majority of the conscripts--seems to be generally effective.

A great deal of literature is devoted to the 1965 putsch led by General Ivan Todorov-Gorunya.[47] Yet, there remain several unanswered questions, all involving party-army relations. In the Bulgarian army, notwithstanding constant protestations to the contrary, putschism has had a long, historical tradition; both before and during the interwar period, the army has been deeply involved in politics and often has acted as an arbiter of political crises. Nor has the 1965 coup attempt been the only such attempt in post war Communist Bulgaria; the 1958-61 rumblings--of the affectionately labeled "coffee-house rebellion"--were led by Yonko Panov, Dobri Terpeshev, and Nikola Kufardzhiev, all of whom have had major connection with army officers and themselves were former partisans.[48] Whereas that rebellion perhaps had as its aim reducing the influence of the party and its main political administration over the army,[49] the 1965 "putsch" was somewhat more complex. Though the regime labeled it as pro-Chinese and attempted to deride its importance, and while many in the West felt that it was simply directed at securing greater independence for Bulgaria to maneuver in foreign and domestic policy, the coup attempt was probably guided by diverse motives among which the diminishing of the strongly pro-Soviet policy of Zhivkov and the strong subordination of the army to the party did play an important, if somewhat unquantifiable role.

Little, of course, is known of the exact nature of the integration of the army with the security forces, with the various departments of army intelligence, and of the infiltration of the army by the GRU and KGB. Persistent reports and rumors of Soviet involvement in discovering or at least assisting in uncovering the plot, seem to indicate some measure of influence, but we do not know whether units of the GRU or the KGB were implicated. The fact that the Ministry of Interior had been reorganized immediately after the coup and that "between April, 1965 and June 1968, eleven out of twenty-eight district first party secretaries in Bulgaria were removed from their posts" only adds to the suspicion that the conspiracy indeed had been very wide ranging.[50]

One interesting source of concern for party and control seems to come precisely from the changing character of the army. As modernization proceeds to create a need for more technically competent soldiers, party control could be--or at least could be feared to be--loosened. It was against such tendencies that Zhivkov himself demanded at the Bulgarian Communist Party's XIth Congress that the party as a whole "must engage in a fight against the technocratists" and continue to emphasize the political direction of the army.[51]

Overall, party control has, since 1965, been reinstated and reinvigorated.[52] The steadily rising party membership and the ever smaller number of officers with partisan background who could challenge the party, the ever closer integration of the top level officers with their Soviet counterparts, the fact that all officers reaching field grade and above since 1966 must study for at least two years in the USSR, and that "all professional officers must learn Russian"[53]--all seem to indicate that the party has at the present time a reliable instrument in the form of the army at its hand and that the army is not likely to engage in the 1980s in domestic offensive action against it.[54]

EVOLUTION OF THE OFFICER CORPS, THE GOOD LIFE, FEAR OF LOSING

It is necessary to recall briefly that the Bulgarian People's Army was established to replace an army whose loyalty to the German cause was unquestionable. The officer corps to a great extent was trained by the Germans, the upper echelon was firmly affiliated with the German military elite, and, in spite of Russia's historic role in the establishment and independence of Bulgaria in 1878, it was allied with the German cause and participated in the Second World War against the Soviet alliance. Even so, it never declared war on the Soviet Union but the USSR, indeed, did declare war on Bulgaria on 5 September 1944--shortly after Romania fell so speedily and so unconditionally on 23 August 1944. Three days after the declaration of war on Bulgaria, the Red Army crossed the Danube into Bulgaria and on the following night the democratic government of Konstantin Muraviev fell and a Communist putsch propelled a Communist-led coalition to power. Under the guise of operating as the local representative of the Allied Control Commission, the overlord of Bulgaria, General S.S. Biriuzov, used his position to thoroughly purge the Bulgarian army and political life of Fascist and pro-German influences.[55] According to the new regime, during the first year in power 2,138 people were sentenced to serve life imprisonment and another 1,940 people were convicted to serve long sentences in jail.[56]

Many of those army officers with pro-German leaning were sent to prison and many other officers with similar leanings, who had been fortunate to be in less exposed or less prominent positions, were also damaged by their expulsion from the army. The new People's Army, created in the wake of the forced dissolution of the old army, drew its officers from two main sources: the partisans and the Muscovites. The partisan movement in Bulgaria during the war was not as strong as it was in Yugoslavia although at least one group of partisans did cooperate very closely with Tito's partisans. It was, nonetheless, certainly stronger than the ones in Romania or in Hungary and hence it had a relatively distinguished record on which consideration for political and army positions was based and expected.[57] Individuals like Slavcho Trunski, Ivan Todorov-Gorunya, Terpeshev, Panov, Kufardzhiev, and others who later participated in two attempted conspiracies or coups, as well as Todor Zhivkov and the current Minister of Defense, Dobri Dzhurov, have all been in the partisan movement.

The second group of officers to whom the reference Muscovites can be justly made had all spent many years in exile in the USSR and, in fact, many of them had served in the Red Army. Such individuals as Georgii Damianov, Ivan Mihailov, and Petur Panchevski began to occupy positions of importance more than commensurate with their general officer ranks. Backed by Biriuzov and the Red Army, just as Vulko Chervenkov gathered power in his hands, the Muscovites in the military also began to squeeze out the partisans. Between 1948 and 1956, they ruled the Bulgarian army totally with one purpose in mind: to make Bulgaria an integral part of Moscow's policy both in the political and in the military sphere.

With the process of destalinization in Eastern Europe, the Muscovites in the military were also losing ground and by the early 1960s nearly all major Muscovites were shifted out of the army; many were pensioned off and others slowly had to yield their jobs to the returning former partisans or to new Communist cadres. The returning partisan cadre, however, that replaced the Muscovites was significantly different from the partisans of 1944, even though they had had partisan background: the sixteen odd years away from the army and influence changed their composition and outlook. Although less subservient than the Muscovites and--as the coup of 1965 and the conspiracy of 1961 amply illustrate--perhaps having had some inclination for greater independence than the leadership was willing to sue for, the newly returning partisans nonetheless all had a keen awareness of Bulgaria's historic ties to Russia and of the necessity for close integration with the USSR. Most of them studied in Moscow at one time or another, and while one could argue that such studies do not necessarily result in having a positive outlook toward the USSR and, indeed, in some cases result in a feeling of contempt for the latter, these men were still cognizant of the necessity of supporting Soviet views while hoping to reconcile them with the Bulgarian raison d'etat. General Dobri Dzhurov, the Minister of Defense, and General Diko Dikov, the Minister of Interior, both of them former partisans, were prototypes of the new partisans who continue to dominate the upper echelon of the military to date and whose legacy of fighting against the Germans during World War II and fighting <u>for</u> Bulgarian independence remains a significant part of the political socialization process of the army and the regime.

The new army after 1947, of course, had to draw on a large number of recruits in order to become the professional force; both noncommissioned officers and officers with proven political loyalty were needed desperately. As elsewhere in Eastern Europe, the largest percentage of new officers and noncommissioned officers had come from the ranks of the peasant class; much as was the case with American blacks in the 1950s and 1960s, this road was the easiest path to achieve upward mobility. The pay in the army was considerably higher than the amount of income that could be earned on the collectivized lands. The class of workers from whose ranks 30 percent of the new officers came, on the other hand, also possessed relatively few convertible skills: most were either semiskilled or unskilled laborers when they joined the new army between 1945 and 1948. And as for the minuscule members of the intelligentsia in the ranks of the new army, all that can be said of them is that they probably joined not because of upward mobility, but for the best, because of a sense of mission and for the majority because of crass opportunism, as they viewed their future in Bulgaria.

As time went by, the rapid transformation of the army slowed down and service schools and academies were established: the Georgi Dimitrov Army Artillery College in 1948, the Georgi Benkovski Air Force College in 1946, the General Blagoi Ivanov and Vasil Levski Army Colleges in 1966 and 1959, the Military Medicine Institute in 1960 and the Nikola Yokov Vaptsarov Marine Officers' College, the General Staff College, and the Georgi Sava Rakovski Military Academy.[58] The educational level of the officers had improved relatively constantly. While data show that between 1969 and 1974 only 40 percent of the officers had completed their higher education (e.g., received a diploma either from a civil or a military college),[59] this figure climbs to 55 percent by 1978,[60] and to 67 percent by 1980.[61]

The professional élan and outlook, the professional improvement, also brought with them greater rewards and greater social prestige. Army officers' pay scales are higher than civilian pay scales by 50-70 percent when all the benefits are taken into consideration, and even without these benefits the pay scales are probably at least 25 percent higher than corresponding positions of responsibility in civilian life. Although exact pay scales are not available to this researcher from public sources, a Bulgarian colonel quoted his salary in 1978 at 800 leva per month; his civilian counterpart, for example, a department head in a ministry, earn only 500 leva monthly.

Moreover, there are sizable fringe benefits that are additional remunerations. The retirement age, of course, is lower than in civilian life; as in all military services of the Pact, men are eligible for full retirement after age fifty, with at least twenty-five years of active service. Housing is either provided in the bachelor officers' quarters of nomcommissioned officers' quarters on or near the base, or the army provides priority housing to officers allocated by the local soviets; officers with families usually can move into an apartment, shortly after being assigned to a new unit. Bachelor officers, if they wish to get married, usually can count on receiving an apartment within half a year of requesting one. In Bulgaria where the average waiting period for an apartment for a young family with two children is four to six years--under optimal circumstances!--such a benefit is not negligible.

Health care and recreation are free and considerably better than services available to the population as a whole. The army's own hospitals are staffed by army physicians whose salaries are higher than those of physicians in civilian life, and who, reasonably, are therefore somewhat more conscientious than their civilian counterparts. Moreover, such recreation units as the army's resorts are situated in the best tourist spots of Bulgaria and are a great attraction for officers with families, although some factories are beginning to provide similar facilities for their employees.

A clothing allotment covering increased expenses for boots, uniforms, and other items, is also given; although exact figures are not known, generally such an allotment is equal to a monthly salary of a major, or around 600 leva. Together with frequent trips to the USSR and other socialist states on exchange visits and officially organized tours, the clothing allotment also acts as an inducement for some to join.[62]

The aforesaid benefits are, of course, also inducements for people to join the specialized units of the Ministry of the Interior on a full-time military assignment basis. Some 12,000 men serve in the security police and the border guards number 15,000; both of these organizations are regarded as elite units.[63] There are no conscripts serving in these services and the benefits extended to the men in these units exceed--by the best estimates available--by 50 percent those which are extended to members of the armed services. Some tension, according to private sources available to the researcher, has indeed come to the surface regarding the inequality of benefits in 1974, although the resolution of the conflict is not known.

All of the information in this section is provided in order to suggest that the Bulgarian army officer and his security police counterpart have a major stake in the system. The benefits, the pride, the mission, as well as the integration with other units of the Warsaw Pact, specifically with Soviet units, render him a reliable instrument, specifically in external-defensive or internal-defensive situations. His personal stake in the survival of the system, therefore, is significant. The component of fear, should the party lose power is equally great. Should communism lose in Bulgaria in the wake of the defeat of the USSR, he realizes that the only way he could escape punishment similar to the punishment meted out at the end of World War II to officers with pro-German leanings, is for the army to be on the victorious side; in internal-offensive action the army has the poorest record in the Southern Tier and because of the Balkan mentality this vulnerability could be further exposed. More about this subject will be said, however, in this chapter's concluding section.

THE EDUCATIONAL PROCESS AND VALUE SOCIALIZATION

Hitherto the picture presented seems to suggest little or no vulnerabilities so far as the army as a whole is concerned. The fact remains, however, that the gap between the well-paid and well-treated officer corps and the conscripts seems to be enormous. Most of the young people, regardless of their participation in DOSO (the Voluntary Association for Cooperation in Defense of the Fatherland in Bulgaria)[64] and of the paramilitary training received in the schools, continue to manifest problems for the political officers and others engaged in the political learning process.[65] No year passes without a mention of the "inadequacy of ideological work" among the conscripts.[66]

What seems to be the greatest problem among the conscripts? Not surprisingly it is the "bourgeois tendencies" that manifest themselves in low morale, desertion, disciplinary problems, alcoholism, suicide, etc.[67] It should not be surprising that the party should warn the army to be vigilant against the presence of such activities as lying, thievery, hooliganism, "alcoholism, nicotinism and rough talk (e.g., cursing)."[68] And while there are undoubtedly positive signs of accomplishments,[69] there is no doubt that the regime itself realizes the problems it is facing in socializing the conscripts.

The major themes of socialization in the army center around patriotic ideals tying history to the current policies of the regime. Thus Christo Botev, the Bulgarian poet (1847-67) is held up as the ideal, for he regarded "patriotism as the greatest human value."[70] Patriotism is also instilled through showing how Bulgarian scholars and the common people kept the culture and the language of the state alive even under 500 years of Turkish rule, and through glorifying 1,300 years of Bulgarian history, Cyrill and Methodius, the Trnovo School, Ivailo's peasant rebellion, as well as such revolutionaries as Karavelov, Vasil Levski, Christo Botev, and Georgi Rakovski. Dimitur Blagoev and Georgi Dimitrov tie the historical process to the current regime and its bases of legitimacy and, curiously, rather frequent mention is made of the Bulgarian army abiding by its international and patriotic obligations in providing support for the "defense of socialism" in East Germany in 1953, Hungary in 1956, and Czechoslovakia in 1968.[71]

Obviously, the Bulgarian authorities are aiming at the youth with a shotgun approach out of which the socialized are expected to pick and choose, as long as the values picked--from among all the positive values--assist in instilling a beneficial, socialist outlook. Irredentist claims toward traditional targets serve as a rallying cry, though the issue of Macedonia is about the only one used by the party as a rallying point.

The question of Macedonia at the southern and western boundaries of the state and located in Greece and Yugoslavia refer to territories that were not incorporated into Bulgaria in 1878. Although Bulgaria suffered losses in both the Balkan Wars and in World War I, she did not recover these territories--including that of South Dobrudja ceded to Romania in 1913--until 1941 when, as a part of her military obligations, she was given control of Macedonia and part of Thrace as well as South Dobrudja. The Bulgarian army, moreover, after the putsch of 1944 had undertaken military activity against the Germans on Yugoslav soil and continued to fight the Germans along with the Red Army through the Austrian and Hungarian campaigns. But, regardless of all that, Macedonia was once again returned to Greece and Yugoslavia; moreover, because of Tito's designs for a Balkan federation the Yugoslavs made inroads even into Bulgarian Macedonia. Only after Tito's break with Moscow were the Bulgarians able to seal the frontier and begin to combat the Macedonian nationalist tendencies that looked somewhat happily toward a greater Macedonian nation as part of an autonomous region in a Balkan federation.[72]

The Macedonian problem continued to dominate the vituperation aimed against Tito and has only lessened during the years of the Thaw. By 1968, however, one saw its re-emergence in the pamphlet <u>The Macedonian Problem: Historico-Political Aspects</u>,[73] that became the standard anti-Yugoslav tract and castigated Yugoslavia as the source of all ills concerning the Macedonian problem. As so frequently in Eastern Europe, history had to play its role in justifying policy and if history did not fit, well, one could always change that. The controversy has continued to date and the issue of Macedonia remains unsettled; it is in fact the only issue where Yugoslavia acts as a traditional enemy and where the socialization process keeps making clear references to blatantly irredentist issues.

It is difficult to gauge what effects thest irredentist issues have among the Bulgarian population as a whole; the people of the Pirin district--the center of

Bulgarian Macedonia--seem to receive every inducement necessary to remain loyal to the Bulgarian state and, in fact, they live nearly as well--though not nearly so freely as far as the freedom of movement is concerned--as their Yugoslav conationalists. The Macedonian issue seems to be a point of vulnerability, but its exploitation would probably tend to increase the nationalistic reliability of the greater parts of the Bulgarian army.

SUMMARY

As stated above, the greatest doubt seems to exist concerning the internal-offensive reliability of the Bulgarian army and the most positive behavior of the army can be expected to occur in a situation when the army would face an aggressive external enemy--specifically Yugoslavia with whom the Macedonian problem remains a burning issue--on its borders. As far as the internal-defensive reliability is concerned, the army is clearly willing to come to the assistance of the party and keep it in power as long as the Communist system exists and as long as the army officers receive the extraordinarily high benefits that accrue to them.

There can be little doubt about the external defensive reliability of the Bulgarian army. Against Yugoslav or Western attacking forces the army is likely to perform exceedingly well and even against a Soviet attack on Bulgaria should such an unlikely situation ever occur, it is unlikely to accept Soviet occupation without a fight. In an external offensive war against NATO the Bulgarian army would more than probably fight either along or integrated with Soviet forces, and their joint mission seems to be the securing of the Bosporus or European Turkey. Initial victories, quick thrusts and quick advances would enhance considerably the chance of external-offensive reliability and would fill the Bulgarian army with pride at their attainment. Should, however, Turkey be able to hold and NATO reinforcements threaten the historic territories of Bulgaria, should such vulnerabilities as Bulgarian Macedonia being attached to a potentially autonomous united Macedonia within Yugoslavia, then the reliability of the opportunistic armed forces would rapidly decrease and the leadership, all their protestations to the contrary, could conceivably engage in an act against the government and, indirectly, in an act of desertion from their Warsaw Pact allies. In such a scenario, the threat to the survival and independence of the nation would reiterate and reinforce the army's traditional Balkan role as a balancer of national policies; a putsch against a national leadership that is presumed to be losing national independence and Bulgarian territories in the East or West would be in the historical character of the army.

NOTES

1. The Military Balance, 1980-1981, pp. 15, 96.
2. Ibid., p. 96.
3. Ibid.
4. Ibid., p. 15.
5. Ibid., p. 110.
6. Trevor N. Dupuy et.al., The Almanac of World Military Power (New York and London: J.L. Bowker, 1974), p. 138.
7. Rabotnichesko delo, 21 September 1975.
8. Dobri Dzhurov et.al., A pårtpolitikai munka a bolgår hadseregben (Budapest: Zrinyi, 1978), p. 103.
9. The various Bulgarian military academies are described in Kratka B'lgarska Entsiklopediia, vols. 2-4 (Sofia: 1964-1967), pp. 158, 445, 57; K.M. Smorgorzewski "Die Militarische Starke der Satellitenstaaten," Neue Zürcher Zeitung, 12 August 1951; Christo Toshkov, "Voenno-technicheskoto obuchenie v stolichnite chilista," Narodna prosveta, 1 (1970) and B'lgraski voin, 9 (1972).
10. A.A. Epishev and Velko Palin, eds., Naveki vmeste (Moscow: Voennizdat, 1969), p. 19.
11. Krasnaia zvezda, 28 September 1969 and Lt. Gen. Mikhail Tsonev in Narodna armiia, 10 October and 11 October 1979.
12. Pirinsko delo, 28 August 1979.
13. Robert Littel, ed., The Czech Black Book (New York: Praeger, 1969), pp. 5, 6.
14. Ibid., pp. 64-69.
15. If one examines the 1961-71 period, however, Bulgaria participated in five, Romania in six, and Hungary in eleven exercises as compared to fourteen, fifteen, eighteen exercises for Czechoslovakia, Poland, and the GDR respectively. Csizmås, Der Warschauer Pakt, pp. 68-71. Figures updated to include the 1980 exercise in East Germany for composite figures see Christopher Jones, "The Warsaw Pact: Military Exercises and Military Interventions," Armed Forces and Society 5 (Fall 1980), 12, 16-17; Dale R. Herspring, "The Warsaw Pact at 25," Problems of Communism (September-October 1980), 7 and Csizmås, Der Warschauer Pakt, pp. 68-71.
16. Csizmås, Der Warschauer Pakt, pp. 68-71.
17. Jones, "The Warsaw Pact," pp. 16-17.
18. Epishev and Palin, Naveki vmeste, p. 190.
19. The Military Balance, 1980-1981, p. 96.
20. Ibid., p. 15.
21. Epishev and Palin, Naveki vmeste, p. 290.
22. Istoricheski pregled, 5 (1964) and 3 (1968) contains good accounts of the coup and the Soviet liberation; cf. Stoian Tanev, Internatsionalnata misiia na

sovetskata armiia v B'lgariia 1944-1947 (Sofia: D'rzhavno voenno izdatelstvo, 1970).

23. The Soviet forces' departure was succinctly analyzed in La Croix (Paris), 30 September 1971.

24. Chicago Tribune, 16 November 1968 and Christian Science Monitor, 2 June 1969.

25. Morgenplast, 23 July 1970; UPI 28 July 1974; Financial Times, 12 September 1974; Kurier, 20 September 1974; Zeri i Popullit, 4 January 1977; Frankfurter Allgemeine Zeitung, 18 April 1977; Reuters, 25 February 1979; Le Figaro (Magazine), 12 January 1980; Rheinischer Merkur (Christ und Welt), 8 February 1980; Frankfurter Allgemeine Zeitung, 8 February 1980 for instance.

26. E.g., Rabotnichesko delo, 10 May 1977; 2 March 1979; 18 January 1980; BTA February 26, 1979; Svoboden naro, 37-38 (1979).

27. Rheinischer Merkur (Christ und Welt), 8 February 1980.

28. Le Figaro (Magazine), 12 January 1980.

29. New York Daily, 16 April 1969.

30. V. Kulikov, in Voenno-Istoricheskii zhurnal, 5 (1980), 25-26.

31. For documentation on the coup see RFE files Bulgaria, 1965.

32. Epishev and Palin, Naveki vmeste, p. 290.

33. Ibid.

34. Rabotnichesko delo, 21 January 1975.

35. Narodna mladezh, 17 March 1968.

36. For accounts dealing with these events see Otechestvenata voina na B'lgariia 1944-1945, 3 vols. (Sofia: 1961-66); Ivan Kirchev, Otechestvenata voina, 1944-1945 (Sofia: 1945) and General Shteriu Atanasov, Kratka istoriia na otechestvenata voina (Sofia: 1958). Cf. the excellent English and German language accounts of Nissan Oren, Revolution Administered (Baltimore and London: The Johns Hopkins University Press, 1973) and Wolf Oschlies, "Die Bulgarische Volksarmee," in Peter Gosztony, ed., Zur Gerschichte der europaischen Volksarmeen (Bonn-Bad Godesberg: Hohwacht, 1977), pp. 227-70.

37. On the party-army connection see B'lgarskata kommunisticheska partiia--sozdatel i rukovoditel na b'lgarskata narodna armiia (Sofia: Durzhavno voennizdat, 1959).

38. Narodna armiia, 3 October 1979.

39. On the command and subcommand levels see Defense Minister Dobri Dzhurov's articles in Narodna armiia, 21 September 1974 and 23 September 1979.

40. Oschlies, "Die Bulgarische Volksarmee," p, 258.

41. Partiinaia zhizn', 2 (1974), p. 27.

42. A Verbitskii, "Bolgarskaia narodnaia armiia," Kommunist vooruzhennykh syl, 11 (1970), pp. 75-76.

43. Rabotnichesko delo, 21 September 1975 and Narodna armiia 21 September 1974 cite 83 percent; Narodna armiia, 16 August 1969 cites 82 percent; while Narodna armiia, 21 March 1975 quotes "around 80 percent" as the appropriate figures for party membership among the officers.

44. It is instructive to note that the Ministry of Interior, both in its Police Academy and at the Georgii Dimitrov Special College located in Strelcha, require around twenty hours of special political instruction weekly and that political instruction seems to be on a par with technical training at the special college that is a unique institution in Eastern Europe. Pogled, 18 June 1973; Otechestven front, 19 October 1971 and Narodna armiia, 16 January 1975.

45. Dzhurov, A pártpolitikai munka, p. 106.

46. Armeiskii pregled, 12 (1976).

47. The plot is best discussed in J.F. Brown, Bulgaria Under Communist Rule (New York: Praeger, 1970), pp. 173-81, although immense documentation is available in the Bulgarian files of Radio Free Europe on this murky affair.

48. Ibid., chapters 6 and 7, pp. 96-172, and passim.

49. See General Vlichko Georgiev's discussion in Narodna armiia, 15 October 1960.

50. Brown, Bulgaria, p. 187.

51. Quoted in an article by Lt. Gen. Tsaniu Bakalov in Armeiskii pregled, 5 (1976) citing Zhivkov's speech at the Bulgarian Communist Party's XIth Congress, in April of the same year.

52. Armeiskii pregled, 11 (1976).

53. P. Ileiv, "V edinstve nasha sila," Voennyi vestnik, 9 (1972).

54. Narodna mladezh, 17 March 1968.

55. For Biriuzov's own account see S.S. Biriuzov, Sovetskii soldat na Balkanakh (Moscow: 1963). Cf. Oschlies, Die Bulgarische Volksarmee, pp. 238-40.

56. Robert L. Wolff, The Balkans in Our Time (New York, 1967), p. 293.

57. According to Oren, at the peak of partisan activity probably around 12,000 partisans operated in Bulgaria. Oren, Revolution Administered, p. 82.

58. Oschlies, Die Bulgarische Volksarmee, pp. 259-60 gives a thorough account of the military academies and colleges as they existed in the 1960s.

59. Narodna armiia, 16 August 1969; Otechestven front, 8 July 1961; Rabotnicheski delo, 20 September 1974; Narodna armiia, 21 September 1974.

60. Zemedelsko zname, 22 September 1978.

61. Literaturen front, 15 September 1980.

62. Dzhurov, A pártpolitikai munka, p. 103.

63. The Military Balance, 1980-1981, p. 15.

64. Doborvolna Organizatsiia za Sadeistvie na Otbranata (Voluntary Association for Cooperation in the Defense of the Fatherland) was established in 1951. The best account of DODO is in Wolf Oschlies, "Paramilitarische Organisationen und vormilitärische Ausbildung in Bulgarien," in Peter Gosztony, ed., Paramilitärische Organisationen in Sowjetblock (Bonn-Bad Godesberg: Hohwacht, 1977), pp. 36-40.

65. I. Rechev, in Utichelsko delo, 22 February 1972.

66. See, for example, Col. Gen. Mircho Asenov, in Literaturen front, 15 September 1980 as well as Narodna armiaa, 10 January and 11 March 1977; 7 and 13 February, 4, 5, and 26 March, 23 April, 13 July, 23 and 31 August, and 15 December 1976 to sample a few of the issues dealing with this problem.

67. See Narodna armiia, 15 August 1961 and 25 June 1964; Narodna mladezh, 16 June and 29 September 1965; Rabotnichesko delo, 31 August 1965; Narodna armiia, 11, 19 January and 3 June 1966, 27 November 1968, 15 December 1970, 6 October 1972, and 28 February 1974 and Svoboden narod, 27-28 (1978) for selected issues dealing with the problem.

68. Dzhurov, A pårtpolitikai munka, p. 115.

69. Armeiski pregled, 5 (1976).

70. Dzhurov, A pårtpolitikai munka, p. 78.

71. Ibid., p. 98.

72. For an interesting account see Dimitar Mitrev, Pirinska Makedoniia vo borba za natsionalno osvoboduvanie (Skopje: 1950).

73. Published by the Bulgarian Academy of Sciences in 1968.

5
Warsaw Pact Reliability: The Czechoslovak People's Army (CLA)

Condoleezza Rice

Czechoslovakia is one of the most developed states of Eastern Europe and the Czechoslovak People's Army, one of the Soviet Bloc's most advanced military establishments. Czechoslovakia forms, with Poland and the German Democratic Republic, the so-called "iron triangle of socialist defense" along the northern tier of East-Central Europe. These front-line states have historically been the center of attention in efforts to train and modernize the forces of the Warsaw Pact. In any calculation of the military capability of the Eastern Bloc, therefore, the Czechoslovak People's Army, Czechoslovak territory and the five Soviet divisions stationed there, must be given due consideration.

While it is relatively simple to obtain measures of military capability based, for instance, on the sophistication and age of equipment, or the extent of alliance standardization, measures of the reliability of these forces--their actual value in conflict--have proved elusive. Though a number of scholars agree that there is reason to question reliability of the East European forces, it has been difficult to pinpoint the grounds on which to judge. The search for indicators of reliability continues, but there is, in the absence of confict, no way to test the potency of the explanations explored. Alternative tests which might increase our understanding, like the Soviet's own calculations of the reliability of their allies, are also not available. In most cases, therefore, we must be content with the construction of indicators based on our best guesses of what ought to constitute reliable armed forces.

Careful study of the Czechoslovak case provides the kind of data, however, which can be useful in exploring

Condoleezza Rice received her Ph.D. from the Graduate School of International Studies at the University of Denver and is now an Assistant Professor of Political Science at Stanford University.

the validity of the indicators of reliability which we develop. The Czechoslovak People's Army was by most accounts the best military in Eastern Europe until about 1966. Operating on the basis of a well-educated population, a sophisticated industrial base, and a heritage relatively free of anti-communism, the armed forces were exemplary of the new socialist armed forces, red and expert. By 1969, this very good military was a broken establishment, ineffective and unsophisticated. The radical change was, of course, caused by the crisis of 1968 which devastated the armed forces. Czechoslovakia, therefore, presents a rare opportunity to see a before and after picture of an East European communist army and to examine the factors which led to the demise of the CLA. Moreover, it is possible in this case to see what the signs of trouble are in the eyes of the Soviet Union and to suggest indicators which show that the Soviets consider an armed force unreliable. Finally, it is possible to examine whether the CLA has "made it back" in the 1980s and to comment on the reliability of the CLA a decade and a half after the cataclysmic events of 1968.

THE CLA IN HISTORICAL PERSPECTIVE

Like all of the East European armies, the Czechoslovak People's Army had an inauspicious beginning. The predecessor to the CLA, the New Czechoslovak Army, watched from the barracks as the Communist Party overthrew the coalition government of Edvard Benes in 1948. The army was called upon neither by Benes or Klement Gottwald, the Communist Party chief, apparently having been dismissed as unreliable by both elements of the coalition government.

The period following the revolution was difficult for the new armed forces. There were a series of attempts to create armed forces more to the Party's liking depending upon recruitment of "workers blood," often at the expense of expertise. The officer corps was purged of most of its expertise, as first pro-Western officers and then a number of communists, were sacrificed in the blood purges which engulfed Czechoslovakia from 1949-1953.

But the fortunes of the CLA began to turn in the early 1950s. Blessed with an educated population (even among the workers) and massive resources, only a few years passed before the CLA was budding into an expert and increasingly "red" force. Both party membership among the officer corps and the level of education and training rose rapidly through the 1950s. By the middle of the 1950s, the emphasis on the professionalization of the armed forces could be seen in several decisions of the Party, downgrading political education, removing police units from the Party cells within the armed forces and, in 1956, selecting the first professional military man to be Minister of Defense. Czechoslovakia also began to draw upon its own substantial armament production capability and by 1954, was virtually self-reliant in small arms. A good deal of equipment was also produced for export to other members of the socialist bloc. When the Warsaw Pact formed in 1955, Czechoslovakia was ready to be an important member.

The golden years for the CLA continued throughout the 1950s. As the CLA grew in sophistication, it found a very important role in the conduct of "socialist" foreign policy. When the Soviet Union, under Khruschev, began to look beyond the Eurasian continent and into the developing Third World for the extension of Soviet power, Czechoslovakia was there to lend a hand. Acting first as the "middle man" in the arms deal with Egypt in 1955, Czechoslovakia went on to become the Soviet Union's junior ally in the Third World. The U.S.S.R. became an important arms supplier, and the CLA participated actively in tutoring Third World military officers. The depth of Czechoslovak involvement can be seen in the fact that at one time there were more Egyptian military men training in Prague than in Moscow. It was also Czech pilots who flew the Soviet-built MiGs out of trouble for the Egyptian air force during the Israeli attack on the Suez Canal.[1]

Czechoslovakia also weathered the storm of 1956. Unlike Poland and Hungary, the de-Stalinization which sent the Soviet bloc reeling left Prague relatively untouched. Stable economically and politically at home and pro-Soviet in orientation, Czechoslovakia and the CLA were perfect allies in the socialist extension of power into the Third World.

The 1960s brought further enhancement of the military capability of Czechoslovakia. As a part of the reorientation of Soviet defense, Khrushchev sought to draw more heavily upon the benefits of the alliance. In 1961, the first efforts to standardize training, including the first joint exercises were taken. Additionally, the equipment of the western-most Warsaw Pact states, long-neglected, was upgraded. Deliveries of newer generation tanks and artillery and aircraft laid the groundwork for a forward based socialist defense. Nuclear delivery vehicles had also been placed in Eastern Europe in 1957, but in the 1960s when new installations were planned, Khrushchev began exploring ways to better use East European territory.[2]

Within these developments which upgraded CLA capabilities, however, were the seeds of conflict with the U.S.S.R. While Czechoslovakia appeared to the outside world a paragon of pro-Sovietism and an efficient military ally, strains were discernible upon the indestructible unity of the Warsaw Pact.

The initial disagreements were about the possible stationing of Soviet troops on Czechoslovak soil. Ever since the revolution, Soviet leaders had attempted to gain permission to station troops on Czechoslovak soil, and leaders from Gottwald to Novotny resisted. The issue was raised anew when Khruschev reputedly approached Novotny and the CLA leadership about stationing warheads near the nuclear delivery vehicles on Czechoslovak soil. A protracted negotiation took place in which the Czechs first suggested that the warheads be placed in the custody of the CLA, but eventually relented and agreed to the stationing of a few specialists to guard the installations.[3] After Khruschev's fall, however, Soviet leadership again initiated "requests" for regular troops, resorting at one time in 1966 to downgrading the performance of Czechoslovak troops and then demanding the permission to station troops on the basis that the CLA was unfit to guard the important western border.[4]

The "troop incidents" were exacerbated by a nascent doctrinal debate within the intelligentsia of the CLA on the question of the value of the Soviet Union's nuclear guarantee. Distressed by what they perceived as a move away from the tenet of nuclear spasm theory or that one nuclear exchange would lead to all-out war, the Czechoslovaks began to wonder whether they were being asked to be sacrificial lambs in a limited conflict in Europe. Reports that casualties along the southwestern front were expected to be 60-70 percent did little to allay their fears.[5] The Czechoslovaks apparently were further distressed by the embarrassment of the Soviet Union in the Cuban missile crisis, undoubtedly wondering about the value of a nuclear guarantee which had been so thoroughly exposed. For these reasons, the Czechoslovak military intelligentsia began to explore by 1966, "alternative" defense postures, suggesting that geographic and cultural factors should determine Czechoslovakia's military posture, not simply class unity with the Warsaw Pact.[6]

This was blasphemy from the point of view of the Kremlin. But the harder that Moscow pushed the military leaders in Prague, the harder the intelligentsia pushed back. Coupled with an intensifying discussion of the creation of a new, national Czechoslovak military-political system, the doctrinal deviation placed the military intelligentsia very close to the edge of Moscow's tolerance. The Soviets, for their part, were disturbed not only by the "renegade" military groups, but by the inability or unwillingness of the central military and political leadership to do anything about the deviation. The split in the Warsaw Pact was growing quite wide long before the crisis of 1968 overtook events in Czechoslovakia. When the freer political atmosphere did emerge, the issues were already on the table for the Czechoslovak military leadership. Although the leadership continually protested that alliance loyalty was not an issue, the Soviets were getting quite a different message in viewing events in Prague. Pro-Soviet officers were being isolated, the "foreign" military-political system was under fire, and theorists like Ladislav Kopecky warned that the Warsaw Pact was a voluntary military alliance in which national circumstances had to be accommodated. "If they are not," he warned, "the possibilities for serious disintegration are great."[7] Finally, in the latter stages of the crisis, the worst fears of the Soviet Union came true. In a nationally televised press conference Vaclav Prchlik, the highest ranking military-political official in Czechoslovakia, criticized the Warsaw Pact openly and in only thinly veiled comments threatened to protect the sovereignty of the Czechoslovak state.[8] The doubts which the Soviets had about the ability of the leadership to deal with renegade elements turned to fear that the renegades were actually in command in Prague. Most importantly, the CLA, a source of trouble for over five years, was now clearly out of Moscow's control.

When the Soviet leadership decided to reverse the reform movement in Czechoslovakia, the army was understandably a high priority. Actually, the Soviets won some concessions on the composition of the CLA even before the invasion. Vaclav Prchlik was removed from his post, though he remained influential in Czechoslovak politics, the moderately radical chief of the MPA Egypt Pepic was "promoted" out of his position, and pro-Soviet general Samuel Kodaj was placed in charge of the Eastern district. The Czechoslovak People's Army did not, of course, resist the invasion, but remained, by Presidential order, confined to the barracks. Whether the Soviets thought the potential for resistance great or not cannot be answered. They did take some precautionary measures, ordering the secret police, for example, to drain aircraft of fuel. For the most part, however, it seems that the Soviets relied upon the leadership of the armed forces to keep the CLA under control. The degree of complicity in the invasion for some of the leading military figures is also difficult to estimate. Rather than actually acquiescing in the decision, indications are that the best the Soviets could get was a promise to neutralize the armed forces. Martin Dzur, the Minister of Defense, has claimed that he did not know of the invasion, but having been notified, moved to notify and protect the political leadership and then to prevent bloodshed. The vote of confi-

change it substantially even today."[12] The communist leadership of Czechoslovakia had attempted to come to terms with its own population and the communist armed forces tried to become a part of the Czechoslovak nation. So abrupt an end to a widely accepted movement for reform produced monumental dislocation in the CLA and shook fundamentally the confidence of the Soviet Union and the Warsaw Pact in the reliability of the armed forces of Czechoslovakia.

MEASURING RELIABILITY

In examining the reliability of the CLA, it is helpful to use the Soviet schema for measuring the readiness of a nation for war. The calculation of "correlation of forces" is a very useful tool in categorizing the various concerns that might be voiced about the reliability of the CLA. Moreover, the schema provides a basis of comparison of the pre-1968, post-1968 and the CLA of the 1980s. The correlation of forces includes economic, military, and what the Soviets term moral-political factors.

Economic measures should include examination of the economic health of the country in order to assess the ability of the state to support defense. It is also important, however, to examine the will or commitment of the state to defense. Defense spending data are useful in addressing this concern. While it is acknowledged that budgetary figures are difficult to verify, several western economists have provided valuable analyses of raw defense data in which the real costs of Warsaw Pact military establishments have been gauged. Moreover, since defense spending varies considerably among Pact members, these data also suggest relative commitment. In the case of Czechoslovakia, the activity of the defense industries is also important, providing a potentially viable second base of production for the Warsaw Pact in any war effort.

Assessment of the military factors can also be based upon available data. Reliable forces must be of sufficient size and composition to play a role in defense, and they must be efficient, well-trained and expert. The age and sophistication of weaponry should be considered as well. Finally, the integration of East European forces for use with their Soviet counterparts is critical.

Most important, but unfortunately most difficult to measure, are those factors that can be classified as moral-political. In the case of the East European forces, these factors are arguably more important than economic strength or military capability. Complicating the measurement problem is the two dimensional nature of

dence which the liberals in the government gave him in electing him to help negotiate with the Soviets may lend support to his argument. He did, moreover, defend reforms for some time, and seems to have tried to rescue the more beneficial changes for the CLA even after the invasion.

Whatever the case, the Soviets and Conservatives within the Party turned, after 1969 and the isolation of the liberal politicians, to the "normalization" of the armed forces. In a series of purges, the officer corps and the military intelligentsia were devastated. Over 11,000 officers were purged between 1969 and 1975;[9] the Klement Gottwald Military-Political Academy, the home of the radical intelligentsia, was closed, and a number of officers were farmed out to reserve duty. Demoralization took its toll as well and by 1971, 57.9 percent of the junior officer corps had failed to reenlist.[10] Recruitment of young men for the officer corps became a constant problem for the leadership as the CLA suffered the ill effects of their failure to defend Czechoslovakia's sovereignty. The senior leadership, for the most part, survived, but they were made to go through a series of humiliating experiences, including political instruction by Soviet and East German political officers in special seminars on Leninism and the Military. The newly purged and now conservative Main Political Administration of the CLA undertook the task of criticizing professional officers for their lapses during 1968, and every officer of general rank was made to rewrite his autobiography, answering prominently for his activities during the period of 1968. These measures taken, the MPA Chief was able in 1975 to say that the consolidation was complete.[11] Interestingly, this was four years after the Minister of Defense Martin Dzur made a similar claim, only to be shouted down by the MPA leadership.

This paper attempts to examine the reliability and efficiency of the CLA following these cataclysmic events. But before turning to this task, it is well to provide a word of caution. The impact of the 1968 crisis on the CLA is partially lost when reduced to a series of measures of size, composition and efficiency. The breadth and scope of the involvement in the reform and the difficulty of recovery is more obvious in the desperate attempts of the leadership to hang on to the vestiges of reform even after the invasion. As the conservative Minister of Defense Martin Dzur stated, "In the past, our army suffered in such sensitive sphere as moral-political unity... and there was a wave of overwhelmingly justifiable criticism and we succeeded in working out an Action Programme which was received in the army with approval. We do not need to

"moral-political" factors in Eastern Europe. It is not enough that these armies support the regime; the CLA overwhelmingly was in support of the Dubcek regime in 1968. They must also support the Soviet Union. One lesson of 1968 is that the Soviets fear considerably militaries which have skirted out of Moscow's control, even if they are good communists and support the domestic regime. The degree of military-political unity is thus exceedingly difficult to judge.

Indications of support for the regime like membership of officers in the Party and participation of officers in the political bodies are useful in addressing the relationship of the officer corps to the regime. Likewise, certain "negative measures" like difficulty in recruiting and retention are indications of demoralization and low moral-political unity. But these measures do not tap key dimensions such as attitudes toward the Soviet Union, Soviet control or the expectation that the military will support Soviet goals. Here, then, it might be better to use "negative measures" which suggest that the military is not considered reliable or morally correct. The existence of viable counterweights to the military--militia or strong police forces--might indicate suspicion on the part of the regime, while the presence and activity of foreign troops would provide evidence of Soviet concern with reliability.

Further, the linkages between the leadership of the armed forces and the rank and file are important and can be examined in terms of the degree to which the values of the military are consonant with those of the society. This was clearly the problem for the CLA in the pre-1968 period. Paradoxically, however, the harmony of societal values and military values might actually be a strike against the armed forces in the eyes of the Soviets. As 1968 clearly showed, the movement of the Czech armed forces toward a more "national identification" was considered a threat to the unity of the socialist bloc. This is one other consequence of the dual identity of the Warsaw Pact forces.

One final "measure" of the degree to which the armed forces are judged to be reliable from the "moral-political" side might be the activity of those forces in support of Soviet foreign policy goals. Presumably, a reliable force would be active in the socialist extension of power to the Third World. This would at least be evidence of confluence of interests between the Soviet Union and an allied armed force. In the final analysis, however, the relationship between the Soviet Union, the communist parties of Eastern Europe and these militaries is so complex that it is very difficult to judge "moral-political unity."

ECONOMIC FACTORS

Czechoslovakia possesses one of Eastern Europe's most advanced economies. During the 1950s, the economic profile of Czechoslovakia was made to conform to that of the U.S.S.R. and heavy industry flourished. In fact, for most of the 1950s, the economy of the new Czechoslovak Socialist Republic was strong and exemplary of socialist economic progress. It came, then, as something of a shock to the leadership when, in 1962, Czechoslovakia became the first socialist state to record growth at less than 1 percent. The impact of this news was so great that a commission of inquiry was formed to evaluate Czechoslovakia's economic problems. Over the next years, several commissions analyzed the situation and in 1966, the most influential of them under Ota Sik, recommended a major overhaul and the inclusion of a market mechanism to help rationalize economic planning.

The economic crisis and the discussion of a cure became major catalysts for the Prague Spring of 1968, though few of the reforms were ever initiated. Since the invasion of 1968, economic reform has been a sensitive issue in Czechoslovakia and the economy has suffered from many of problems characteristic of centrally planned economies; stagnation, low productivity and inefficiency. Czechoslovakia's GNP consistently trails that of East Germany and Poland, though per capita income continues to rank high. The 1981 Czechoslovak GNP was estimated to be about 110 billion dollars.[13] The economic profile still favors heavy industry, although poverty in raw materials, especially in petroleum, makes the Czech economy very dependent on shrinking Soviet oil deliveries. It is not surprising that Czechoslovakia is the key country in an effort to find alternative fuel sources, particularly through the use of nuclear power. The most important industries are machine tools, electronics and a few chemicals, all important basic industries for defense.

Defense spending pressures have always been high for Czechoslovakia. Prior to 1968, Czechoslovakia's commitment to defense generally exceeded 4 percent of GNP. In 1966, 3.9 percent of the GNP was devoted to defense, a higher percentage than any other East European state that year.[14] The figure is also significant because it was in 1965 that the Warsaw Pact's Political Consultative Committee first met to consider targets for defense spending. Reportedly, Antonin Novotny, then President and General Party Secretary of Czechoslovakia, was enthusiastic about Czechoslovakia's ability to meet her alliance commitments.[15] Unfortunately for Novotny, the tide was beginning to turn in

Czechoslovakia and, returning home, he met considerable opposition from within his own Party. Over the next two years, there was an open and candid debate about defense. Czechoslovakia's outlays for defense began to decline and have never recovered their pre-1968 levels. The impact of the crisis is, therefore, quite clear. The early commitment to defense spending, reversed by sour economic news and internal opposition, reached a low in 1974 of 3 percent and has hovered around 3 percent since that time. Moreover, Czechoslovakia's unwillingness to spend more is often defended. In 1980, Oldrich Behounek warned that new defense demands would be inappropriate by the alliance and should not be made.[16]

Defense spending data alone, however, understate Czechoslovakia's economic contribution to the Warsaw Pact. The heavy industrial profile of Czechoslovakia supports an active arms industry which should be considered an asset to the military strength of the alliance. Czechoslovakia's arms producing heritage was strong before communism and, with the exception of a brief period immediately following the war, has remained so. This is also one area in which the crisis of 1968 left few scars. Though several lines of weapons licensing were discontinued in 1970, Czechoslovakia continues to produce a wide array of small arms, armored vehicles, light aircraft and artillery pieces both by indigenous design and under license. The Czech arms industries are distinguished from other producer in Eastern Europe both by sophistication and quantity, and Czechoslovakia is still the only non-Soviet producer to develop and market a "standard weapon of the Warsaw Pact," the L-39 AERO. Czechoslovakia's active arms industries are used not only to supply the Warsaw Pact, but to support the efforts of the socialist bloc in the Third World.

The activity of arms industries in Czechoslovakia has not been without costs for the Warsaw Pact. First, there are some indications that Czechoslovakia is not always attentive to standardization of features, particularly in small arms.[17] Second, there is an ulterior motive for the sale of arms in the Third World and it is not always consistent with the political aims of the Warsaw Pact. Czechoslovak officials have, on occasion, been very candid about the profitability of arms sales. In more than one instance, Czechoslovak arms have been found in the hire of South African forces, and other less than desirable quarters.[18] Although the Czechs argue that it is impossible to track and control the flow of arms to guerilla fighters, there is at least one instance in which Czechoslovakia was actually guilty of contracting for the sale of arms to Pinochet in Chile.[19] The Soviets were furious and not only vetoed the deal, but ordered the government of Czechoslovakia to rein in its arms merchant "Ominpol" and place it under strict surveillance of the Ministry of Interior.[20]

Therefore, the economic contribution of Czechoslovakia to the Warsaw Pact is somewhat mixed. The degree to which defense spending can be held, even at its present level, depends on the health of the economy. The picture is bleak, given heavy reliance on imported oil from shrinking Soviet reserves, aging plants, continued inefficiency and little hard currency in reserve. Czechoslovakia may also be one East European state which will be hurt, perhaps unfairly, by Poland's credit rating. While Czechoslovakia has borrowed very little and has an excellent record of repayment, Western fears of another Poland are bound to hurt the ability of the leadership to obtain credit. The arms industry, however, is one place where Czechoslovakia can continue to make an important economic contribution to the Warsaw Pact. It has not gone unnoticed that arms can be sold for hard currency. In 1980, 8 percent of all Czechoslovak exports were in arms.[21] Given the appetite of the Third World for military goods and Czechoslovakia's ability to produce very good weapons indeed, armaments may represent one of the few growth industries in Eastern Europe.

MILITARY FACTORS

The impact of the 1968 crisis was immediate upon the military reliability of the Czechoslovak armed forces. The clearest indication was in the declining size of the Czech forces. As a result of purge and resignation in the officer corps, personnel in some branches was 10-30 percent below normal. In the air force, it was admitted to be 20 percent below normal, making it impossible in the first years of 1970 to even hold proper training and evaluation exercises.[22] The overall strength of the Czechoslovak armed forces also began to decline after 1968, dropping from a high of 240,000 in 1966 to a low of 168,000 in 1969.[23]

Another measure of the effect of 1968 on military reliability was the changed status of the Czech armed forces relative to Poland and The German Democratic Republic. Christopher Jones has noted that on measures of mobility--including the frequency of maneuvers outside the home territory--Czechoslovakia's forces now score lower than the other forces of the Northern Tier.[24] From descriptions of several exercises, the Czechoslovaks have been used repeatedly in a garrison-like fashion, backed up and fronted by other national forces.

Additionally, throughout the 1970s, there was reason to doubt the military efficiency of the Czechoslovak forces as well as their reliability. Not only were numbers below the pre-1968 levels, but Czech forces fell behind the Poles and East Germans in age and sophistication of equipment. No longer were deliveries of advanced Soviet equipment made to Czechoslovakia first or concurrently with similar deliveries to Poland and East Germany. This lag in modernization of the forces continued until late in 1979.[25] At least one further problem was the low level of expertise in the officer corps, perhaps leaving Czechoslovakia without sufficiently trained personnel to man new equipment. In an effort to replenish the decimated officer ranks, young men were rushed through officer candidate school in half the normal time.[26] Further, in order to bring "loyal" officers into the corps, men of working class backgrounds were allowed to go to officer candidate school even though they might lack requisite education. Finally, so much time was devoted to political education and training in an effort to "normalize" the CLA, that military commanders were chastized for complaining about the balance between military training and political work.

On most measures of military efficiency and reliability, the CLA seems to have made a comeback in the 1980s. Long-delayed deliveries of new equipment are now being made and weapons like the T-72 are entering service with the Czechoslovak armed forces. The total force strength of the Czech forces has also stabilized, but well below the 1968 levels. The forces now number just under 200,000 (195,000 in 1982).[27] Leaner Czechoslovak forces, better equipped and trained, may represent the trend for at least the near future. Czechoslovakia's smaller troop strength is also sealed by one important demographic factor. Czechoslovakia's birth rate has been declining modestly, but steadily, over the last several years. It has, however, stabilized at over 1.1 percent since a period of drastic decline between 1966 and 1969.[28]

Nevertheless, Czechoslovakia's contribution to the Warsaw Pact's military strength has increased in one sense as a result of the events of 1968. There are now five Soviet divisions stationed on Czechoslovak territory. Consequently, the Soviets now enjoy another forward base with the Central Group of Forces. Moreover, the smaller Czechoslovak forces increasingly have been used as a supplement to the Soviet forces. Christopher Jones has suggested that the augmentation of the Central Group of Forces by Czechoslovak units is an important alternative way of viewing the contribution of these forces.[29] This means that the Czechoslovaks now exercise with the Central Group of Forces in ways that blur distinctions between them and call into question the integrity of discreet national groupings. The "Druzhba Exercises" of 1982 are exemplary of this phenomenon. Functional units, for example, artillery units of the Soviet, Czech and Hungarian forces, exercised together. This was also true of bridgelaying units of the same forces which did not exercise at all with their national armies. Finally, there was extensive training of chemical troops of the Soviet Union and Czechoslovakia during Druzhba 1979 in isolation from the maneuvers in which the national armed forces participated.[30]

The military reliability of the Czechoslovak armed forces is therefore mixed. It would appear that the smaller Czech forces are being equipped and modernized more rapidly than during the 1970s. This suggests that the CLA's recovery is well underway. With the problems which now face the armed forces of Poland, the Czechoslovak forces may well be pressed to assume more responsibility for the "iron triangle" along the Northern Tier in any case. Nevertheless, the modernization of the equipment of the CLA barely disguises what continues to be Czechoslovakia's most pressing military concern; the "moral-political" unity of the military forces and continuing difficulty in the recruitment and maintenance of qualified personnel.

THE PROBLEM OF MORAL-POLITICAL UNITY

Czechoslovakia's leadership has long experienced difficulty in attracting the best young men to the officer's profession. This was due, in part, to the anti-military attitude of the Czechoslovak population and the resultant dismal level of prestige of officership in Czechoslovakia. The crisis of 1968, which led to massive purges and resignations in the officer corps, exacerbated this problem. Although actual figures on personnel problems are not available, the continuing concern with recruitment and retention is evident in the total preoccupation of the military press with enticing young men to choose the profession. The Czechs go to great lengths to show that enrollment in military schools and military training are superior because, according to one journal, "While it is not difficult to obtain information about civilian schools, finding out about academic conditions in the military ones is a bit more complicated. Young men sometimes have incomplete, often distorted ideas about military schools, the military occupation and the like."[31] Because competition with the civilian sector for qualified technical students is so stiff, attractive allowances are given to young men who will enter military education and service. In the case of young men enrolled in military high schools or colleges, families are given an allowance and a deduction from "income taxes."[32] The effort extends, then, from the recruitment of boys 13 or 14 years old to military high schools, to the recruitment of those already in the work force, ages 18-25, into officer candidate schools. There is still a heavy premium on working class background, however, with special arrangements for workers who left high school concurrently to obtain both military training and a high school diploma.

The "moral-political" problems reflected in these recruitment difficulties are also evident in relations between the Party and the professional officer corps. Party membership which hovered around 85 percent in 1967 dropped drastically as a result of recall of party cards after 1968. Recent numbers for party membership are unavailable, but in 1975, only 72 percent of the officer corps belonged to the Party.[33]

Since 1968, the Party leadership has made political unity a very high priority. The Main Political Administration is extraordinarily active in arranging "political education seminars" on a regular basis to guard against the "lapses of moral-political unity evidenced in the political crisis." This is quite a change from the role of the Main Political Administration under Vaclav Prchlik, when respect for a certain distance of the Party from military affairs was held. Moreover, in order to assure that the political indoctrination is not only in Marxism-Leninism, but in pro-Sovietism, there are frequent contacts between political workers of the CLA and of the Soviet Central Group of Forces. The contacts are not limited to political workers either. As one Czech spokesman explained,

> Our commanders and soldiers as well as working people from industrial plants, agricultural cooperatives, schools and institutiosn are deepening close ties and internationalist friendship with the Central Group of Soviet forces. They are thus expressing their gratitude for the freedom the Soviet Army brought us in the days of May of 1945 and for the assistance extended to socialist Czechoslovakia in foiling the plans of counterrevolutionary forces in August 1968.[34]

These efforts are apparently not always well received. Members of the political administration have lamented the less than enthusiastic attitude of the officer corps toward political work which borders on "apoliticism."[35]

Another indication of the continuing crisis of

confidence of the CLA is the relative weight of other power instruments in the society. After 1971, the border guard and the military counterintelligence service were transferred to the Interior Ministry and efforts were begun to strengthen and enhance the role of the militia. The growth of the militia, which numbered 70,000 in 1967, to about 140,000 is remarkable in itself.[36] Moreover, the militia, equipped with light arms in the past, began using much heavier weapons, including tanks and armored personnel carriers after 1970. Specialized units, among them anti-tank and air defense units, and large territorial units were developed after 1971. It should be noted that this historical counterweight to the CLA was praised by the Soviet Union during the 1968 crisis, when the CLA was considered unreliable and its leadership vacillating and untrustworthy. While it is not clear how this massive buildup has been accomplished, it is indicative of concern about the CLA's problem of consolidation.

One final indication of concern about the effectiveness and reliability of the CLA is in the activity of Czechoslovakia abroad. In an era when the Soviet Union is involved heavily in the Third World, Czechoslovakia's military personnel are conspicuously absent. The pervasive activity of Czechoslovakia in the 1960s has been usurped and surpassed by East Germany. Arms sales and military assistance continued into the 1970s, but after 1970, the emphasis has shifted decidedly toward transfer. There are a number of possible explanations, but the most compelling is that the CLA was unfit for extra-national duty following the upheaval of 1968. One other explanation is also potent, however. Having become deeply involved in Egypt, the Czechs were burned badly by the break in Egyptian-Soviet relations after 1973. The Czechoslovaks had invested a great deal of money, expertise and political capital in Egypt and were beginning to reap the benefits when the break between Moscow and Cairo occurred. It is unlikely that Czechoslovakia, having once devoted resources to the "socialist extension of power" which were lost in a turn of events outside Prague's control, is now more circumspect about involvement.

There is some recent evidence, however, that Czechoslovakia's military activity is picking up, including the dispatch of military advisors. Although Prague denied the presence of advisors in Angola in 1976, there have been reports of advisors in Yemen and Afghanistan since 1980. There is at least one report of Czechoslovak soldiers fighting along side Bulgarian, East German, Cuban and Vietnamese forces in Afghanistan, but the veracity of these reports is unclear.[37]

In sum, the dislocation of 1968 has not passed,

though the efforts of the Party to strengthen the "moral-political unity" of the CLA continue. This was a tremendous price of the 1968 invasion, shaking to its very foundation the effectiveness and reliability of the best forces of Eastern Europe. Problems of officer retention and troop morale continued to be important indications that the big question mark in Czechoslovakia is neither economic nor military, but the elusive moral-political factor, which is undoubtedly difficult for both the Party and the Soviet Union to assess.

CONCLUSION

Czechoslovakia provides an interesting look at a force that was once considered both red and expert. Several indications of the Czechoslovaks fall from that lofty position are apparent. The forces are now smaller and buttressed by foreign troops and a number of more politically reliable counterweights like the militia. What Czechoslovakia has lost in the direct military contribution of her forces both to European missions and abroad has been largely replaced by an emphasis upon her contribution through the production and sale of arms. Although the forces finally have been modernized in recent years, the most pressing problems continue to be morale and prestige of the forces, reflected in the desperation of the leadership to attract young men to officership. Residual concerns with political loyalty, manifested in still lower standards for those of "workers' blood" and intensive political training, call into question the efficiency of the forces.

The most difficult piece of the puzzle is still the degree to which the CLA has managed to regain some semblance of unity in the post-invasion period. The armed forces were considered foreign and anachronistic within the society prior to the crisis of 1968. In an effort to strengthen the position of the CLA in the society and to create a bond between Czechoslovak tradition and the armed forces, important reforms were taken by the leadership. Unfortunately, these reforms set the CLA and the Soviet Union on a collision course and when the CLA failed to defend the popular reformation of the society it was plunged deeper into a crisis of legitimacy. Whether it will recover in the foreseeable future is difficult to predict. The kind of dislocation from which the CLA still suffers must be of concern to the leadership of Czechoslovakia and the Soviet Union for some time to come.

In the final analysis, the reliability of the Czechoslovak forces will be dependent upon what they are asked to do. The key question of scenario of conflict must be kept in mind (as discussed in the Nelson chapter in this volume). But in any conflict, an overarching concern must be the malaise which continues to haunt the CLA. It is still the only military to undergo revitalization and rejuvenation in pursuit of a place in the Czechoslovak nation only to have the reform aborted by its ally to the East. And it is still the only force which must confront a legacy of doubt about its ability and willingness to defend the sovereignty of Czechoslovakia and the popular reforms which the Communist Party and people had begun.

NOTES

1. Stockholm Peace Research Institute, The Arms Trade With the Third World (Stockholm: SIPRI, 1979), p. 522.

2. For a full discussion of these developments, see Thomas Wolfe, Soviet Power in Europe 1945-1970, pp. 148-150 (Baltimore: Johns Hopkins Univ. Press, 1971).

3. Josef Hodic, "Military Political Views Prevalent in the Czechoslovak Army: 1948-1968" From Research Project: The Experience of Prague's Spring, directed by Zdenek Mlynar (Vienna, 1979), p. 19.

4. Ibid., p. 19.

5. A. Ross Johnson, et.al., East European Military Establishments: The Northern Tier (Santa Monica: Rand, 1980), p. 160.

6. Lidova Armada, July 2, 1968.

7. "Unity in Military Alliance," Mezinarodni Politika, no. 9, September 1967.

8. The report of the press conference can be found in Obrana Lidu, July 16, 1968.

9. A. Ross Johnson, et.al., East European Military Establishments, p. 161.

10. Ibid., p. 161.

11. Lidova Armada, no. 16, 1975.

12. "Speech at the All-Army Conference," Martin Dzur, Obrana Lidu, October 1968.

13. The Military Balance (London: IISS, 1982), p. 14.

14. Thad P. Alton, et.al., "East European Defense Expenditures 1965-1978," East European Economic Assessment (Part II) submitted to the Joint Economic Committee of the Congreee of the U.S. (Washington, 1981), p. 179.

15. Michael Kaser, Comecon (London: Oxford University Press, 1967), p. 19.

16. "RVHP and the defense capability of socialist states," Historie a Vojenstvi, no. 1, 1980.

17. See the discussion of standardization by John Erickson, "Military Management and Modernization Within the Warsaw Pact," in Robert Clawson and Lawrence Kaplan, eds., The Warsaw Pact: Political Purpose and Military Means (Willimington: Scholarly Resources, 1982), p. 222.
18. UPI, "The Guns of Brno" November 5, 1979.
19. Ibid.
20. Ibid.
21. Arms Control and Disarmament Agency, World Wide Military Expenditures and Arms Sales (United States Government Printing: Washington, 1980), p. 130.
22. Lidova Armada, July 5, 1970.
23. The Military Balance (London: IISS, 1968-1982).
24. I am grateful to Christopher Jones who pointed this out to me at a recent symposium on the Warsaw Pact at Cornell University, May 1982.
25. The Military Balance.
26. Prace, March 5, 1981.
27. The Military Balance.
28. United Nations Statistical Yearbook, Historical Supplement (United Nations Publishing: New York, 1979), p. 391.
29. Discussion with Christopher Jones.
30. See reports of the exercises in Obrana Lidu and Rude Pravo, February 5, 1979 and Obrana Lidu, February 2, 1982.
31. Prace, February 15, 1980.
32. Letectvi a Kosmonautika, vol. 57, 1981.
33. I.I. Yakubovsky, Boevoe sodruzhestvo bratskikh narodov i armii (Moscow: Voenizdat 1974).
34. "They Are Fulfilling the Commitments They Adopted; The Soldiers are Celebrating Their Holiday With New Successes," Obrana Lidu, October 5, 1978.
35. Lidova Armada, no. 12, 1975.
36. Nova Svoboda (London), January 25, 1975.
37. "East Bloc Boosts its Military Aid to Africa," The Christian Science Monitor, July 19, 1979 and The New York Times, December 20, 1982.

6
German Democratic Republic

Henry Krisch

INTRODUCTION

Peace in Central Europe rests on a balance of forces. Both politically and militarily, it is important for each side to know the potential for military and political strength not only of the other side but of its own forces as well. An important element in these calculations is the availability and reliability, both militarily and politically, of the "allied" forces, i.e., the European NATO states and the non-Soviet WTO states. From the Soviet standpoint, this calculation has three dimensions. Like their counterparts in the United States, the Soviet planners need to know whether the East European armies can be mobilized effectively to fight against NATO forces, both offensively and defensively. Unlike Western prognosticators, however, the Soviet planners also need to know whether or not the armed forces of their allies can be mobilized against domestic uprisings, and, indeed, whether these armed forces might perhaps be used against Soviet forces themselves.

All of these considerations apply particularly to the German Democratic Republic (GDR) and to its armed forces. The GDR not only is the westernmost salient of Soviet-controlled or influenced territory in Europe but also lies athwart the main avenues of attack and defense in the North European plain between the USSR and the industrial centers of Western Europe.[1] Together with Polish and Soviet forces, the GDR armed forces constitute the northern salient of formations likeliest to be involved in the early stages of European fighting.

Henry Krisch is an Associate Professor of Political Science at the University of Connecticut, Storrs. He received his doctorate and Russian Institute Certificate from Columbia University.

For the GDR, however, this scenario is far more delicate politically and psychologically than for Poles or Russians, for it would involve a direct military clash between Germans. Thus the most probably occasion for the use of GDR troops outside their state territory is also the most problematical in terms of their reliability; the definition of the enemy--his intentions, social essence, moral standing--is a key element of GDR military capability.

A second potential scenario for the employment of GDR armed forces is to keep domestic order. While such duties may from time to time become the task of any armed forces (as in Little Rock in 1957 and Watts a decade later), the potential for a direct challenge to the regime that would have to be put down by military force is much greater where the regime lacks legitimacy.[2]

Any estimate of the future role of the GDR armed forces, therefore, must deal with the possibility of their internal employment. As we shall see, two major crises in 1953 and 1961 saw very different patterns in the role of the armed forces. For the immediate future, the possibility of popular uprising in the GDR seems remote, while the increasingly close ties between the military and everyday life in the GDR suggest that, in the event of serious domestic turmoil, the armed forces themselves might be internally divided. Finally, a special GDR contingency is the formal prerogative of the commander of Soviet forces in the GDR. Without consulting GDR authorities, the Soviet commander may institute "all necessary measures" to combat any threat to the security of his forces.[3]

The GDR armed forces might also be used while allied with Soviet Forces against other WTO states. This has, of course, already taken place once: in the invasion of Czechoslovakia of August 1968. Studies of this operation have shown the important part played in its <u>political</u> preparation by the GDR leadership under Ulbricht.[4] Although the military contribution of GDR armed forces was symbolic rather than essential, the political symbolism of their participation was powerful, both in certifying the GDR's full membership in the Soviet bloc and in the readiness of the GDR to employ its armed forces in Soviet interests. There is some evidence to suggest that the GDR authorities took special precautions against unwelcome political effects of the intervention among members of the armed forces,[5] but there is no evidence of any difficulties in carrying out the invasion. Similarly, there seems little question but that the GDR armed forces would have carried out effectively military action against Poland in 1980-81.

A final possible use for GDR forces is against the

Soviet Union itself, or, more probably, against Soviet forces on the territory of the GDR and possibly in nearby regions of Eastern Europe. During the postwar period, Soviet troops fought East European armies at least once, in Hungary in 1956; and they were threatened with such action in Poland in that same year, in Yugoslavia after both 1948 and 1968, in Romania in that year as well, and in Albania at various moments. An armed Soviet-East German conflict, however, seems unlikely as long as the GDR armed forces and regime remain closely linked. An East German-Soviet conflict makes sense only within the context of a GDR initiative toward German unification that does not win Soviet approval. But an anti-Soviet unification of Germany cannot sustain the present GDR regime, the leading party, and the careers of its chiefs. They can have no interest in a fundamental anti-Soviet position; all of the other actual or potential confrontations listed above clearly had their origins in an assertion of nationalism. Despite all the often ingenious efforts at development of a GDR national identity, or at reinterpretations of the German historical heritage, any anti-Soviet German nationalism is incompatible with the maintenance of the GDR.[6]

These various scenarios for the possible use of GDR military forces must be judged as to their intrinsic probability (or political plausibility), the extent to which mobilizing forces for such purposes would be acceptable in terms of GDR elite and mass perceptions and to what extent physical constraints on action, especially resources, limit the "mobilization potential" of the armed forces. The size, organization, and political relationships of the armed forces themselves must also be considered. What follows in this essay is an application of general considerations of mobilization potential to the case of the GDR.

Notwithstanding unknowable circumstances and the interaction of personalities, institutions, and external forces during a given time of crisis, one can, nevertheless, stipulate the likelihood of occasions when the armed forces might be engaged (as indicated above). Furthermore, it is possible to identify political, economic, and ideological factors that figure in the decision-making process of the East German leadership. This interaction of situation and perception can suggest the varying extent to which the GDR's military potential can be made actual.

SCENARIOS OF POSSIBLE MILITARY ACTION

The meaningful possibilities of using GDR armed forces are:

1. Participating in armed conflict between NATO and WTO forces (offensively or defensively--as we shall see, this is not an important distinction);
2. Suppressing an internal revolt against the regime, or aiding in its overthrow;
3. Participating in a Soviet-directed action against another East European state; and
4. Participating in Soviet-directed actions in other parts of the world.

Conflict in Central Europe

In the event of superpower conflict in Central Europe, the armed forces of the GDR necessarily would be engaged on the main fronts of the war. The distinction between defending the GDR from attack (as in retrospect GDR political-military leaders claim to have done in 1961) and participating in a Soviet-led assault on West Germany is, at least theoretically, a moot point. As a recent GDR analysis of just wars has argued, all wars conducted by the proletariat are just wars because the moral evaluation of a given conflict depends on the class interests being served.[7] Any war in which the working class takes part* is therefore one necessary for defense of its class interests. All the just wars of the working class have come about due to aggression by Imperialism, and thus "a just war by the working class is only thinkable and practically speaking possible as a defensive war." It is awareness of this fact that serves to heighten the morale of working-class armies.

Such reasoning suggests that, as far as desired attitudes are concerned, the distinction between defensive and aggressive military action is not significant. In this respect, GDR military thought parallels Soviet views. The GDR armed forces must be prepared to counter NATO's plans with "heightened combat and mobilization readiness ... prompt discovery and effective counteraction of new weapons," and expanded conventional warfare capability.[8]

Such military conflict would involve Germans fighting Germans. It has therefore been a standard feature of GDR propaganda to deny the existence of any special, common bonds between the Germans of the GDR armed forces and those of the West German state. The closer general relations between the Federal Republic of Germany (FRG) and the GDR became in the wake of Bonn's *Ostpolitik*,

---

*More precisely, is *justified* in taking part in. Presumably, a properly led working class, i.e., one under acceptable Marxist-Leninist party direction, would not conduct any other kind.

the more urgent became the military need for psychological demarcation (Abgrenzung). In 1972, for example, Erich Honecker, in a speech to East German troops, declared the Federal Republic to be not only "a foreign country, but an Imperialist foreign country (Ausland)" at that.

A recent (1979) GDR soldiers' manual makes the same point in sharp and candid detail:

> For soldiers of socialism, the enemy is always concrete. Whosoever carries weapons against us is our enemy. Therefore ... enemies are not only the bosses of banks and monopolies ... the NATO generals .... Enemies are also the mercenaries of Imperialism, stuffed full of anti-communism and drilled for an aggressive war, who would not hesitate for a second if ordered to fire upon us. It is all the same what language they speak, German or English, which uniform they wear ... whether they are volunteers or not, it is even all the same what class they come from--who serves Imperialism with arms is our enemy.[10]

After this it is hardly surprising to be told that "hatred for Imperialism is the same as love for Socialism." As far as anyone can tell from external indications, therefore, the armed forces of the GDR could be mobilized in a war involving West Germany.[11]

Domestic Conflict

Would the regime, in response to an internal political crisis, call upon the armed forces to suppress unrest? If it did so, would the armed forces act to support the regime? Such questions cannot be answered meaningfully without knowing the precise circumstances surrounding such a crisis, but one can note two highly relevant factors. One is the historical record; the other is the availability of instruments of repression other than the military.

Twice in the GDR's history the regime has had to contend with actual or potential episodes of civil unrest: the first was the outbreak of rioting and strikes around June 17, 1953; the second was at the building of the Berlin Wall on August 13, 1961. In the first instance,[12] when a protest demonstration by construction workers in Berlin turned into semipolitical disturbances in many cities and towns of the (then) Soviet Occupation Zone, order was restored by action of the Soviet army. Local police units (Volkspolizei) were ineffective in crowd control, seemingly unable to restore public order. The East German regime already had at its disposal more heavily armed and better trained units of the "barracked" police (Kasinierte Volkspolizei, KVP), but did not call them out.* Order was restored by the action of Soviet commanders invoking martial law. In East Berlin this took place as of 1:00 P.M. on the seventeenth; there and in Leipzig, martial law was not lifted until July 9. Of 217 urban and rural districts (Kreise), the occupation authorities proclaimed martial law in 167 of them. Although the Soviet military authorities did make use of KVP elements, the burden of restoring order fell chiefly on Soviet shoulders.

While the regime already had, in the KVP, armed detachments that had been recruited on a politically selective basis, the decision not to rely on indigenous forces may have resulted in part from the confusion and irresolution of the regime, as well as Soviet nervousness about international relations in the wake of Stalin's death. In any case, the failure of the regime to enforce its own authority engendered a severe loss of political legitimacy, which economic and social reforms could not hide.

Although the building of the Berlin Wall was not accompanied by popular disturbances, the atmosphere was such that unrest was certainly to be feared.[13] The ten weeks prior to August 13 had seen an unprecedented outflow of refugees from the GDR, and the reaction of the West Berlin populace was such that the West Berlin and Western occupation authorities believed it necessary to take steps to prevent violent incidents along the sector border. Approval for building the wall was secured from the Warsaw Pact as a whole, and particularly from the Soviet Union at a meeting of party leaders from in Moscow on August 3-5. The actual organization of the project, as well as its execution, was left to the GDR authorities themselves. The operational chief of the project was Erich Honecker, at that time the second man in the party hierarchy and responsible for military-security affairs in the SED Secretariat. The implementation of his directives was in the hands of both regular NVA units and GDR para-military formations, the Kampfgruppen der Arbeiterklasse. The use of this factory-based militia was a powerful political symbol of the regime's ability to mobilize popular support; its use of the NVA was an equally potent symbol of the degree to which the GDR military forces could regard West Germans as hostile elements.

The WTO approval of the Berlin Wall project expressly authorized the GDR to take measures to secure its borders; the GDR was seen, and has continued to see itself, as acting on behalf of the entire bloc, safe-

---

*Compare this to the Polish regime's reliance on special para-military units to enforce martial law after December 13, 1981.

guarding its most exposed Western salient. Participation in this enterprise, and identification with it, have become a matter for pride among GDR leaders. Honecker, for example, in his memoirs describes his personal direction (under Ulbrichts' mandate) of the operation, mentioning by name some of the other leading participants, who are still politically prominent.

For the NVA, the wall is now a quasi-military "victory" over American-West German plans to invade the GDR after first provoking an uprising. Lacking glorious victories about which to boast--the invasion of Czechoslovakia in 1968 seems still to be insufficiently popular to be glamorized--such action in Berlin has become the NVA's "heroic" precedent.[14]

Although the NVA seems entirely capable and reliable in this regard, the regime does have other forces available to it for internal security purposes. Under Defense Ministry jurisdiction, but organized separately from the regular army, are the frontier troops (*Grenztruppen*). There is a special guard regiment of 5,300 men under the Ministry of State Security (which provides the ceremonial guard at the memorial to victims of fascism on *Unter den Linden*); special police riot forces of the Interior Ministry and the workers' militia (*Kampfgruppen*) account for about 400,000 more. Service in the border troops, SSD regiment, and some police units are regarded in law as equivalent to regular military service, and represent service alternatives for young GDR men. These units are armed with weapons at the level of mortars, armored personnel carriers, antitank guns, as well as small arms.[15]

The utility of these forces in upholding the regime seems to be quite high. In the event of war, therefore, rear-area security (for both Soviet and GDR forces) would seem assured.

It is difficult to imagine an effort by the GDR armed forces to overthrow the regime. Neither Prussian, Imperial German, Weimar Republican, nor Nazi history provide any effective examples for the armed forces to follow. Furthermore, the Leninist principle of military subordination to party command has been consistently applied in the GDR. As we shall see below, the interconnection of party and military, the continuity in strict party supervision of military affairs, and the increasing attention paid to the military's policy preferences reduce the chances for a military coup to a negligible level.

Against Other WTO Members

For the GDR leadership, the prospect of military action against one of the other WTO states presents a mixed perspective. Such actions may awaken embarrassing echoes of the Nazi era, both abroad as well as among GDR citizens. There may also be long-term costs in terms of trade and future political relations. However, participation in such actions may also produce useful results. Chief among these is the opportunity to serve Soviet purposes and thereby win advantages in bilateral Soviet-GDR relations; such advantages may range from generally closer political ties to deliveries of superior weapons.[16] More immediately of concern is the GDR's fear of domestic political consequences of liberalizing or anti-Soviet tendencies in other East European countries.

Therefore, GDR responses to political developments in East Europe displeasing to the USSR have been uniformly hostile. Already in 1956, for example, the GDR loosened ties with Poland and the Polish party, banning the sale of Polish party newspapers in the GDR. As noted previously, the evidence shows that GDR hostility to the Czech experiments of 1968 was a factor in furthering the invasion of that August. In this case, the presence of many party officials and members in the GDR who had been residents of the CSSR before 1945--in some cases party members there--gave Czechoslovak events an unwelcome resonance in the GDR.

The GDR reaction went beyond political criticism and extended to participation in the military invasion of the CSSR. There seems to have been no special difficulty in carrying out the invasion; GDR troops were tactfully kept away from major population centers. Nevertheless, in the armed forces and in the population at large, there was some opposition to the invasion.[17]

The GDR response to the campaign for Polish "renewal" in 1980-81 was predictably hostile. Aside from particular, especially economic difficulties, such as shortfalls in Polish deliveries, the rise of Solidarity was viewed as the consequence of weakness and foolishness by a succession of Polish party and state leaders. At every stage of the turbulent political struggle that climaxed with the imposition of martial law in December 1981, the GDR took the side of conservative elements in the Polish party and state, and it identified reform with Western-sponsored subversion of socialism.

Honecker himself was relatively restrained in his public comments, but other party officials of lesser rank were allowed to denounce Polish lack of enterprise and Polish ideological errors. An unfortunate consequence of this was a revival of anti-Polish ethnic prejudice among East Germans. It seems clear that, had the occasion arisen, the GDR would have been willing to participate in military action against Poland.[18]

Poland and Czechoslovakia are, for historic, geographical, and economic (trade) reasons the East

European countries of most concern to the GDR. At times, however, the GDR has had cool relations with Yugoslavia, Romania (especially after Bonn-Bucharest diplomatic ties were established in 1967), and Albania. Token GDR military participation to uphold the Brezhnev Doctrine in such countries is certainly plausible.

Third World Intervention

The deployment, at Soviet behest, of GDR military personnel, advisers, and equipment in Third World countries has grown steadily in recent years. The larger subject of GDR involvement in the Third World[19] cannot be examined here. But a GDR military source has cited five types of aid extended to Third World armies--presumably examples of GDR practice: (1) supplying weapons and technical equipment; (2) training military cadre; (3) helping the development of an armaments industry; (4) licensing local production of advanced weapons; and (5) engaging in field training of local forces. In addition, there may be the "temporary presence in a few liberated countries of troop contingents from particular socialist states." (Contrary to "malevolent slander," such troops are there by invitation of the host country in accordance with Article 51 of the U.N. Charter.)[20]

How many GDR troops are serving abroad? Unfortunately, there are no GDR sources, and outside estimates vary widely. A general impression of the GDR's effort may be gained by comparing GDR troop-level estimates with estimates of the Soviet and Cuban military presence (see Table 6.1). The GDR military commitment may be seen as an autonomous effort at building diplomatic support and economic ties in the Third World, or as deliberate subordination to Soviet policies. In either case, the mobilization of GDR military forces for such purposes should be relatively easy.

The least likely scenario for the employment of GDR forces is in defense of GDR interests against the USSR. There are two reasons for this. First, the most likely motive for such action, the defense of GDR interests, is difficult to imagine in the absence of an ideational basis in nationalism. As we shall see below, GDR policy on the national question has not produced a "national" consensus apart from a common German identity which would be strong enough to provide the basis for military action. Even if one could imagine a purely "statist" anti-Soviet enterprise--for example, blocking the Berlin access routes by way of armed resistance to some future Bonn-Moscow deal--the close integration of GDR and Soviet forces, and the sheer physical presence of a Soviet force in the GDR larger than the NVA, make such a contingency highly improbable.

TABLE 6.1
GDR Troops in the Third World

Country	Butler-Valenta	Military Balance 1982-83
Angola	350	450
Guinea-Bissau, Cape Verde	100	-
Ethiopia	300	250
Mozambique	200	100
PDRY (S. Yemen)	300	325
Algeria	-	250
Guinea	-	125
Iraq	-	160
Libya	-	400
Syria	-	210
Total	1,250	2,270
USSR Total	3,020-3,120	19,650 (not counting Afghanistan)
Cuba Total	41,440-42,440	36,100 (of which 33,000 are in Ethiopia, Angola, Nicaragua)

Sources: Shannon R. Butler and Jiri Valenta, "East Germany in the Third World," Proceedings (September 1981), p. 61; International Institute for Strategic Studies, The Military Balance 1982-83 (London: IISS, 1982), pp. 17, 22, 103.

INTEGRATION WITHIN THE WTO AND WITH THE SOVIET UNION

Despite being one of the original signatory parties to the Warsaw Treaty in 1955, the GDR then had only "national armed forces," a designation that had been applied to the para-military "barracks police" (KVP) since 1952. After the formal establishment of the "National People's Army" (Nationale Volksarmee, NVA) in January 1956,* the WTO's Political Consultative Committee, on "application" of the GDR, approved incorporation of all East German armed forces into the WTO.[21] Although it is unclear whether this formal total incorporation of its armed forces into the alliance structure has great practical significance, given the NVA's frontline location in the likeliest future conflict, the symbolic importance of this provision remains great. Such a step may well have been introduced as a sop to anti-German feelings in Eastern Europe (analogous to the motives underlying the EDC, WEU, and other Western "safeguards"); it also emphasizes that the NVA is committed, by its own regime, to be a policy instrument of the Soviet-led alliance.

The relative weight of the GDR within the WTO organization possibly is enhanced by the status of Defense Minister Hoffmann as the senior defense minister in the WTO; this may give his views extra resonance within the WTO Council of Defense Ministers. Hoffmann is a politically active defense minister, traveling on politico-military missions to both Communist and non-Communist nations (such as India). He has commanded at least three major WTO maneuvers: in 1963, 1970, and 1971.[22]

For the regime, GDR participation in WTO activities is seen as a legitimating activity; the detailed and widespread coverage given to such maneuvers as "Armed Comradeship 80" (Waffenbruderschaft 80) in the fall of 1980 is an indication of this. The purely military activities were accompanied by political meetings not only among troop contingents from various countries but also between such military units and the civilian population of the GDR.[23]

The integration of the NVA with the WTO command structure extends beyond the multilateral level to bilateral arrangements with, especially, the Polish and Soviet armed forces. The number of NVA officers[24] training at Soviet military academies had by 1981 reached 2,400 active officers, while 175 more have attended the Soviet General Staff academy (paralleling the assignment of high SED officials to Soviet party schools), and Polish officers (and possibly others?) train at the GDR's "Friedrich Engels" military academy

*For origins and organization of the KVP and NVA, see below.

in Dresden.[25] In addition to WTO maneuvers as such, maneuvers are held involving just two or more WTO member states, especially the "Northern Tier" forces; joint Soviet-GDR-Polish Baltic coast landing exercises are an example.[26]

During the decade of the 1970s, the GDR increased its defense spending to a relatively greater extent than did WTO member states, other than the Soviet Union. In terms of WTO goals, especially as articulated at the 1978 Moscow WTO meeting, GDR policy as more fully integrated into the WTO framework (see Table 6.2).

GDR-USSR

Integration with the Soviet Union in the military field is difficult to separate from the general trend of GDR policy, particularly in the Honecker era.[27] This "assimilation" (Annäherung) was seen in GDR acceptance of the Soviet plans for a Berlin settlement and detente with Bonn in 1970-72 (the issues over which Ulbricht had lost his position), in ever-closer social and economic ties (some of these are discussed below), and in a series of programmatic and ideological pronouncements. For example, the 1974 revision of the GDR Constitution of 1968 contained the provision (Article 6) that the GDR would be "forever and irreversibly allied with the Soviet Union"; such ties were said to guarantee to the people of the GDR "further progress on the road to peace and socialism.[28]

One year later (October 1975), a new Soviet-GDR treaty contained the declaration that "the all-around strengthening" of Soviet-GDR relations would contribute to the "further assimilation of the socialist nations." Language equivalent to the "Brezhnev Doctrine" pledged the GDR to intervene against untoward political developments in Eastern Europe. Regarding specifically military obligation, the treaty provides (in Article 8) that the GDR shall aid the USSR with all means, including military, if the latter is attacked by any "state or group of states." Unlike the Warsaw Treaty text, this obligation is not limited geographically to Europe.[29]

To provide these formal state actions with suitable ideological foundations, the SED party program adopted in 1976 (at the 9th Party Congress) declared that the "most important" task in foreign affairs was the "development of all-around fraternal relations between the GDR and the USSR," based on the "law determined qualities (Gesetzmässigkeiten) of the flowering and assimilation (Aufblühen und Annäherung) of socialist nations."[30]

A critical factor in shaping the attitude of the GDR leadership toward compliance with Soviet policy is the GDR's dependency on the USSR, especially for fuel,

TABLE 6.2
GDR Military Expenditures, 1971 and 1980 (non-Soviet WTO)

Item	GDR Ranking
Milex/GNP	1971: fourth 1980: second
Milex/CGE	1971: fifth 1980: fifth
Milex per capita	1971: second (tie) 1980: first
Armed forces/thousand population	1971: fourth 1980: third

Source: USACDA, World Military Expenditures and Arms Transfers, 1971-1980 (Washington, DC: Government Printing Office, 1983).

Note: Milex = military expenditures; CGE - central government expenditures; GNP = gross national product.

energy sources, and equipment generally, which of course also have direct implications for the operational capacity of the GDR's armed forces. Insofar as GDR-Soviet economic relations are of an interdependent nature, they act as well to constrain Soviet ability to enforce its will against GDR objections.[31]

The overall structure of GDR-Soviet trade is a striking confirmation of the importance of trade between developed economies: Each is the other's leading trade partner. The proportions are quite different, however, and reflect the difference in importance of this tie to the respective partners. Soviet trade forms about 37 percent of all GDR foreign trade, while the GDR accounts for almost 10 percent of total Soviet foreign trade. (The former represents a diversification of the GDR's trade over the past two decades; the comparable figures for the Soviet share of GDR trade were [in 1970], 40 percent, and [in 1960], 43 percent). (See Table 6.3.) The increase of GDR-Soviet trade in successive Five Year Plans is likewise evident (see Table 6.4).

Moreover, Soviet-GDR trade is essential to the GDR and important to the USSR in terms of the commodities exchanged. As of 1980, the GDR supplied 65 percent of Soviet imports of oil refining equipment, 62 percent of construction cranes, and 98 percent of railway cars. The special position of the GDR as a major supplier of advanced industrial commodities to the USSR has gradually declined as the Soviet Union has expanded its range of suppliers and has gained (through oil and gas production) the means to pay for them. Especially important from the GDR perspective is that one of its chief rivals in this trade is the Federal Republic. Total GDR-Soviet trade in 1980 amounted to 9,200 million rubles, while West German-Soviet trade reached 4,780 million rubles. However, although GDR deliveries of machinery to the USSR, which in the 1950s had amounted to over 40 percent of such Soviet imports, had by 1976 declined to 17 percent, the GDR remains the Soviet Union's largest supplier of machinery and the second-largest importer of Soviet machinery.[32]

The GDR's close trading relationship with the Soviet Union has in recent years become a source of dependence with the increasing trade deficit incurred by East Berlin. In 1980-81, while GDR foreign trade grew by 10.7 percent, trade with the USSR grew by 16.1 percent.[33] This bilateral GDR-Soviet trade accounted for over half of all GDR trade with CEMA member states; at the same time, the GDR's deficit in bilateral trade with the USSR grew in 1980 to 540 million transfer rubles. In 1981, this was reduced to 380 million, and in the first nine months of 1982 to 320. The accumulated foreign trade debt to the USSR, however, now stood at 2.39 billion transfer rubles in 1981, and 2.71 by September

TABLE 6.3
Trends in Soviet Trade With the GDR

Year	Total GDR Trade (millions of VMS)	Soviet-GDR Trade	As Percentage of Total
1960	18,487.4	7,907.4	42.7
1970	39,597.4	15,484.5	39.0
1975	74,393.6	26,539.4	35.6
1980	120,100.8	42,608.8	36.0
1981	132,926.9	49,888.3	37.5

Sources: *Statistisches Jahrbuch der DDR 1979, 1980*; *Statistisches Taschenbuch der DDR 1982*.

TABLE 6.4
Soviet-GDR Trade in Successive FYPs (in billions of VMs)

FYP	Amount
1971-75	99
1976-80	177
1981-85	275 (planned)

Source: *Neuer Weg* 37, 2 (1982): 64.

1982. (It should be noted here that the GDR maintained a positive trade balance with the other CEMA states.)

The main source of this debt is the slowly rising price of Soviet oil. Even with the reduction of Soviet deliveries from 19 to 18 million tons* in 1982 and 1983, with its consequent lowering of the cost of oil imports, the indebtedness of the GDR to the USSR did not shrink appreciably. In 1970, the GDR paid for Soviet oil with 7 percent of its Soviet export earnings; by 1981, this had risen to 33 percent.[34] This led as early as 1978 to the granting of substantial credits to a number of CEMA states, including the GDR, to allow these states to pay for imports of Soviet oil beyond their capacity for increased exports to the USSR.[35] The need to pay for oil will continue to foster a concentration of trade on the USSR, especially in specialized machine production; this necessarily means less ability to pay for Western imports.

The material dependence of the GDR on Soviet supplies is most evident in this instance of oil. As shown in Table 6.5, the USSR has supplied almost all of the GDR's petroleum imports over the past several years, including the Honecker decade of increased dependence on oil as an energy source. Even the reported recent reduction of Soviet oil supplies will only increase the GDR's economic difficulties by forcing the GDR to buy oil in hard-currency markets.

Although the amount of oil to be delivered over the life of the current five year plan is less than that of the previous period, the decrease is small, significant mostly as a sign that the former steady increase in deliveries will not take place. As the comparison of figures for 1981 and the immediately preceding years show, the cost of Soviet oil for the GDR has increased, the amount delivered has remained the same or may indeed fall slightly, and the share of oil imports provided by the USSR has dropped somewhat. Indeed, given the possible long-term decrease in oil prices due to global oversupply, and in view of the fact that the price of Soviet oil, under the "Bucharest formula," represents the average of the immediately past five years, the GDR could be paying above world prices for Soviet oil.

The dependence on Soviet oil can be extended to a range of important raw materials[36] as shown in Table 6.6. For energy and other raw material supplies generally, and for natural gas in particular, the GDR (like other East European states) must supply labor and investment capital.[37]

*Most sources refer to 17 million tons, but Honecker's confirmation of reductions in deliveries came in a reference to "about 36 million" tons for a two-year period.

TABLE 6.5
GDR Oil Imports, Total and From USSR, 1971-85

Year	Total Imports (millions of tons)	Imports From USSR (millions of tons)	Oil Imports From USSR as Percentage of Total Imports From USSR	Oil Imports From USSR as Percentage of Total Oil Imports
1976		16,000,000	15.8	88.7
1977	19,042,000	17,007	18.3	89.3
1978	19,925	17,760	22.4	89.1
1979	20,694	18,536	24.6	89.6
1980		19,001	29.2	86.9
1981		19,000 (ca.)	31.5	83.7
1982		18,000 (ca.)		
1983		18,000 (ca.)		
1971-75		63,200	11.3	84.0
1975-80		88,300	23.0	88.6
1981-85		87,000 (ca.)		

Sources: Statistisches Jahrbuch der DDR 1980, 1981; Ronald Francisco, "East German Foreign Policy: An Economic Perspective" (unpublished paper); Maria Haendcke-Hoppe, "DDR-Aussenwirtschaft unter neuen Vorzeichen," Deutschland Archiv 16, 4 (April 1983): 382; Erich Honecker, quoted in Neues Deutschland, December 18-19, 1982, p. 3.

Note: Between 2 percent and 4 percent of the annual total is unaccounted for in the sum of deliveries listed in GDR statistical sources, and presumably comes from "spot market" purchases or unannounced deals with oil-producing countries.

TABLE 6.6
GDR and WTO Military Expenditures, 1971 and 1980

Country and Year	Percentage: Milex of GNP	Percentage: Milex of CGE	Milex Per Capita (Current Dollars)	Milex (Current Dollars)	Armed Forces per Thousand Population
GDR 1971	5.6	14.1	342	5,840	11.8
1980	5.7	11.1	451	7,537	13.8
Poland 1971	5.9	23.0	222	7,298	9.6
1980	5.4	13.8	243	8,654	11.8
CSSR 1971	5.3	16.2	342	4,926	15.4
1980	4.9	15.5	362	5,550	13.9
Hungary 1971	5.3	11.6	219	2,280	14.0
1980	4.4	8.7	215	2,304	11.1
Romania 1971	5.8	17.4	151	3,114	10.6
1980	4.4	11.2	153	3,406	10.4
Bulgaria 1971	9.8	26.8	250	2,131	22.2
1980	12.4	33.3	381	3,393	18.2
USSR 1971	14.4	67.3	575	140,948	15.9
1980	14.6	48.3	708	188,032	16.2
WTO 1971	11.8	46.5	477	166.6 bill.	14.9
1980	11.8	35.1	583	218.9 bill.	15.1

Source: U.S. Arms Control and Disarmament Agency, World Military Expenditures and Arms Transfers, 1971-9980 (Washington, DC: Government Printing Office, 1983).

Note: Milex = military expenditures; GNP = gross national product; CGE = central government expenditures.

The USSR is also the GDR's sole supplier of generating equipment and enriched fuel material for nuclear power generation. Thus a major alternative source of energy is no less vulnerable to Soviet pressure than are oil and natural gas. In 1981, GDR electricity was generated primarily from lignite (79.3 percent) and nuclear power (11.8 percent).[38] The one energy source that is under domestic GDR control is coal; as recently as 1977, coal (almost all of it bituminous and lignite) accounted for 71 percent of primary energy consumption (in barrels/day oil equivalent) and 92 percent of domestic energy production.[39]

While coal is useful for generating electric power, it cannot propel military vehicles. Without Soviet oil and oil products, the GDR armed forces would literally come to a halt. One need not expect that there would ever be such a shutdown. It is rather that this dependency gives the Soviet authorities a means of continuously checking GDR military mobility. It also reinforces the tendency of GDR political and military planners to coordinate their activities as closely as possible with their Soviet counterparts.

The material relationship that most closely influences Soviet-GDR military ties is that of weapons supplies. The armed forces of the GDR are almost entirely supplied (especially in major weapons categories) with Soviet equipment. The NVA, for example, has some 1,500 main battle tanks of the T-54/55 and T-72 varieties (with about an equal number in storage), twenty-four FROG-7 and eighteen SCUD-B surface-to-surface missiles, and quantities of artillery, mortars, armed personnel vehicles, wire-guided missiles--all of these are of Soviet manufacture. The naval forces (Volksmarine) have no ships larger than frigates of 2,000 tons displacement (Soviet-built Koni class), in addition to several varieties of patrol boats and corvettes, especially the new (1981) Parchim-class corvettes.* Small naval craft are the one item of military equipment of domestic manufacture. The air force has between 300 and 400 MiG aircraft of various vintages: twelve of the newest MiG-23, over 300 MiG-21, and thirty-five of the older MiG-17.[40]

The GDR supplies its own basic logistical items. Yet, as Dale Herspring has pointed out, the armed forces leadership and the civilian party leadership must lobby in Moscow for weapons, rather than engaging in intra-GDR allocation conflicts.

An indicator of political outcomes of intra-WTO bargaining is the relative stocks of modern weapons among the East European WTO members. Although discussed earlier by Daniel Nelson in this volume, it is worth

---

*The Military Balance and Janes Weapons Systems give differing numbers for Parchim-class corvettes.

noting the symbolism for the GDR of modern weapons systems such as high-performance aircraft. The GDR, after the abandonment of a domestic aircraft industry in the 1960s (on Soviet direction?), has been totally dependent on the Soviet Union for an air force; the record shows that it has been given only a very modest one (and no naval air arm at all).[41]

The relationship suggested by trade and armaments policies is seen clearly in the structure of military forces as well. To begin with, the NVA is outnumbered on its own territory by the "Group of Soviet Forces in Germany" (GSFG). The NVA has a total troop strength of 113,000 (the total for the GDR armed forces comes to 166,000), while the strength of the GSFG is 380,000.* Thus the close relationship of GDR forces with the "regiment next door" partakes of the nature of a scarcely avoidable embrace.

The frequency of integrated exercises (see Chapter 1 of this volume), when coupled with the organizational subordination of the GDR armed forces to WTO/Soviet commands, suggests that the activities of the GDR armed forces, including future actions, are best understood as coordinated bilateral activity. The GDR military leadership is, at every turn and in its own interests, an advocate of close ties to the Soviet Union. That the military is an important legitimating agent to the regime itself means the self-interest both of the GDR armed forces and of the political leadership tend to increase their reliability as instruments of Soviet policy.

GDR MILITARY EXPENDITURES

The commitment of the GDR regime to an extensive military establishment may be seen in the amount of money spent on military objects. Of the WTO member states other than the USSR, only Bulgaria allocates a higher proportion of GNP to military expenditures. Military expenditures per capita are second only to the USSR in the WTO. Both its economic potency and its demographic limitations are perhaps revealed in figures that show it to lag with regard to military expenditures as a proportion of total central government expenditure, and to rank in the middle to high with regard to number of armed forces per thousand of population. Its economic potential allows the GDR to outspend its East

---

*Organized in twenty divisions (nine tank, ten motorized rifle, one artillery). By contrast, the total Soviet troop strength in the Northern, Central, and Southern Commands (Poland, Czechoslovakia, and Hungary) comes to 185,000. International Institute for Strategic Studies, The Military Balance 1982-83 (London: IISS, 1982), 14.

European neighbors in military matters on a per capita basis, while devoting a relatively smaller share of the national budget to this purpose; the military burden is thus a bearable one as far as central government financing is concerned.

Given its defense commitments, however, the GDR must devote a substantial share of military-age manpower to this purpose, with some 8 percent of military-age males under arms. The result has been a difficult tradeoff between industrial and military manpower needs. The GDR has sought to relieve these demographic pressures by extending the term of service for active reserve duty from twenty-one to twenty-four months (for all those who have served at least one year's active duty). On the other hand, the length of the active duty service remains at eighteen months--less than the two years demanded in the USSR, Bulgaria, Poland, and the CSSR.[42]

The regime's commitment to military expenditures has remained consistent throughout the Honecker era. In fact, the GDR increased the proportion of its growing GNP that it spent on defense throughout the past decade. Some studies suggest an even greater such expenditure than is shown by the ACDA figures. Recent calculations by William Reisinger indicate that the ratio of defense to GNP for 1980 had reached 6.22 percent, the highest total among non-Soviet WTO members; it has also had the sharpest rise among these states over the past several years.[43]

Reisinger further shows that this GDR commitment to military expenditures is best explained as the outcome of a bilateral Soviet-GDR bargain, in which Soviet material and financial subsidies to the GDR (i.e., a Soviet version of the "Swing" forgiveness for clearing debits) and the volume of mutual trade are directly related to the military expenditures. Thus the military readiness of the GDR armed forces is both a result and an occasion of the close political ties of the GDR leadership to its Soviet connection. (See Table 6.6.)

As these figures show, the GDR's military expenditures have reached the highest non-Soviet WTO levels in a number of crucial indicators: military expenditures per capita, and as a percentage of GNP. In these two measures, the GDR closely approximates the Federal Republic, despite the latter's much greater size, population, and total GNP.

The increasingly stringent economic situation, together with an increased WTO commitment, has made fulfilling this dual commitment to economic welfare and military buildup, this WTO guns-and-GDR butter policy, increasingly difficult.[44] While open debates on this score are not available from published sources, we have some indications that the drain of military

TABLE 6.7
GDR and FRG Defense Expenditures, 1980 and 1981

Year	Total (US $, millions)	Per Capita (US $)	Percentage of CGE	Percentage of GNP
		GDR		
1980	4,793	286	8.2	5.5
1981	6,953	415	8.6	7.7
		FRG		
1980	33,611	548	28.3	3.7
1981	29,047	471	28.2	4.3

Sources: International Institute for Strategic Studies, *The Military Balance 1982-83* (London: IISS, 1982), p. 124; U.S. Arms Control and Disarmament Agency, *World Military Expenditures and Arms Transfers, 1971-1980* (Washington, DC: Government Printing Office, 1983).

Note: CGE = central government expenditures; GNP = gross national product.

needs on the resources of the GDR does not please everyone. For example, Defense Minister Hoffmann recently noted that, in order to be sufficiently armed for the defense of peace and socialism, the people of the GDR would have to sacrifice some comfort and leisure.[45]

Thus far, satisfactory economic performance has muffled potential conflict over such issues. With a recently emerging slowdown in the rate of growth of the economy, however, the possibility of such conflict must be judged to have grown. Certainly any estimate of the _future_ ability of the GDR to finance high levels of military expenditures, even if it does suit regime policy, must take this into account. Furthermore, reduction of the economic margin needed to pursue social goals and WTO military commitments simultaneously may lead both to mass disaffection and to policy and personal conflict at the apex of the political system.

GDR ARMED FORCES

The GDR armed forces, viewed in terms of their presence and standing in society, have come a long way from the early days of the GDR and of the beginning of politics in the Soviet occupation zone. While the German Communists, like Leninists everywhere, had not been pacifists or nonmilitarists on principle, their political stance in the 1930s "against war and fascism," and their political revulsion against the militarist-Prussian elements of the German past, made it seem unlikely that a Communist German army would soon have a place of honor in a state like the GDR.

The current status of the NVA, however, is best summed up by a 1981 headline in _Neues Deutschland_: "The National People's Army of the GDR is the sole German army worthy of the name."[46] What are these armed forces that have won so esteemed and central a place in the life of the GDR? How does their role affect their mobilization potential?

Origins of the Armed Forces

The armed forces of the GDR--principally the National People's Army (_Nationale Volksarmee_, NVA) are an increasingly important instrument of the regime's statecraft in both the foreign and domestic policy arenas. In origins, structure, and purpose, the NVA is a product of several factors: German military traditions and recent German history, Soviet security and foreign policy interests, and typical Communist patterns of civil-military relations. Thus we have today a military force self-proclaimed as different from its immediate German predecessors and West German counterpart, yet in much of its ceremonies, material symbols (uniforms, medals, etc.) an evocation of the German past.

Alone among the member states of the WTO, the GDR did not possess armed forces at the time of its accession to the Warsaw Treaty (January 1956). Nevertheless, the regime in East Berlin did dispose of military units long before the formal proclamation of the NVA on January 19, 1956. As far back as 1946, Soviet authorities in their zone of occupation authorized creation of a "barracks" (kasernierte) police. This force, known after 1952 as the Kasernierte Volkspolizei, KVP, by 1950 consisted of some 50,000 men and included both tanks and artillery. In 1952, reacting to the planned incorporation of West German units in the abortive European Defense Community force, the KVP was designated as the "national armed forces" of a democratic Germany. When after the Federal Republic's admission to NATO and the GDR's entry into the WTO, the NVA was formally established, the KVP consisted of 100,000 men plus security and border guard detachments.[47]

The shift from KVP to NVA allowed the regime to be especially selective as to the officers staffing the new army. The officer corps of the NVA was recruited largely from two sources: veterans of politically "approved" military campaigns (Spain, Russian front), and politically reliable young officials drawn from civilian political pursuits. According to Defense Minister Hoffmann, of the twenty-nine generals and admirals who occupied "leading positions" in the GDR armed forces as of March 1, 1956, seven had served with the International Brigades in Spain, and twenty-one had "actively" fought Hitler in World War II--either in the ranks of the Red Army, in (presumably Soviet) partisan detachments, with the National Committee "Free Germany,"* or while in prisons and concentration camps.[48]

These veterans were assigned the task of rapidly training their successors in the buildup of the GDR armed forces; the new officers were "young workers, members and officials of the Free German Youth, who in the fifties had volunteered for ... the KVP ...." The average age of these newcomers was 27.7 years, and 78.7 percent of them had had no more than an eighth-grade education. Such politically reliable volunteers still represent the bulk of the NVA officers corps; the present military leadership of the GDR is drawn in large part from this first generation of Communist officers. Yet, four of eight military members or candidate members of the SED's 10th Central Committee had served in Hitler's army, and one was a member of the Nazi party. All of them had served on the Soviet front, had been

*Those who came from the NK"FD" were largely captured Wehrmacht officers.

captured, and were subsequently politically "reeducated" (two through the National Committee "Free Germany"). But the defense minister and the career officer who heads the SED Central Committee's security affairs department (Hoffmann and Scheibe) have a Communist rather than a military background, and the head of the army's political administration (Kessler) was a member of Communist youth organizations prior to military service.

The political reliability of the NVA was enhanced, then, by a recruitment process that stressed social-political background, including KVP service. Scheibe tells us (and describes his own career in the process), that some two hundred officers staffing the NVA at its formation had been members of the KPD or of another "organization of the German working class" prior to 1933. Typically, class origin and party membership were regarded as essential criteria for officers.[49] Recruitment of soliders for the ranks was a great problem as well. "Pacifist feelings," acknowledges Scheibe, were "understandable", but had to be overcome through inculcation of a "class-based" attitude toward military service.

NVA: Structure, Equipment, Military Role

The GDR military establishment is notable for the degree of its integration into Soviet and Soviet-directed military commands. The NVA, uniquely in Eastern Europe, is in peacetime under direct command of the WTO commander-in-chief. GDR naval forces along with some Polish and Soviet units, are under operational command of the Joint Baltic Fleet, headquartered in Leningrad. Air and air defense forces are integrated with the air arm of the GSFG and the WTO air defense command in Moscow, respectively. On its own territory, the NVA is greatly outnumbered by the GSFG, which has freedom to maneuver, and which may be used in internal crisis situations without prior GDR approval.[50]

Personnel strength of the armed forces totals 167,000 (an increase of 10,000 over five years), of which 113,000 represents the NVA. There are an additional 70,000-75,000 men in border, security, transport, and other special formations, plus about 350,000 in factory militias (Kampfgruppen der Arbeiterklasse), who train with mortars, machine guns, armored tracked vehicles, but whose members are not full-time military personnel.[51]

About half (67,000) of the NVA consists of conscripts (the naval and air units also have conscript troops), whose term of service is eighteen months. Reservists have active duty obligation until the age of fifty (sixty upon declaration of an emergency). Women are exempt from compulsory service, but may be called up for various support and (since 1982) possibly combat service under emergency conditions.

The NVA consists of two armored and four motorized infantry divisions, as well as various ancillary formations. As noted previously, the heavy equipment of the GDR armed forces, such as T-54, T-55 and T-72 tanks and all combat aircraft, is exclusively Soviet in origin; the logistical support of the NVA and other GDR forces in this regard is in line with Soviet support for all WTO forces. The GDR produces, and equips its forces with small arms, coastal vessels, all manner of quartermaster stores and various specialized electronic and optical gear (some of the latter is supplied to the Soviet space program as well).

PARTY, ARMED FORCES, AND SOCIETY

The personal and institutional arrangements to secure party control over the armed forces are in a familiar Soviet and East European pattern. There are effective party controls at every level of the military command structure; high-ranking party personalities occupy key positions of general military policy making.[52]

It would be very misleading, however, to picture party-military relations entirely in an adversarial light, and to focus attention only on party control mechanisms. More than in some other East European states (such as Poland), the NVA is a creation *of* the party rather than an autonomous representative *of* national values. The military plays a valuable role as a foreign policy instrument and more importantly as an instrument of domestic legitimation. For these reasons it is more appropriate to think of a party-military symbiosis; the party is clearly in charge, but its goals and those of the politically reliable and technically proficient officers are largely the same.

Political direction of the armed forces is centered in the State Council (*Staatsrat*), which is charged with the constitutional function of "taking fundamental decisions regarding the defense and security of the country." More immediately (and especially from 1971 to 1976, when the positions of First (General Secretary) of the party and State Council chairman were not united), the supervision of military affairs fell to the National Defense Council. It has been headed by successive party chiefs.

Walter Ulbricht and Erich Honecker. Administrative control of the armed forces is exercised through the Ministry of National Defense, which has had but two heads since its creation: Willi Stoph to July 1960, and Heinz Hoffmann since (Stoph had previously, as minister of the interior, controlled the KVP.) Hoffmann is a veteran of the Communist movement and has been a Politburo member since 1973. Both of these governmental agencies are subordinate to the party leadership in the Politburo and the Secretariat.

Honecker, Stoph, and Hoffmann are all Politburo members, as is Paul Verner, who along with Honecker is a Secretariat member and has assumed Honecker's former position as party secretary in charge of security matters. (As mentioned previously, the operative head of this section is a career officer and Central Committee member.) Despite the growing importance of the military establishment in GDR affairs, the actual participation of professional military officers in the central policy-making structures of the regime is quite limited. For example, the GDR's two defense ministers, Stoph and Hoffmann, are essentially civilian politicians with extensive party backgrounds, although Stoph served in the Wehrmacht in the 1930s and 1940s, and Hoffmann fought in Spain with the International Brigades.

The most prominent GDR leaders, including the SED General Secretary and Head of State Erich Honecker, have eschewed recent Soviet models and have not personally assumed military rank and its formal trappings. However, the GDR has followed Soviet precedent in awarding military rank to the head of the uniformed police (Interior Minister Friedrich Dickel), the chief of the security services (Minister of State Security Erich Mielke), as well as to Defense Mininster Heinrich Hoffmann, a party official with a semi-military background.

In the Central Committee of the SED, membership by military officers has never exceeded the current level of 4 percent of the total membership.[53] Of the eight military members or candidates of the Central Committee aside from Hoffmann, three are concerned with the political relationship of party and armed forces, one is a staff officer, and the remaining four command the border troops, naval, air, and ground forces, respectively. Unlike the Soviet Union (where the membership of professional officers in the Central Committee is roughly twice as high as in the GDR), no commanders of troop units (below this high command level) are represented.

Within the NVA itself, an astounding 99 percent of the officers are SED full or candidate members (this figure has been constant since 1975), which is the highest total in the WTO.[54] These officers are, of course, expected to be highly qualified military professionals but must display a conscious political commitment and "devotion" (Ergebenheit) to the "Marxist-Leninist party." Note that this refers to the military commanders, not their political affairs deputies. Of course, a military career has its rewards: It is a "many sided, interesting and pleasant career, with good opportunities for advancement."[55]

During the first decade of the NVA's existence, the SED moved in successive stages to strengthen its political presence throughout the military ranks. Basic party organizations (Grundorganizationen) were established down to the battalion level; sections (Parteigruppen) reached down to the company and platoon level; each commander (at company levels and higher) had a political deputy; finally, a Central Political Leadership was set up at the company level so as to "watch over the political activities of officers down to a very low organizational level."

In recent years, the main problem for this political control and indoctrination system has been to maintain the soldiers' "proper" image of the country's foes --especially West Germany. As noted previously, this is a particularly delicate issue, given that the likeliest external-warfare scenario involves troops from both German states.

Despite this problematic relationship--and it is impossible to tell in advance just how the NVA would actually react to the prospect of fighting other Germans--the soldiers of the NVA have not defected in large numbers (as opposed to the frontier troops, who of course have greater opportunities in this regard). Most defectors have been enlisted men; of the few defecting officers, who are mostly in junior grades, most have nonpolitical motives, except for dissent regarding the 1968 invasion of Czechoslovakia. A West German survey of military defectors (1967-72) found that 95 percent of officers and 55 percent of NCOs "fully identified" with the regime from which they had just fled.[56]

The reliability of the GDR armed forces for use in both internal and external military operations is enhanced by traditional German and Prussian elements of a "strategic culture," all of which act to bind the regime and its armed forces closely together.[57]

These elements include, first, the perception of the armed forces as creative and innovative, revitalizing or safeguarding the state and its values. Moreover, while there were certainly major examples of German-Russian hostility, there were also--especially in the period from Tauroggen to Waterloo--examples of Russian-German military and political cooperation.

Second, the socializing force of the military (for good or ill) was seen throughout the Prussian and German experience of the nineteenth and early twentieth centuries. Service in the armed forces, and especially the role models provided by the officer corps, were looked upon as generators of positive models for citizens' behavior.

Despite such episodes as Soviet use of military symbols during the period of the "National Committee 'Free Germany'" (1943-45), military values generally were regarded as contrary to values of the new revolutionary regime. Gradually, however, the GDR made greater use of national and military symbols. Evident in the military parades every October 8, the GDR's national holiday (violating Allied agreements), and highlighted by the ceremonial guard (by a special regiment of the Ministry of State Security) at the Memorial to Victims of Fascism on Unter den Linden. Statues of great men of the Prussian and German pasts are prominently displayed.

This rediscovery of virtue in the German past has become a widespread phenomenon in the GDR; clearly a major decision was taken to appropriate as much of German history as possible, and to use it for buttressing the legitimacy of the GDR.[58]

In general, the new view of the German past that is current in the GDR is exemplified by a statement of historian Ingrid Mittenzwei, herself a leading practitioner of this "new history" in the GDR: "A people cannot pick out its traditions: it must confront them, and it should do so in a differentiated manner." This more nuanced approach to historical events and persons received Erich Honecker's explicit blessing: We cherish and carry forward various traditions that have contributed to the growth of world culture "without caring about their social or class position." A good example of the political use to be made of this revised approach to historical events is the treatment of the 500th birthday of Martin Luther.[59] The celebration of Luther, while the most elaborate, is but one of a series of public acts designed to show the GDR as a worthy curator of the German past.

The legitimating and integrative functions of the military are also observable in such diverse policy fields as education and foreign affairs. Over the past five years, the GDR has extended paramilitary training to the two highest grades of secondary school, and has made this instruction compulsory for males. (Females have been restricted to such "supportive" training as civil defense and first aid.) The consequences of this policy for mass attitudes toward the military will be considered below; its significance, particularly for the Honecker era, lies in its demonstration of the mutually legitimating effect of state and military. Indeed, the institutionalization of a military presence in GDR schools and in society at large has been one of the major developments of the Honecker era.[60]

In foreign policy, the armed forces are a legitimating institution both in relation to the Soviet Union and the WTO as well as in the larger world arena. The military importance of the NVA to Soviet strategy in the "Northern Tier" is at the same time a source of political influence for the GDR within the alliance framework. Recent events in Poland have served to heighten this importance of the GDR armed forces, including its naval forces, which had hitherto lagged behind those of Poland in strategic significance. Involvement in the Third World, insofar as it serves Soviet aims, has the same effect as the GDR role within the WTO. From the GDR's perspective, its involvement in Africa and the Middle East is a source of prestige, a possible encouragement to desired economic relationships, and an outlet for ambitious and energetic GDR citizens. In a society with extremely restricted travel opportunities, the wider horizons available to NVA personnel are not a negligible legitimating factor.

Given such a role for the armed forces, it makes sense from the regime's perspective to regard military service as not only an obligation--both to the GDR and to the entire socialist community--but in fact a "right," albeit one that, for males, is difficult not to exercise. Commenting on the 1982 version of the military service law, Hoffmann declared that "such a constitutionally guaranteed right to safeguard the peace and the achievements of the toilers can exist only in ... a state ... that for the first time is truly the fatherland of workers and peasants."[61] Such a state, as Neues Deutschland declared on this same occasion, may properly demand "from every male citizen ... that he be ready at any time to perform his service."[62]

To insure proper attitudes toward military service, the regime has since 1978 made paramilitary instruction compulsory for boys in the last two years of secondary school. Despite considerable opposition led by the Evengelical Church, the regime was adamant in maintaining this system and has continued to insert military themes into GDR life. The military is to become a presence in the life of the community, to encourage enlistments and application for officer training, to propagate desired values regarding the WTO and NATO--in short, to do much of the work of political socialization that had once been the exclusive domain of the party.[62A]

How this increasing amalgamation of political and military leadership will be received by a citizenry exhorted to struggle for peace remains to be seen. As an instrument of statecraft, however, the armed forces of the GDR remain strong, firmly in the party's hands, and almost an ubiquitous presence in GDR life.

The response of elements of the population to the

heightened militarization of GDR life has taken the form of an unofficial peace movement. The importance of this movement for our theme is in the light it sheds on popular attitudes toward military commitments, and thus on constraints which may inhibit the regime's ability to mobilize the country's armed forces.

Several aspects of the peace movement are especially noteworthy. Participants in this informal social activism seek autonomy from the official and officious guidance of the authorities; such an attitude, if widespread, would impair the regime's ability to mobilize the population for centrally set goals in the classical Leninist mobilization style. Moreover, by finding an organizational and spiritual basis in the Evengelical Churches, this otherwise somewhat incohate movement assures itself a structure and, given the regime's reluctance to enter into a direct church-state confrontation, a degree of protection. Finally, in terms of the issues as such, the peace movement challenges one of the fundamental rationales of GDR and WTO military activity. It does this by rejecting the official contention that only Western weapons are dangerous.

Uniquely among Communist states, the GDR allows some forms of conscientious objection to regular service. The struggle over the extent and forms of non combatant service will have an important effect in the future on the ability of the regime to mobilize the population.

The problem of an alternative to the universal (male) military service arose with the latter's introduction in the GDR in 1962.[63] There must have been considerable opposition, especially from church sources, for after negotiation between state and church figures, a decree of the National Defense Council permitting modified alternative service was issued as early as 1964.*

The decree provided for the creation of construction units (Baueinheiten) within the NVA. An inductee, upon petition, could be assigned to such a unit. In the first decade of the Baueinheiten's existence, some three thousand to five thousand young men appear to have chosen this form of service;** from the beginning, but with mounting intensity since 1978, there has been dissatisfaction with this alternative. For the most part, these units built military installations--airfields, for example, and thus directly supported the GDR defense

---

*That this was the form of dissemination chosen--a decree of the NVR published only in the official law register--indicates the political reluctance of the regime to allow such options.

**Exact figures have never been published.

effort. Demands for a truly alternative service crystallized in a plan devised at Evangelical youth meetings in Dresden in spring 1981. Under the label "social peace service" (Sozialer Friedensdienst) it foresaw two years of service (deliberately longer than the eighteen months of active military duty) in social services, health care, disaster relief, and environmental action, together with "political" training in such topics as peaceful conflict resolution.

The reaction of the regime to this proposal was swift and has remained uncompromisingly hostile.[64] Politburo member Werner Walde snapped that, after all, the GDR was itself one gigantic peace service. The regime's official responsible for church affairs, Klaus Gysi, rejected such a service as unsuitable for GDR conditions on the grounds that it qualified the constitutional obligation for universal military service, called into question the GDR's ability to fulfill its Warsaw Pact obligations, and finally that it defamed (!) GDR soldiers by suggesting that service in the NVA was "unsocial war service."

Subsequent official and unofficial statements have not added substance or detail to this initial rejection. That the brusque rejection of this initiative has not ended the controversy is clear from the continued propaganda drumfire in favor of armed service. In the spring of 1982, for example, the FDJ staged large rallies with the slogans "Peace must be armed" and "Secure the peace against NATO arms." Individuals came forward to testify to their willingness to defend socialism with arms--or to bear the sacrifice of having a loved one in the service. Defense Minister and Politburo member Hoffmann summed up the regime's viewpoint as follows: Service in the NVA or with the frontier troops, whether as a young recruit or as a reservist, "is the most effective way of serving peace."[65]

A more general peace movement has also found support within the church because the churches have provided an opportunity for groups to meet and discuss questions of nuclear strategy, including alternatives to present-day security arrangements. For a Communist country it is exceptional to find an unofficial forum for public discussion of such important issues.

An excellent and rather poignant example of such an expression is the Dresden Peace Forum of February 13, 1982.[66] Organized by an unofficial group of young people, it was given official church sponsorship to forestall official prohibition. Scheduled for the anniversary of the destructive allied bombing of Dresden in 1945, it was attended by four to five thousand persons, and it included a candlelight march to a war-damaged church. A highlight of the forum was a frank question-and-answer session between Evangelical and

Lutheran Church officials and members of the audience. All of the themes mentioned above were raised and discussed. Church leaders reminded the audience of the limits to the churches' influence, and urged their listeners not to rush to political martyrdom.

A church-sponsored meeting in late 1981 produced a slogan, "Create peace without weapons" (Frieden schaffen ohne Waffen) a badge "Swords to ploughshares" (Schwerter zu Pflugscharen), and a program that called for GDR and WTO contributions (unilateral gestures, if need be) to nuclear disarmament. As indicated, the notion of GDR disarmament or arms reduction has been met by counter-slogans and political hostility. It is not significant, of course, that arguments are presented in favor of armed defense of the GDR; in East as in West, one may make a good case for policies of nuclear deterence. The GDR response to its unofficial peace movement is striking, however, because of the denial that Soviet-bloc policies might need correction, or that GDR and Soviet arms might be a threat to peace. "We need both the sword and the ploughshare," Hoffmann declared--and this has remained policy.

Symptomatic of the official attitude toward this development is the banning of public display of the "Swords into ploughshares" badge; ironically, the badge depicts a statue of a man fulfilling the biblical injunction to transform the former into the latter (with appropriate biblical chapter-and-verse citation); the depiction is that of the statue presented to the United Nations as a gift by the Soviet government. Nonetheless, the authorities, in the person of State Secretary Gysi, met with clerical and lay leaders of the Evangelical and Lutheran Church on March 22, 1982, to tell them that public display of the badges would be prohibited.

Under such circumstances, church leaders had to advise especially their young parishioners not to wear the badges, for the regime's opinions were backed up by action. Church authorities reported such measures being taken as: "Dismissal from universities and academic secondary schools ... being barred from earning the Abitur (secondary school academic diploma), refusal of apprenticeship, suspension from school and being barred from factories.[67]

An example of the peace movement's spreading from its church basis to wider social circles was presented at the Dresden Peace Forum of February 1982. This is the "Berlin Appeal" (Berliner Appell) of January 25, 1982.[68] Modeled on a number of similar petitions circulated in West Germany on aspects of strategic policy, it was initiated by an East Berlin evangelical clergyman involved in pastoral work with young people, Reiner Eppelmann. Among its more than two hundred signatories were writers, workers, clergy, and the since-deceased dissident Communist physicist, Robert Havemann. Typically for the GDR peace movement, it was addressed equally to East and West (for example, it called for the denuclearization of both German states), and it supported alternatives to the "balance of terror" and upheld the propriety of unofficial peace protests.

As of autumn 1983, the unofficial peace movement (both church related and otherwise) still exists, as does the regime's hostile response. These two forces are likely to continue into the middle-range future, at least as long as there are prospects either for a Soviet-American agreement on strategic and theater nuclear forces, or for as long as there seems a possibility of mobilizing West European opinion against NATO nuclear procurement and deployment policies; in either case, the regime will hesitate to crush this political force, if only for propaganda reasons.

What are the likely effects of this situation on the mobilization of the GDR armed forces? As has been shown, the regime has a strong and self-interested commitment to an active military policy, and there is strong support for this in German tradition. Does the evident disenchantment with military service and its rationale among some elements of the GDR population mean that there might be mass disaffection if the regime sought to mobilize GDR armed forces? Or is today's "peace movement" the historical heir of earlier German pacifist and antiwar elements who ultimately represented only an ineffectual minority?

In a warlike situation where the NVA could be depicted as defending the social and economic arrangements of the GDR, it would probably have the support of at least a large plurality of the population; studies have shown that there is acceptance of the basic socioeconomic order in the GDR. An offensive war, especially one against the Federal Republic, might be harder to "sell" to the population. A military move into another East European country would presumably not require massive mobilization and would, as in 1968, provoke only scattered ideological opposition.[69]

The great unknown in all of this is the effect of the awareness of nuclear weapons on mass attitudes toward military matters. Given the subject political culture of Communist states, it seems unlikely that serious opposition to regime policies could arise. The postwar history (e.g., Poland 1976-1980, Czechoslovakia in the mid-1960s) of Eastern Europe teaches us, however, that quite widespread and fundamental opposition to the premises of official policy can arise and spread into numerous sectors of the population to be activated by the onset of a crisis within the regime. At the very least, GDR and Soviet policymakers will have to be aware of the spread of antimilitary sentiments among the GDR population, particularly because so many young people have been involved.

CONCLUSIONS

As stated at the outset of this essay, any assessment of the mobilization potential of the GDR armed forces has to focus on scenarios, regime interests and policies, and social, economic, and attitudinal setting. Having these criteria in mind, to what extent does the evidence suggest that the GDR armed forces would, from a Soviet perspective, be a reliable instrument of policy in a major conflict in Europe, within the GDR, in Eastern Europe, and in the Third World?

As far as scenarios are concerned, the reliability of the GDR's armed forces is likely to be inversely proportional to the scenes of action listed above, that is: being inserted in Third World situations would be easy; being used against an East European country feasible, with precautions against ideological unrest (the purpose, after all, of the "Brezhnev Doctrine" rationalizing such intervention); being used domestically depends so much on the particular circumstances of internal unrest as to make prediction impossible; finally, in a NATO-WTO conflict in Central Europe, the NVA might well fight in defense of the GDR's existence as a socialist German state, but would perhaps find it difficult to fight to prevent German reunification. Germans East and West may say _now_ that they care about their common heritage, or that _they_ would prefer reunification, but in a time of crisis they might prefer other, more immediate values, such as their careers, or the security of their homes--things that might be more immediately at hazard in a crisis. The time when feelings of all-German solidarity might be most influential in shaping decisions might therefore be _before_ the onset of a crisis. It is during "normal" times that policymakers--in Moscow, East Berlin, Bonn, and Washington--must ponder the tantalizing factor of German loyalties.

In a material sense, the GDR would find it difficult _not_ to respond to Soviet pressures for armed forces mobilization. As we have seen, both trade patterns in general and weapons procurements in particular tie the GDR closely to the USSR. The broader pattern of cooperation in research and development, of academic and political collaboration, all make it difficult for the GDR to break away from its Soviet alliance.

Finally, from a political perspective, the GDR, particularly in the Honecker era, is governed by a party-state leadership that has clearly defined its own interests and political future as requiring the closest possible identification with Soviet policies. This regime closely controls its armed forces, and could and would mobilize them for Soviet-approved purposes to the widest limits of its considerable ability. The military leaders themselves, closely bound to their Soviet counterparts by training, equipment, supply needs, and operational integration (both multilaterally in the WTO and bilaterally through the GSFG), would support such policies.

Uniquely in East Europe, the regime in East Berlin cannot (easily) assert its national interests against Soviet direction; a "national" GDR resistance to Moscow would inescapably raise the question of dealing with the West German support that would surely be presented. A joint German policy, however, would harbor so many risks for the party-state system in the GDR and its leaders that any minimally prudent policy would seek to avoid such contingencies.

NOTES

1. John J. Mearsheimer, "Why the Soviets Can't Win Quickly in Central Europe," International Security 7 (Summer 1980): 20-26; Viktor Suvorov (pseud.), Inside the Soviet Army (New York: Macmillan, 1982), pp. 41-44, 128-30; A. Ross Johnson, Robert Dean, Alexander Alexiev, East European Military Establishments: The Warsaw Pact Northern Tier (R-2417/1-AF/FF; December 1980) (Santa Monica: RAND, 1980), pp. 79-82. Cited hereafter as RAND 1980.

2. Henry Krisch, "Political Legitimation in the German Democratic Republic," in Political Legitimation in Communist States, ed. T.H. Rigby and Ferenc Feher (London: Macmillan, 1982), pp. 111-25.

3. A convenient source is: Melvin Croan, "Entwicklung der politischen Beziehungen zur Sowjetunion seit 1955," Drei Jahrzehnte Aussenpolitik der DDR, ed. Eberhard Schulz et.al. (Munich: Oldenbourg, 1979), p. 376. Cited hereafter as Drei Jahrzehnte. See also the discussion in Studiengruppe Militärpolitik, Die Nationale Volksarmee (Hamburg: Rowohlt, 1976), p. 55.

4. Jiri Valenta, Soviet Intervention in Czechoslovakia 1968 (Baltimore: Johns Hopkins University Press, 1979), pp. 113-16.

5. Reiner Kunze, The Wonderful Years (New York: George Braziller, 1977), pp. 96-99.

6. Henry Krisch, "Nation Building and Regime Stability in the DDR," East Central Europe 3, 1 (1976), 15-29.

7. Quoted from Wolfgang Scheler, Gottfried Kiessling, Gerechte und Ungerechte Kriege (Berlin: Militärverlag der DDR, 1981), in DDR-Report 12, 10 (1981), 682-83.

8. Defense Minister Heinz Hoffmann, quoted in Neues Deutschland, February 5-6, 1983, p. 2.

9. Neues Deutschland, January 7, 1972, p. 3.

10. Quoted from Vom Sinn des Soldatseins. Ein Ratgeber für Soldaten (Berlin, 1979), in Michael Richter, "Kann man Frieden Kreigen?" Deutschland Archiv 16, 3 (March 1983), 259.

11. "The Armies of the Warsaw Pact Northern Tier," Survival 23, 4 (July-August 1981), 177-78.

12. A convenient recent reference work is: 17. Juni 1953. Arbeiteraufstand in der DDR, ed. Ilse Spittmann and Karl Wilhelm Fricke (Cologne: Edition Deutschland Archiv, 1982).

13. A convenient recent reference work is: 13. August 1961. Die Mauer von Berlin, ed. Jürgen Rühle and Gunter Holzweissig (Cologne: Edition Deutschland Archiv, 1981).

14. Karl Greese and Wilfred Hanisch, "Der 13, August 1961--ein Erfolg der Sicherheits--und Militärpolitik der SED," Militärgeschichte 20, 4 (July-August 1981), 389-98, cited in DDR-Report 14, 9 (1981), 581.

15. International Institute for Strategic Studies, The Military Balance 1982-83 (London: IISS, 1982), pp. 21-22; Die Nationale Volksarmee, pp. 56-61.

16. For military and financial reasons, the Polish navy has allowed its ship roster to age as compared with the Volksmarine of the GDR; most of the latter's ships entered service after 1972, most of the former's earlier. Moreover, the Volksmarine has been lobbying effectively with the Soviets for a naval air arm, which would significantly upgrade its politico-military importance in the Baltic region. See Dale R. Herspring, "The Changing Role of the East German Navy in Soviet Baltic Strategy" (unpublished paper presented at Wingspread Conference on the GDR, April 15, 1983), esp. pp. 15-19.

17. Karl Wilhelm Fricke, Politik und Justiz in der DDR (Cologne: Verlag Wissenschaft und Politik, 1979), pp. 558-62.

18. See the surveys in Deutschland Archiv 13, 10 (October 1980), 1013ff. and ibid. 14, 1 (January 1981), 4-8; coverage of the SED 10th Congress, with its anti-Polish remarks in discussion is in Neues Deutschland, April 13-17, 1981.

19. Michael Sodaro, "The GDR and the Third World: Supplicant and Surrogate," in Eastern Europe and the Third World: East vs. South, ed. Michel Radu (New York: Praeger, 1981), pp. 106-41; Melvin Croan, "A New Afrika Korps?" Washington Quarterly 3, 1 (Winter 1980), 21-37.

20. Klaus-Ulrich Schloesser, "Zur Rolle der Armee in den national befreiten Staaten Asiens und Afrikas," Deutsche Aussenpolitik 27, 10 (October 1982), 72-74.

21. Die Nationale Volksarmee, pp. 47-51.

22. Melvin Croan, *East Germany: The Soviet Connection*, Washington Papers No. 36 (Beverly Hills, Sage, 1976), p. 60.
23. *Neues Deutschland*, September 13-14, 1980.
24. Heinz Hoffmann, "Die Nationale Volksarmee--eine moderne socialistische Verteidigungsmacht," *Einheit* 36, 2 (February 1981), 144.
25. *Neues Deutschland*, October 9-10, 1982, p. 3.
26. Dale R. Herspring, "The Warsaw Pact at 25," *Problems of Communism* 29, 5 (September-October 1980), 1-15; *Neues Deutschland*, March 23, 1981, pp. 1-2.
27. Henry Krisch, "Soviet-GDR Relations in the Honecker Era," *East Central Europe* 6, 2 (1979), 152-72.
28. *Verfassung der Deutschen Demokratischen Republik*, 2d ed. (Berlin: Staatsverlag der DDR, 1975); a synoptic text of the 1968 and 1974 texts is in *Deutschland Archiv* 7, 11 (November 1974), 1188-1224.
29. The treaty text may be found in *Neues Deutschland*, October 8, 1975, and *Deutschland Archiv* 8, 11 (November 1975), 1204-6.
30. *Program der Socialistischen Einheitspartei Deutschlands* (Berlin: Dietz Verlag, 1976), pp. 83-85, 89-90.
31. Gert Leptin, "The East German Economy Under Ulbricht and Honecker," *East Central Europe* 6, 2 (1979), 200-217; Philip Bryson, "The GDR in the International Economy," ibid., pp. 187-99; Doris Cornelsen, "The GDR in a Period of Foreign Trade Difficulties: Developments and Prospects for the 1980s," *East European Economic Assessment, Part 1: Country Studies* (Washington, DC: Government Printing Office (Joint Economic Committee), 1981), pp. 299-324; Arthur A. Stahnke, "The Economic Dimensions and Political Context of FRG-GDR Trade," ibid., pp. 34-76.
32. *Drei Jahrzehnte*, p. 400; *Narodnoe Khoziastvo SSSR v 1980g*. (Moscow: Finantsy i Statistiky, 1981), pp. 538-39; *Vneshnyaya Torgovliya SSSR v 1979g* (Moscow: Statistika, 1980), p. 45.
33. Maria Haendcke-Hoppe, "DDR-Aussenwirtschaft unter neuen Vorzeichen," *Deutschland Archiv* 16, 4 (April 1983), 380-81.
34. Ibid., pp. 383-84.
35. Gerhard Brendel and Hans-Joachim Dubrowsky, "Tendenzen im Handel zwischen den RGW-Ländern," *Deutschen Aussenpolitik* 27, 10 (October 1982), 34-37.
36. *Never Weg* 37, 2 (1982), 64.
37. Hans-Joachim Dubrowsky, "Vollständiges Bild des Jahrhundertgeschäfts," *Die Wirtschaft*, Nr. 10 (1982), 24; Cam Hudson, "East European Media on Their Participation in the Gas Pipeline Project," Radio Liberty Background Report/229 (November 2, 1982); Erich Honecker, in *Neues Deutschland*, December 18-19, 1982, pp. 3-4.

38. Statistisches Taschenbuch der DDR 1982, p. 56.

39. CIA, National Foreign Assessment Center, Energy Supplies in Eastern Europe: A Statistical Compilation, December 1979, ER-79-10624, esp. Tables C-1 and C-3, pp. 40 and 41.

40. IISS, Military Balance, pp. 21-22.

41. Herspring, "Changing Role of the East German Navy."

42. The text of the revised military service law of 1982 is in Neues Deutschland, March 27-28, 1982, pp. 9-10 (the earlier version: ibid., October 14-15, 1978, p. 4). For an analysis, see Karl Wilhelm Fricke, "Volkskammer beschloss neues Wehrdienstgesetz," Deutschland Archiv 15, 5 (May 1982), 458-61.

43. William M. Reisinger, "East European Military Expenditures in the 1970s: Collective Good or Bargaining Offer?" International Organization 37, 1 (Winter 1983), 143-55.

44. For recent surveys, see Hans-Dieter Schulz, "Korrektes Schuldenzahlen als Erfolg," Deutschland Archiv 16, 2 (February 1983), 116-19; "Die Krisenspuren werden deutlicher," ibid., 16, 1 (January 1983); 1-5. See also the report of a November 1982 sumposium on the GDR economy in Franz-Lothar Altmann, "Die DDR-Wirtschaft unter dem Zwang von Engpassen und Instabilitäten," Osteuropa-Wirtschaft 28, 1 (January 1983), 62-68.

45. In Neues Deutschland, March 26, 1982, p. 3.

46. Neues Deutschland, February 17, 1981, p. 1.

47. Die Nationale Volksarmee, esp. chaps. 1 and 4; Gero Neugebauer, "Militärpolitik und Streitkräfte," Politik, Wirtschaft und Gesellschaft in der DDR, ed. Günter Erbe et.al., 2d ed. (Opladen: Westdeutscher Verlag, 1980), pp. 174-91.

48. Hoffmann, "Die Nationale Volksarmee."

49. Herbert Scheibe, "Sozialistischer Offizier--Klassenauftrag und Verpflichtung," Einheit 36, 2 (February 1981), 149-50; data from Günter Buch, ed., Namen und Daten wichtiger Personnen der DDR, 3d ed. (Berlin: Verlag, J.H.W. Dietz Nachf., 1982).

50. As a symptom of the degree of Soviet-GDR military integration, it may be noted that all NVA/Air officers must know and use Russian. It is estimated that at work in the GDR Ministry of National Defense are some 900 civilian employees, 3,200 NVA officers and enlisted men, and eighty Soviet staff officers. As in other WTO member states' military commands, there is a Soviet officer present at GDR military headquarters as a WTO staff representative. In 1980, this was Col. Gen. Magomed Tankayev (RAND 1980, pp. 83-85); in 1982, it was Army General Ivan Shavrov (Neues Deutschland, October 9-10, 1982, p. 1).

51. IISS, Military Balance, pp. 21-22.

52. The basic study is: Dale R. Herspring, East German Civil-Military Relations: The Impact of Technology, 1949-1972 (New York: Praeger, 1973).

53. See the chart in Dale R. Herspring, "Die Rolle der Streitkräfte in der Aussenpolitik der DDR," In Drei Jahrzehnte, p. 318.

54. "Armies of the Warsaw Pact Northern Tier."

55. Scheibe, "Socialistischer Offizier."

56. "Armies of the Warsaw Pact Northern Tier."

57. Trond Gilberg, "The Balkan Strategic Culture: A Preliminary Analysis" (paper presented at the International Studies Association, Mexico City, April 1983).

58. See, inter alia, stories in the Frankfurter Allgemeine Zeitung, November 8, 1981, p. 26; February 6, 1982, p. 9; February 17, 1982, p. 9; Eckart Förtsch, "Preussen-Bild und historische Tradition in der DDR," Deutsche Studien 19, 75 (September 1981), 176-87; Kurt Hager in Neues Deutschland, July 22, 1981, p. 4.

59. The SED's official theses on Luther were in Einheit 36, 9 (September 1981), 890-903. Honecker's speech at the founding of the official Luther commemoration committee is in Neues Deutschland, June 14-15, 1980, pp. 3-5. A survey is Ronald D. Asmus, "The GDR and Martin Luther" (unpublished paper presented at the Wingspread Conference on the GDR, April 1983).

60. Hoffmann, "Die Nationale Volksarmee."

61. Ibid.

62. Neues Deutschland, March 29, 1982, p. 2.

62A. Nawrocki, "Bewaffnete Organe," Ch. 14.

63. Die Nationale Volksarmee, pp. 155-76.

64. See the documentation in Deutschland Archiv 15, 5 (May 1982), 530-54.

65. Neues Deutschland, June 14, 1982.

66. See note 64, supra.

67. Ibid.

68. See the continuing coverage of this phenomenon in the Radio Liberty dispatches of Ronald Asmus.

69. Krisch, "Political Legitimation"; a basic study is still Gebhard Schweigler, National Consciousness in a Divided Germany (Beverly Hills: Sage, 1975); Thomas A. Baylis, "Economic Reform as Ideology," Comparative Politics 3, 3 (1971), 211-29.

7
Hungary

Ivan Volgyes

THE NATIONAL ENVIRONMENT

The military historically has been one of the most highly regarded classes within Hungarian society, even if during the period between World War I and World War II the officers from the good families and from the nobility of "seven plum trees" (impoverished gentry or nobility owning only enough land to barely support seven plum trees) had already suffered greatly from the effects of the depression and from a lack of economic certitude. Many of them--specifically the badly paid junior officers of the infantry--could not keep up with the expenses of the rich military caste characterized by the bubbling champagne and the glittering crystal and chine of the officers' casino.

Was this group already declassé in the interwar period? Perhaps yes. Beyond the glitter, the decorations, the pomp and circumstance, slowly there began to emerge a more sober awareness of the existing system's artificiality. In the army of the 1930s one witnesses the beginnings of a questioning attitude; in the army modernization debates in the 1930s one already senses the recognition that the outmoded social system cannot provide the necessary wherewithal for the efficient operation of a modern army.[1]

These attitudes, however, were all submerged in the great event engulfing the nation between 1938 and 1945. In the first part of the war the great jubilation, caused by the army's assistance in recapturing the lost territories, had slowly replaced the earlier questioning attitudes. The Soviet army, of course, viewed the

---

Ivan Volgyes is Professor of Political Science, University of Nebraska, Lincoln. This chapter first appeared as "Hungary: Problematical Performer," in Ivan Volgyes, The Political Reliability of the Warsaw Pact Armies: The Southern Tier Copyright 1982 by Duke University Press, Durham, N.C., pp. 60-86.

participation of the Hungarian army in the war with extreme concern. The so-called Carpathian group of the Hungarian army--a group containing around 40,000 men--had been given the task of maintaining the role of occupation troops behind the advancing German army as it entered Soviet territory after the outbreak.[2] The group distinguished itself by its extreme cruelty against the local population, although some officers had refused to participate in these events and some had even joined the partisans. Even though they suffered the loss of some 200 officers and 4,500 men, the vast majority served the German cause unhesitatingly.[3] The initial Carpathian group itself was replaced by the end of October 1941 by other units, and on 12 November 1941 the Hungarian government acceded to the German requests, thereby thrusting Hungary into the anti-Soviet military effort.[4] During the winter of 1942-43, nearly 200,000 members of the Second Hungarian Army perished on the Russian front.[5] That army, doomed from the beginning, was purposely sent to certain doom in Russia as a token payment for the return of Hungarian territories. It was composed of people largely between thirty-five and fifty years of age, having only one machine gun for every kilometer of front line. They were bereft of warm clothing and adequate oil for the normal operation weapons.[6] As a result of the destruction of the Second Army it was not until 1944 that the army as a whole was able to recover sufficiently from the morale problems resulting from the death and destruction of the 200,000 unfortunate soldiers on the Don.[7]

The recovery, however, was a mixed blessing. With the Soviet army's approach to the Hungarian border, the Hungarian army officer faced his greatest dilemma; although many had refused to support the Germans, they were suddenly forced to choose between Hitler and Stalin. The choice of subjugation by Russia or nominal independence under Hitler was an empty choice, a false dichotomy, the very artificiality of which was proven by the German occupation of Hungary on 19 March 1944, and by the ascendance of Szálasi and the Arrow Cross party to power on 15 October 1944.[8]

With the culmination of these events, history left little maneuverability to many Hungarian officers and noncommissioned officers. Although not anxious to support Hitler or Szálasi, many Hungarian officers continued to fight tooth and nail, because they perceived the imminent destruction of Hungary at the hands of the Soviet army; they were willing to give their lives in the defense of the nation. While some had surrendered or simply deserted at the first opportunity because they saw seemingly inevitable defeat, only a very small group, whose efforts were doomed, attempted to fight the Germans.

Thus, the respect and influence of the professional army by the war's end had totally eroded. It had ignominiously lost the war and, as far as the general population was concerned, had been unsuccessful in preventing hostile powers from occupying Hungarian lands. It had also, once again, lost the lands that Hitler had given back to Hungary. And more importantly, with his participation in a war fought by machines, in a war where his role was regarded as clearly secondary to that of the heroic ally, the Hungarian army officer--even though the roster of prisoners of war captured by the Soviets contained a disproportionately high percentage of officers--could not even show his personal bravery to the population as the raison d'etre for the army.

For the occupiers and for the Communists soon to become influential in the new government, the Hungarian army officers clearly represented a hostile force. The officers were regarded as members of the former ruling class, deemed irrevocably hostile to the Communists' professed egalitarian attitude, and they represented a possible rallying point against the new order. Fearing the loss of their previous privileges, status, and wealth, the army officers as a rule, in turn, regarded the Communists as natural enemies; their fears, confirmed by the continuous ascent of Communist influence and the concurrent losses of their own positions, compelled them to retreat from political life. When the Communists gained control it was the army officer who was punished most severely, judged most harshly, and sent to the worst type of forced labor camps.[9]

The Soviet troops considered the Hungarian army officer merely an extension of his German counterpart and assumed that he had committed crimes just as serious as those of the most of the Wehrmacht officers. For the Soviets, too, the Hungarian army was not merely a defeated army, but also one that deserved no respect for its hesitation, for its spinelessness, for its tragic misunderstanding of history. In 1945 the Hungarian army had reached the abyss of respect, morale, and social status.

It was in this atmosphere that the new army was officially created in 1946. Although since January 1945 there had existed military units made up of troops that had earlier surrendered to the Soviet Union and joined the fight against the Germans, Zoltán Vas claims that in some fighting on front-line units of the Red Army, Hungarian Communists and prisoners of war had been integrated since 1942.[10] The organization of the Hungarian army in Hungary was not fully undertaken until the second part of 1946. Most of those senior officers willing to fight against Hitler were not willing to become a part of an organization subservient to the party. Nevertheless, the new Communist-led army came into existence following the signing of the Paris Peace Treaty of 10 February 1947. On 9 September 1948, the army received its new Communist Minister of Defense, Mihály Farkas, one of the most ardent Muscovite Stalinists. It was he who, until 1953, molded the new People's Army, and who, more than anyone else, was responsible for the development of the Hungarian armed forces.[11]

The Hungarian People's Army officially came into existence in 1948, organized in a manner reflecting closely the Soviet pattern and a conscious desire on the part of the Communist leadership to Sovietize the army. After an initial hesitation, reflecting a lack of clear directives, the Communist army elite went to work to emulate the Soviet army; even ranks and insignia were based on the Soviet usage as were decorations and the general privileges given to the cadres.[12] The new Communist army also copied the Soviet practice of assigning political officers in the form of <u>nevelo tiszts</u> ("teaching or training officers"). The first and most important problem facing the organizers of the People's Army, however, was the need for officers who were both qualified for command positions and who were trusted by the party. Consequently, in 1949 the Political Department of the Hungarian Ministry of Defense issued a directive which attempted to fill the gap of missing personnel. The temporary solution designed to meet shortages of qualified, politically reliable personnel was the creation of a dual command structure divided between a political commissar and a military commander.[13] Although the structure and function of the dual command system has been maintained since 1949, stringent controls on the military commanders were placed during the period of 1949-55.[14]

An additional important element in the Sovietization of the army was the arrival of Soviet military advisers in Hungary and the sending of Hungarian military cadres to the USSR.[15] In November 1948, hundreds of Soviet military officers began to be assigned to duty at all Hungarian command headquarters down to the regimental level.[16] Although theoretically these officers were supposed to fulfill only advisory functions, practically they were able to influence all important command decisions. There is some debate on the nature of the connection between these advisors and the KGB; in the absence of reliable data one can only conclude that some of these Soviet advisors did have intimate ties with the Soviet security organs.

The sending of Hungarian military cadres to the Soviet Union was another part of the deliberate Sovietization process. Starting in December 1948, literally thousands of young cadres (both military and civilian) were sent to Soviet military and political academies and dozens of general staff officers were sent to the Soviet general staff schools. The obvious and most frequently stated goal was to have them acquire both the technical proficiency required for their job and the desired Weltanschauung needed to keep ideology in the proper perspective.

Prior to the 1956 revolution the party also actively engaged in a recruitment program designed to create a loyal officer corps. Officers and noncommissioned officers recruited during these years came largely from those elements previously discriminated against by former army recruitment procedures. The army specifically recruited from the working class and the peasantry. Indeed, by 1953 nearly eighty percent of the army officers were children of manual laborers and peasants, with an inordinately high thirty-five percent of the officers claiming to have come from the peasantry.[17]

There are no exact figures of the breakdown of the officer corps during these years. According to one source, 52.8 percent of the officers in 1954 claimed to have come from the working class while thirty-five percent claimed to have peasant origins.[18] It is interesting to speculate, however, about the remainder of the officer corps, the twelve percent nonworkers and nonpeasants. Undoubtedly, among them there was a large number of former officer specialists whose views for various reasons coincided with the regime. A good example was Colonel Pál Maléter who later on, during the Hungarian revolution, became the Minister of Defense and was executed in 1958. Maléter had finished the Ludovika Academy in 1940 and as a first lieutenant went to Russia in 1941. Instead of the boredom of the POW camp, after his capture in 1943, he chose the life of a guerilla and signed up to harass Axis units in Transylvania. After the war he remained in the army and within the military-party hierarchy he was regarded as and acted like a Stalinist party official. He was sent to the Zrinyi Academy in 1950 as one of the most trusted young cadres. Throughout the purges of the 1950s and in the following years he managed to survive as an armored unit commander in Budapest.[19] Although again exact figures are not known, one can estimate that at least one-half of those officers, not of peasant or worker origin, had been like Maléter, former army officers in various capacities. The remainder of that twelve percent probably were central party cadres who were simply political personnel sent to supervise the political reliability of the army.

Why so many workers and peasants joined so willingly such a disrespected force, of course, is easily understandable in the light of history. After all, the upward mobility offered by the army was attractive to formerly dispossessed elements of society. It certainly was preferable for those worker and peasant lads who otherwise could expect to perform only physical labor. It required limited intellectual work, at least in the beginning. It furnished respect in a society where respect was scarce and it gave them both a sense of power and of participation in a process in which many of them believed. The tangible benefits were also enormous. Aside from security and food, the chance of having an apartment or at least a private room, free boots, and free uniforms were all highly welcome benefits in a modernizing society characterized by the scarcity of consumer goods. And finally, it was the path of least resistance to material security and safety.

The political education of the new army was in the hands of the company's political officers directly assigned by the Main Political Administration of the Ministry of Defense and guided by the Administrative Department of the Party Central Committee Secretariat. In this sense the Main Political Administration was a dual organization. It controlled and directed the relatively sophisticated education of the army by recruiting for and supervising the political schools and by maintaining control over these processes and institutions through the assignment of political-educational leadership posts to such trusted leaders as, for instance, Sándor Nográdi. The most important political-ideological training institution under the control of the Main Political Administration was the Petofi Academy in Huvosvolgy in Budapest.[20] Until 1953, however, due largely to the purges and to the instability of the command structure, the political work was not considered as having reached high enough levels to be regarded as a truly effective instrument of political socialization.[21]

The year 1953 can be considered a turning point in Eastern European history for various reasons. First, this was the year Stalin died and, second, it was in this year that some tentative changes began in the Eastern European societies, eventually culminating in the revolts of 1956. In Hungary both Mátyás Rákosi's and General Mihály Farkas's powers were curbed and a new educational effort began under the new Minister of Defense, Lieutenant General István Bata. The various military academies, such as the Gyorgy Dozsa (infantry), the Mátyás Rákosi (armored carriers), the Lajos Kossuth and Gábor Aron (artillery), the Mihály Táncsics (engineering), the Máté Zalka (intelligence), the Gyorgy Killián and Pál Vasvári (air force), and the Endre Ságvári (communication) colleges began training professional officers, and regular six-month training courses were also established within the major divisions of the army. Similarly, the Miklos Zrinyi Academy, the equivalent of the Command and General Staff Colleges, reestablished a highly professional military curriculum.[22]

The emphasis on professional achievement was reflected in political education as well; it began to shift away from the primitive "let us love the Soviet Union" to the cautious view of regarding Hungary's past in a far more positive light than before.

It was during the years 1953 through 1956, however, that the greatest amount of stress also appeared within the army units. Because of the necessity of maintaining a modern armed force, those recruits formerly welcome for their background were, during these years, forced to acquire significant new knowledge and become proficient in organization, management, and modern warfare techniques. As education, despite original intentions, spread among the more intelligent officers, more questions were posed to the leadership and many of these questions could not be dogmatically answered. It was necessary, on the one hand, to instill patriotism and, on the other, to maintain the fiction of socialist brotherhood. The officer was torn between these two extremes in searching for an acceptable middle-of-the-road position. The incipient nationalism, so characteristic of both the peasant and working classes of Hungary prior to the war, was also reflected among the officers who had come from those classes. The cognitive dissonance between the theory of socialist internationalism and one's natural nationalism, aggravated by the unique position of the Soviet troops and special privileges given to Soviet officers, for many became too much to bear. When the revolution of 1956 broke out, the army seemed to melt away.

The nonparticipation of the army in the revolt is, of course, a contradictory phenomenon in itself. Indeed, it is true that the army cannot be equated with individual units; for instance, the regular army detachment ordered to put down the riot at the Radio Building on 23 October 1956 refused to abide by the orders and the requests of the AVO to fire on the demonstrators; in fact, they joined the revolutionaries. The ten battalions of Soviet forces sent from the Soviet bases surrounding the capital, taken from units of the Second Guards Mechanized Division at Cegléd, were unable to defeat the Hungarian army units in the Killián Barracks and at the Corvin Cinema nearby in three days of heavy fighting; the fact was that here as elsewhere, some three divisions of Soviet troops "sent to restore order in an East European capital" were simply defeated.[23] It is also true that the sporadic defense of the nation against an overwhelming force of some 120,000 men, taken from eleven fully-staffed category one divisions in Romania and the Ukraine, had produced many desperate, individual acts of heroism; the sad--though perhaps politically wise and humanly understandable--fact that Imre Nagy refused to give an order to the armed forces, unfortunately or fortunately limited such acts to the discretion of those individual commanders.[24]

Much has been written on the reasons for Soviet intervention and the West knows now that the political decision to intervene with the Red Army, more than likely was made a long time before 1 November 1956. November 1, of course, was the date when the Imre Nagy government declared in desperation its withdrawal from the Warsaw Pact and János Kádár, the future leader of the Communist party that had disintegrated by 23 October 1956, disappeared from the capital to form the new revolutionary government on Soviet territory in Uzhgorod. By 31 October 1956, however, in the afternoon hours, Soviet troops in heavy concentration already entered the territory of Hungary from the USSR.[25] Orders had to be given for such a large scale assault much earlier and the coordinated nature of the attack through Záhony and Szeged, the positions taken up by other Soviet units near Szombathely, makes it amply clear that notwithstanding Khrushchev's protestations to the contrary, it is more than likely that the USSR had not ever thought of allowing to see the defeat of its army or the installation of a "democratic" government in which the role of the party would be diminished.[26] Without central orders to defend the nation against such incredible odds, the Hungarian army could not and would not put up a certainly hopeless stand to stop the invasion by vastly superior forces.

Immediately after the revolution the army was purged. Its leadership was thoroughly revamped and one of the most significant changes concerned a new role definition for the army. The emphasis in socialization slowly shifted from the defense of the "great socialist fatherland" to the defense of Hungary. Although integrated activities continued with the Warsaw Treaty Organization armies, the role of the army as the defender of the country became paramount.[27]

The first task of the new regime was to "purge the entire army and specifically the officer corps of the traitors, those who had taken part in the counter revolutionary events, who were politically unstable and who were cowards."[28] All officers joining the army had to sign an officers' declaration condemning the revolution, announcing their desire to fight against it, accepting the necessity of Soviet military intervention, and unconditionally accepting the Kádár government.[29] Those who refused to sign the statement were expelled from the officer corps within twenty-four hours; in spite of the obvious threat of violence used against them, twenty percent of the former officer corps still refused to sign.[30] In 1956 Kádár emphasized that the army must be under extremely strong supervision by the party and the party, in turn, during these years--aside from the obvious assistance rendered by the Soviet Army and the Soviet Secret Police--could count almost solely on the backing of the Workers' Guard and not the army.[31] In 1957 new guidelines were established for the direction of the military.[32] The 1957 guidelines structured the military political apparatus along the same lines as the party organizations operating in civilian life. It reinforced the power of the Communist military commander, thereby implying an abolition of the old dual structure and subordinating these commanders' work to higher party authorities. In spite of all these efforts, it took a full year to reorganize the army, and not until November 1957, could one speak of a relatively complete party control over the army.[33] Since that date, however, it is clear that the army has been a solid partner in the control of the party over society.

SIZE OF THE ARMED FORCES

The Hungarian armed forces number 93,000, the smallest in size of all the East European armies. The army includes 0.87 percent of the entire population in 1980.[34] Except for Romania, no state has spent proportionately less on defense during 1975-80 in the Warsaw Treaty Organization than Hungary and in 1980 its defense spending with 1.08 billion dollars was the absolute lowest figure in the bloc. Its reservists and its paramilitary forces are the smallest in the region (143,000 and 75,000 respectively); in spite of the strong pressures on the political leadership from the Soviet Union, its contribution to defense as a percentage of total government spending has not increased appreciably between 1975-78 (3.5-3.8 percent). Although Pravda in 1978 carried the lukewarm Hungarian endorsement of the Soviet desired increase in defense spending,[35] actual Hungarian defense spending from 1979 (900 million) has only increased by two-tenths of a percentage of the total GNP.

Military service is now eighteen months for all men (reduced from two years in 1980) with more than thirty percent of the entering conscripts having reached twenty-two years of age as a result of Hungary's large pool of recruits and rather minimal defense needs. Conscripts number sixty-two percent of the total military force, not an inordinately large percentage compared to other armies of the WTO. Compared to other southern tier armies, however, 11,000 men, fully seventy-three percent of the 15,000 borderguards directly under the Ministry of Interior, are also conscripted soldiers; moreover, there are no significant numbers of armed security police in uniform as a part of the state's monopoly of force.

EQUIPMENT AND TRAINING

As far as Hungary's armed forces are concerned, the equipment in their arsenal is distinctly middle level; only during 1980 did the airforce receive twenty MiG-23s to replace some aging MiG-17s. The mainstay of the motorized forces still are some 1250 T-54/-55s, although 60 T-72s and 100 PT-76s have also been recently incorporated in its arsenal.[36] The army is unique in the southern tier as far as having a SAM regiment equipped with SA-6s. The unique emphasis on the importance of the military engineering branch should also be noted.[37]

The training of the armed services, especially the enlisted men, leaves much to be desired. In spite of the relatively low period of service and the large pool of available men, there are contradictory pressures at work. While Hungary seems to have the manpower at first glance to have a larger army or a larger pool of conscripts available for service, it is astounding to note that some twenty-five percent of those who have reached the conscript age cannot be called up because they are unfit for service; this percentage is the highest among the Warsaw Pact armies.[38] Moreover, a very large percentage of the young people drafted for the service (twenty to thirty percent) have already been sentenced for a crime committed before their enlistment and, consequently, serious disciplinary problems hamper the work of the army as a whole.[39]

Ample evidence indicates that the training period is severely limited by the contribution the army is expected to make to construction work in Hungary, which suffers from severe labor shortages. More than ten billion forints of work--2.4 million workdays!--have been performed by the army conscripts precisely in such civilian work between 1974 and 1979 alone.[40] Other figures also reinforce this perspective; in 1979, for instance, five billion forints were produced by the army,[41] and for the period from 1964 to 1979 this figure has amounted to at least thirty billion forints.[42] Such construction work takes up valuable time and--with the importance of the political-educational work also being emphasized--there is precious little time left for much needed technical-military training. The conscripts themselves are aware of this deficiency; according to one study, while during the first year of the service forty percent of the recruits thought that their technical preparation was adequate, by the time they left the army only seventeen percent agreed with this proposition.[43] Hence, the general impression one gets from the literature and the available evidence all point in the direction of inadequate training as far as the average conscript is concerned.

MILITARY DOCTRINE

It is very difficult to discuss Hungarian military doctrine without discussing Soviet military doctrine regarding the role assigned to Hungary; within the Warsaw Pact, at first glance, the doctrines advanced by the USSR and Hungary seem to be inseparable.[44] The basic doctrine regarding the army's role has been enunciated at the Eighth Congress of the Hungarian Socialist Workers Party and has been reaffirmed in all major documents since then. Hence, Hungary "is an integral part of the Warsaw Pact and according to (its) strength and its potentialities (it) will do everything possible, (it) accepts all duties necessary for the guaranteeing of the security of the country and of all those states that belong to the socialist community."[45] The bases of these policies lies in rejecting any attempt that can be construed as anti-Soviet activity or attitude and following the dictates of the USSR in all areas of defense activity.[46]

If there are disagreements between Soviet and Hungarian doctrinal considerations, they are likely to be in two areas: (1) the emphasis on defensive activity, qua the defense of the Hungarian homeland; and (2) the amount according to which Hungary is capable of supporting defense expenditures. Regarding the first area, one should call attention to the fact that Hungarian doctrine is based on the concept of honvédelem ("national defense"); the purpose of its military doctrine is "the defense of the fatherland" or haza ("homeland").[47] Though one always attaches the adjective socialist to modify the term, and always extends it to the defense of socialism everywhere socialism has come to exist,[48] the entire educational effort of the country tends to inculcate the necessity of the defense of the country proper by bringing the entire brunt of Hungarian history to bear on the values to be possessed.

Regarding the amount necessary to be spent on national defense, within the leadership there has been cleavage between those who wanted to raise military spending in accordance with the demand of creating a stronger army and those who emphasized the necessity of strengthening the domestic economy. While the USSR demanded at the Political Consultative Committee meeting on 23 November 1978 that the member states raise their defense outlays by three percent, the Hungarian leadership, though agreeing in principle on 7 December 1978 to the proposition, in reality has increased its military outlays insignificantly. In fact, it has acceded skillfully to the demands of its own military establishment by placing the burden on them to secure more modern or up-to-date weaponry from the USSR, including new MiG-23 squadrons. While this reluctance is not significant as a deviation from Soviet dicta, it does indicate considerably less importance for the military than is evident in the USSR; similarly, it also shows a greater emphasis on the necessity for domestic construction and the provision of a relatively high standard of living than exists elsewhere in the region.

It is an interesting question whether or not any specific mission has been assigned to the Hungarian military in the event of a conflict with the West. The earliest mission known directs the army to occupy--in a possible confrontation with Yugoslavia--the cities and areas surrounding Szabadka (Subotica) and Ujvidék (Novi Sad), areas where there is a large concentration of Magyars. From September 1949 to May 1950 the commander of the units that prepared for such a task was General Béla Király who, during the 1956 revolution, was to become the commander of the Budapest garrison and the head of the newly established National Guard.[49]

Judging from the fragmentary evidence of the maneuvers the Hungarian army has participated in since the 1960s to date, several conclusions emerge: (1) The heavy emphasis on military engineering and the enormous concentration in engaging in such exercises that nearly always involve water-crossings, as well as the equipment possessed by the army proper, appear to indicate that a primarily military engineering role and the securing of military bridge-heads, seem to be significant parts of the mission of these forces;[50] (2) The secondary mission of the army seems to be a defensive role concentrating on coordinated antiaircraft activities where the army's equipment is most modern to defend the area from possible incursion from the west or southwest;[51] (3) The heavy emphasis on the theory that under contemporary conditions there exists no difference between the front and the rear areas, seems to indicate that the Hungarian regime intends to inculcate in its professionals the acceptance of roles that do not envision a significant part of the army in front line activities.[52] The disposition of forces--together with the above considerations--therefore, indicates that the mission of the Hungarian army would be one in which it would be expected to serve a secondary support role. At best its tasks would be to assist in trying to open a bridgehead to the south or southwest toward Ljubljana or Novi Sad. These findings are at best inferential, however, since no concrete evidence is available on the subject.[53]

SOVIET CONTROL

In the southern group of forces, among Hungary, Romania, and Bulgaria, Hungary is in the position that it alone has a large contingent of Soviet troops, euphemistically called whenever they are mentioned in the press as the "Soviet forces temporarily stationed in the country." Although they are generally sequestered in their quarters located in the vicinity of Veszprém, Cegléd, Kecskemét, Szentendre, and Kiskunfélegyháza, the two tank and two mechanized infantry divisions act just as much as integrators for the Hungarian armed forces as for displaying the barely visible presence of an occupation army.

The presence of the Soviet army, of course, can be explained by 1956, the one violent event that so far has resulted in a defeat--even if a temporary one--of Soviet forces. But the fact that the Hungarian army has never been trusted by the Soviet Union, even before 1956, and we have no reason to believe that they are any more trusted today, is amply illustrated. Khrushchev, for example, has stated flatly to Micunović, the Yugoslav ambassador to Moscow that the army leadership "has not trusted" the Hungarian army and its leadership,[54] regardless of the high percentage of working-class recruit officers and the predominance of Muscovites in command positions.[55] He regarded the Hungarian army as "heroic" only in cruelty against civilians and submissive to the point of "self-destruction" at the hands of its officers at the Don in 1942; such an army can never be trusted. Nineteen fifty-six just added to the past sins of the fathers.[56]

The new Hungarian army, since 1948, has been under the control and command of Soviet-trained officers who either have received their training in the USSR during the interwar period as trusted Communist refugees from Hungary and Czechoslovakia--who were lucky enough to escape death in Stalin's periodic purges--or were former POWs captured from 1942 to 1944 who were sent back to Hungary after a successful indoctrination period. Men like Mihály Farkas, the Stalinist Minister of Defense between 9 September 1948 and 2 July 1953, who primarily owed his allegiance and his career to Stalin or Rákosi, subordinated the Hungarian army and its mission to Soviet needs and desires and molded the army into an instrument of Soviet power.[57]

Moreover, Soviet advisers also permeated the system; beginning in October 1948 thousands of Soviet advisers arrived and were assigned to Hungarian units down to the regimental level.[58] Although in theory they were only supposed to act as advisers, in reality they controlled both the lines of communication to higher levels and had their own channels through which to report on the army. With the assistance of the KGB-GRU and their predecessors, and with the full cooperation of Hungarian military intelligence and the infamous AVO, the Hungarian army became a thoroughly infiltrated and controlled tool of the Soviet military.[59]

The establishment of the Warsaw Pact, at least

theoretically, had given somewhat greater stature to the Hungarian army officers;[60] they had, in fact, begun to distance themselves to some degree from the Soviet stance. In 1956 and during the revolution, of course, Soviet control in reality had melted away, but the time when such relative independence was practiced was far too short.[61] It became clear during the revolution that--in spite of Soviet control--the army could not be trusted; only the top elite seemed to remain loyal, and even their neutrality was the best the Soviet army could hope for. Colonel Maléter and General Király were, of course, exceptions among the top military elite, but even the Soviet and the Communist historians are hard put to find any example of heroic army activity against the revolution.[62]

Soviet control was reimposed immediately after the final defeat of resistance. The very fact that the army, and especially the officer corps, had to be purged in order to be rid of "the traitors (and) those who had taken part in the counterrevolutionary events," indicates the extent of the distrust of the army by the new government and by the USSR's military establishment.[63] The army command structure was revamped under the watchful eyes of the Soviet troops in Hungary and liaison officers began the long and arduous work of integrating Soviet and Hungarian command structures into the Warsaw Pact as a whole.

Since 1957 Hungarian troops have been thoroughly integrated into the Warsaw Pact at all levels; Hungary plays a role in all areas of the WTO command structure.[64] The USSR, however, has taken Hungary out of the Mutual Balanced Force Reduction negotiations; nowhere is there an indication that the Soviet forces would ever consider their mission truly temporary and thus leave their permanent bases and apartments in the various cities of Hungary. Although Hungary, at least in theory, claims that it possesses a sovereign army, unlike Romania or Poland, we have no reason to accept that claim. Indeed, to date it is one of the most heavily integrated and controlled, and one of the least trusted armies in the WTO.

Since 1962 Hungary has participated in the Warsaw Pact's military exercises; in that year Romanian and Soviet forces participated in joint exercises on Hungarian territory and Hungarian troops went to Romania where Soviet-Bulgarian and Hungarian troops were employed in a joint exercise, for the last time on Romanian territory. Exercises in which troops other than Hungarian and Soviet have participated and which were located on Hungarian territory have been relatively rare; in addition to the 1962 exercise, only the 1971 ("Opal-'71") that included Soviet and Czech forces and the 1979 multilateral exercise were held in Hungarian territory.[65] Most other exercises (usually held twice a year) include units of the Hungarian and Soviet forces stationed in Hungary.

Hungarian troops have also participated in exercises held on the territory of the other Warsaw Pact states, including the "Vltava" (Czechoslovakia) in 1972, and the 1980 troop exercise in the GDR and Poland.[66] Moreover, there have been several coordinated map exercises in which only command structures were integrated.[67] From the evaluation of all these exercises, one can draw the general consensus that the Hungarian troops--and especially the artillery, rear services and antiaircraft components--perform relatively well.[68]

The integration is also enhanced by the relatively large percentage of Hungarian army commanders (especially majors and above) who have attended some Soviet schools, most notably the Voroshilov General Staff Military Academy in Moscow.[69] In fact, if one can believe an informed source available to this researcher, whose present position is still within the Hungarian armed forces at a staff level, for command positions of colonel and above, attendance at the Voroshilov and Malinovskii Academies and at the Zhukov Air Defense and General Staff Academy for varying periods ranging from two to eight years is mandatory. Christopher Jones called attention to this phenomenon and to the existence of an "old boy" network; it certainly seems to apply to Hungary.[70] Since the language of instruction in Moscow obviously is Russian, knowledge of Russian is a prerequisite for commanders desiring advancement; thus further adds to the control of the USSR over the Hungarian forces.

Soviet control in Hungary exists on three different levels. First, the Soviet representative of the commander of the united forces of the WTO on the territory of Hungary--until 1980 Colonel General Iurii Naumenko--and his staff exercise daily and operational control over the Soviet and Hungarian armies as part of the southern group of forces. While, theoretically, only the three category one divisions (one tank and two mechanized motor rifle divisions) are designated as part of the WTO forces, Naumenko, or his successor, Fiodor Ishchenko, can request additional forces any time they desire.[71] Second, the Soviet military attaché and his staff, working out of the Soviet embassy, has a special liaison office directly with the Central Committee's Administration Department, the main political department of the Ministry of Defense, and the Executive Committee of the army's Hungarian Socialist Workers Party organization.[72] Finally, the local representative of the GRU and his staff maintain constant contact with the appropriate military and civilian authorities.

In this sense, there has developed a permanent and

institutionalized relationship between the Soviet commanders and their Hungarian partners; whether one needs cheap vodka, or spare parts for MiG-23s, or even newer weapons, these direct ties are more important than the ties that exist between the official authorities at the level of the Ministry of Defense in Budapest and their counterparts in Moscow. In fact, an officer in the Hungarian army confirmed that it was finally Naumenko who succeeded (upon Hungarian urging) to get the MiG-23s, rather than Defense Minister Lajos Czinege and his official contacts. All of these factors, of course, also imply the amount of leverage the Soviets possess in the military sphere.

PARTY CONTROL

The Communist party--the Hungarian Socialist Workers Party since 1956 and the Hungarian Workers Party between 1948 and 1956--has always placed a great deal of emphasis on the role of the party as the direct supervisor of the army. The supervision takes place both through the closely integrated work of the party's Central Committee and its administrative division and through the "direct subordination of the armed forces to the party's policies under the direction and control of the CC."[73] The formal control work takes place through the Central Committee Secretariat's Governmental and Administrative Department. Cooperating with the main political department of the Ministry of Defense, whose head reports directly both to the Minister of Defense and to the administrative department of the CC Secretariat, are the political departments at the division level and, at the subdivision levels, the political deputies of the commanding officers. The Central Committee, moreover, possesses another committee whose task is to evaluate the work of the army's political work, namely the Army Committee of the Hungarian Socialist Workers Party, whose head in 1978 was Major General Dezso Papp.[74] This body seems to be unique in the Warsaw Pact, and its existence also seems to indicate the concern of the army for the supervisory work of the party over the army.

Party membership among the members of the army professional ranks is very high; from the beginning of one's service career, party membership is regarded as essential for advancement. Intensive recruiting begins already at the specialized military high schools, located at Eger, Nyiergyhaza, and Tata, where students are screened according to political reliability, and continues through the service colleges.[75] The percentage of party members in the army is not known, but most sources agree that the "vast majority of the officers are party members."[76] Even if the percentage of party members is probably the lowest among the southern tier armies, among those finishing military colleges in the 1970s, the majority had probably already joined the party. Thus, for example, fifty-seven percent of those finishing the Máté Zalka Technical Military College in 1978 had already become party members prior to their graduation,[77] and that rate seems to hold for the other schools as well. At the same time, party membership is very low for enlisted men and NCOs; at one unit that seems to be representative of the whole party membership among nonofficers was only 1.6 percent.[78] The role of the party cells is directly subordinated to the deputy commanders for political affairs, and at the very top, joint control is exercised by the Ministry of Defense's main political administration and the party's Army Executive Committee, acting directly under the supervision of the CC's administrative department.[79]

The role of the party looms very large for the professional cadres, especially for the officer corps,[80] but "for the vast majority of the conscripts the KISz cells (the local units of the Communist Youth League) are perhaps even more important."[81] The work of the KISz is also subordinated to the Army Executive Committee and the Youth Division of the Ministry of Defense main political administration, but control is also exercised through the Central Committee of the KISz.[82] The heavy emphasis on political work on this level also shows up in the fact that, while for those enlisting or drafted in the age cohort for KISz membership, the rate of KISz membership is thirty-five to forty percent; among those who have just completed their military training this rate is estimated at sixty to sixty-five percent.[83] For the military as a whole, KISz membership is estimated to be fifty percent, or slightly more than for the KISz membership of the age cohort at large.[84] It should be noted, however, that the ratio of party membership among those who are drafted is lower than that of their age cohort for the population in general; 0.5-0.8 percent compared to roughly four percent for the population as a whole.[85] It should also be noted that the cleavage between the officer corps, with very high party membership, and the enlisted men and the NCOs, with very low party membership, can be regarded as an important gap that certainly causes worries for the party leadership.

Unlike the other states of the southern tier, in Hungary there exists no security police or uniformed political police. One of the Kádár regime's important contributions has been the disbanding of the AVO and it is to the regime's credit that it has not reinstated it. This is not to say that there are no political acts against political recalcitrants, or those who are viewed as recalcitrants by the regime; the Ministry of

Interior's own Department for Political Affairs under the control of the Administrative Department of the CC Secretariat deals with them with a very extensive non-uniformed apparatus. Nonetheless, security police connection with army units can only be undertaken, due to the lack of an institutionalized basis, on a covert basis and this fact alone limits this control function. Needless to say, Hungary's military intelligence apparat has a close and certainly time-tested cooperation both with the KGB and the GRU; the internal links, for purposes of control, however, are weakened considerably.

In one area there exists strong and very important ties between the USSR and the Ministry of Interior. The Border Patrol consists of 15,000 men, the vast majority of whom (11,000) are conscripts. It is subordinated to the Ministry's Party Political Committee, to the commander-in-chief of the Border Guards and the Hungarian Socialist Workers' Party Central Committee Secretariat's Administrative Department.[86] The tasks of the Border Guards are outlined in Decree Number 40 (1974),[87] which states emphatically that the border guards are parts of the armed services of the country but vests their supervision and operation within the Ministry of Interior. The law regulates everything concerning the range of the border zone,[88] including the heights of plants that may be grown in a zone fifty meters from the border;[89] all these regulations conform to the general features passed by the Soviet and other WTO countries regulating their own border patrol work, thereby suggesting a close cooperation between the ministries of interior and the state security agencies of the Warsaw Pact countries.[90] While we do not have exact figures for party membership of the border guard, it is known that party membership is a requirement for professional border guard service and that both party and KISz membership is higher than that of the army.[91] The elite nature and the higher-than-average party and KISz membership, probably render this unit more reliable in some sense than the army as a whole, although the high percentage of conscripts suggests significant problems that could conceivably develop.

Mention must be made briefly of the role of the Worker's Guard (munkásorég) as an auxiliary organization.[92] In 1980 there were approximately 80,000 members of the Workers Guard (or Workers Militia), a part-time--para-military organization that came to existence in 1957 to bolster the military strength of the Kádár regime. Theoretically, their function is similar to that of the United States National Guard, but in practice they possess only small arms and their activities are limited to the maintenance of general control over the population and the factories in the event of internal disturbances. Party membership among the various units, however, is surprisingly high: in 1980 it was eighty to eighty-two percent.[93]

PROFESSIONAL MILITARY EDUCATION; THE GOOD LIFE

Training for the military as a profession reflects to a very great extent both the prestige and the commitment of the army officer corps, on the one hand, and the enlisted men and draftees, on the other. Since the government tries to project the army toward the citizenry as a force "of the people," not as an elite, the democratic nature of the army is constantly emphasized.[94] At the same time, however, the role of the army as a special force and its mission as a special mission is also constantly emphasized, especially through the system of defense education, which began in 1964 and is in full force at present.[95] Its task is to integrate in all grades of secondary schools some aspects of defense education with the avowed aim of making the people proud of fulfilling their role in the defense of the fatherland by willingly and voluntarily enlisting in the army.[96]

The defense education offering in the schools, however, was only the beginning of an increased emphasis on military-political education. A concomitant step was taken in 1964; the renewal of political education for the draftees who entered the army without previous defense or political training. It had been known, of course, even before the reorganization that most of the draftees, entering the army exhibited "political knowledge that was terribly weak."[97] It was clear that their ideological training was minimal, their world view was constrained by unwelcome influences and that they joined the service not because they felt it their duty, but because they were compelled by law and by the political order to do so.[98] The political education courses offered draftees on an extensive scale since 1964 have attempted to provide the missing positive world view through compulsory lectures offering, in a sense, an in-service training for them.[99]

The political training of the draftees begins during the initial period of the training camp. Seventy percent of the initial training camp period has been allocated for specifically military topics, twenty percent of the time is spent on the application of social sciences to military activities, and the remaining ten percent is devoted to strictly political subjects.[100]

The clear aim of training is to "strengthen the interest of the draftees in politics, to introduce them to the Marxist Weltanschauung and to strengthen their experience in public life and in the Communist movement."[101] But, in addition, the army seemed to have another goal in mind as well: namely, the encouragement of the most intelligent of the draftees to join the professional military through a variety of inducements. Consequently, the army has been offering several incentives to those draftees who would be willing to dedicate their lives to being professional military officers. Those willing to study and who possess adequate intellectual capacity have been receiving twenty-eight hours of free time per week in order to prepare themselves for the university.[102] The army has even established scholarships for the most promising draftees who, during their service time, attend the universities. These draftees receive more than twenty-four days additional annual leave and considerable financial remuneration as well.

While all of these activities were directed toward the draftees, within the officer corps large scale educational changes were also introduced. Between 1964 and 1969 the army officer corps was entirely altered and consequently the army itself became an instrument of force which was widely different from its predecessor: it had become once again a truly professional military system.

The first of the significant changes was the downgrading of the Unified Officers' School and the upgrading of the system of military colleges. The most important of these colleges soon became the Lajos Kossuth Military College in Szentendre, the purpose of which is to train and commission infantry officers for the Hungarian army.[103]

The Kossuth College is on an equal level with other four-year institutions of higher learning, such as teachers' colleges. Here, however, the final degree is a commission as an officer of the army.[104] The commission itself is regarded both as a license and as a recognition that the individual is politically advanced enough to be trusted in a leadership position. The requirements of the college are relatively stringent, including learning two languages in four years, one of which must be Russian and the other may be German, English, or one of the other languages that are occasionally offered. Military subjects and technical subjects naturally abound, but there is also strong emphasis on the social sciences. A large number of courses in this field deal with ideological questions.[105]

Above the level of the military colleges, the most prestigious army institute in Hungary is the Miklos Zrinyi Military Academy. In the past many students were sent there as political necessity dictated, without even having completed their secondary education or officers' training course. By 1968, however, the system was significantly altered and, as of that year, students could enroll only after the successful completion of either the Kossuth College, other military colleges, or an equivalent officers' training school. Without having graduated from the academy one cannot pass to high command in the Hungarian armed forces. In some respect the academy resembles the United States Army Command and General Staff College, except that the breadth of the program is somewhat greater. The course of study at the Academy takes three years during which the students cover from thirty to forty different subjects. Languages once more are emphasized as is the continuous perusal of at least 100 technical language periodicals.

It is interesting to observe that within the course offerings one can find such modern fields as organization theory, leadership technology, and management techniques. But by far the most important nontechnical subjects are those related to politics. In a curious and fundamental departure from memorization, students are encouraged to advance their own theories and to deal with topics "openly," all within the Communist frame of reference, of course. But even within this frame of reference the values instilled in the professional military leaders seem to contain elements of genuine intellectual curiosity and an openness to debate difficult propositions.[106]

Those who leave these institutions are professional soldiers, devoted to their line of work, knowledgeable about their technical subjects, and specialists in their military area, possessing some skills in the social sciences and aware of the political limits of the system. They have little in common with their counterparts of the early 1950s and wear their uniform far more proudly than others had worn it in those days. The values they are to possess have been outlined for them in advance by the party, and it is those values they must strive to attain, instill, and maintain. It is relatively easy to discern those values that should be possessed by the people who undergo these socialization processes. It is more difficult to ascertain the type of personnel who undergo the socialization process in the professional schools, and it is to this question that our attention must now turn.

The political socialization as well as the training of the professional military officer is determined, to some extent, by the type of student who volunteers for the officer training institutions.[107] The volunteer for the military colleges is usually between eighteen and twenty-one years of age.[108] Generally speaking, there seems to be little regional variation among those who volunteer, while draftees are predominantly non-Budapest personnel, volunteers for the officer training academies represent the entire country.[109] For many secondary school students not accepted by the universities, the military schools represent a chance to receive at least some form of higher education. Although it is not known exactly what percentage of the applicants originally chose the military colleges as the first choice, it is known that: only 4.1 percent of the students in these schools had "A" or "A-" averages in their high school studies; that 33.9 percent of the students came with "B" averages; an absolute majority of 50.7 percent of the students had "C" averages; and 11.3 percent of the students had "D" averages.[110]

Other indirect evidence seems to indicate that same picture for the cadets. According to a second study by the same author, 40.7 percent of the cadets had an average score on IQ tests and a further 16.3 percent had less than an average IQ; consequently, only 43.0 percent possessed a higher-than-average IQ score.[111]

Generally speaking there seem to exist three different types of motivation for joining the army as a professional military officer. According to the official figures, seventy-three percent of the applicants chose the military officer corps as a profession because they desired to work in the military field, because they liked the lifestyle, and because they liked the societal role played by the military.[112] These students chose the military in order to "serve the security of the power of the people" and were motivated to become professional officers as a result of the following considerations: "the social importance of the profession; the possibility of attaining technical knowledge; the possibility of attaining a materialist world view and lifestyle; the desire for closer community life; the social respect and high regard of the profession; the possibility of a continually changing type of work; and the possibility for getting a further education."[113]

Although there are rather confusing motivations here, such as service to the state contrasted with self-serving motives, this mixture of motivation can be accepted as appropriate for most applicants. In this respect the motivation of three-fourths of the applicants would be comparable to those of applicants to military academies in other countries. A healthy blend for any academy is certainly one combining idealistic motives with a desire for personal gain.

What is more troublesome for the regime is the remaining twenty-seven percent of applicants to the military colleges motivated by other reasons. Thus, for example, sixteen percent of the applicants applied because of the following factors: the attractiveness of the military environment; good earning potential and possibility for high material remuneration; the possibility to exhibit physical strength; good opportunities for relaxation and enjoyment; a chance for success; good-looking uniforms; free lifestyles and the possibility of relatively free movement during work hours. Such motivation again can be said to be extremely mixed, but here one can only discern an unhealthy mixture dominated largely by selfish motives. The military for these people provides a chance to attain status and in some instances enrich personal lives. In others, the choice is made deliberately; because of the lack of possibilities for advancement through acceptance into other academic institutions, the military is viewed as a spring board toward the attainment of a skill, a degree, a social position, or simple material benefits. It is this group specifically that desires the choice noncombatant assignments within the military, such as those of military historians, army psychologists, or researchers.[114]

Unlike the previous group, eleven percent of the applicants to the colleges were motivated by totally incoherent or inconclusive goals. Among this group very frequently one found students who became military officers because of the following motives: the "existence of a military tradition in the family; the ease of the profession (sic); the desire of parents; friends who had joined the army; desire for adventure and a proclivity toward romanticism; and desire for an 'easy' course of study."[115] The military tradition in the family, as a category, provides us with an interesting perspective. While one notes that of those who join the army to become professional military officers, only 1.7 percent had fathers who prior to 1945 had been members of the armed forces, the number of those students whose fathers have been professional military personnel since 1945 is vastly greater. By 1974, for instance, fully 16.4 percent of the cadets who volunteered for professional service had fathers who--at the time the youngsters applied to the college--were serving in the professional ranks of the military.[116] This figure is considerably higher than that in the report prepared on the basis of a survey commissioned and administered by the army's Main Political Directorate in 1973, which only listed ten percent for this category. At the same time, one must also note that of those studying at the various other service academies the higher ratio is more in accordance with Gruber's findings: at the Kilián Air Academy this ratio was 14.2 percent, at the army's Máté Zalka College it was 10.4 percent and, most significantly, of all those students who have been sent to study in the various army colleges of the USSR fully 19.1 percent boasted parents with a professional military background.[117]

The social composition of the contemporary Hungarian army is greatly varied. While the army officers are presumed by officials to belong to the social category of the intelligentsia, their background and their social traditions are highly differentiated. Those in their forties and still on active duty had come almost exclusively from the ranks of the workers and peasants; according to one figure in the 1960s, fully seventy-one percent of the entire professional corps and about the same percent of the NCOs are still recruited from the ranks of the above two groups.[119]

Consequently, it seems that today's professional military represents a chance for upward mobility for some, the continuation of a heritage for others, and a chance for status maintenance for still others. Few, if any, join the professional military today for purposes of accomplishing such a large leap as their forefathers; in a society where social mobility essentially came to a close by the late or mid-1970s, accomplishing such a large jump is nearly impossible anyway.

Given these parameters, however, the life of the army officers and even that of the professional non-commissioned officers seems to be relatively well rewarded. Although we do not have exact pay scales, the beginning lieutenant in the Hungarian army started out earning 3,000 forints per month in 1977, when the average wage for the Hungarian population was 3235 forints per month.[120] According to our figures, after five to six years of service, that salary increases to 4000 forints per month and doubles in fifteen to twenty years. Such an income is naturally supplemented with an additional 6500 forints annual clothing allotment and the provision of an apartment within the housing area if it is available on base (usually it is) and interest free provisional loans for those married soldiers who desire to build apartments where there is none to be had within the officers' compounds.[121] Retirement at age fifty-five instead of sixty with an average of sixty to ninety percent of the last five years' average income is also an inducement, as are the twenty-five to thirty-seven days of annual vacation, well in excess of the vacation provided for the average Hungarian citizen.

Military life, however, also results in major drawbacks as well, drawbacks that provide a counterweight to the projected benefits of the system. First, while it is true that the income of the officers is higher than those of their civilian counterparts, the fact that they are unable to engage in the second economy--an economy whose weight affects at least every second wage earner in Hungary--results in serious income deprivations.[122] Moreover, as is clear to anyone who has ever visited the housing provided by the military for the professional soldiers and their families, since these units were built mostly in the 1950s and 1960s the level of comfort does not reach the full comfort level of the new civilian housing units. Hence, for the vast majority of the professional cadres there exists a distinction between military housing and its civilian counterpart in terms of attractiveness; drabness and the total uniformity that characterizes most military complexes compares unfavorably even with the "silo-style" of nonmilitary Hungarian complexes built in the civilian sector.[123] The greatest problem, of course, remains the provision of apartments for families with two or more children; these families have a lower per capita income and, as a result of the family size, their quarters are considerably less spacious to accommodate every individual.

Another problem relates to the provision of adequate rest and recreation opportunities the army is supposed to provide for its professional cadre. Only seventeen percent of the total number of army children below eighteen years of age have an opportunity to spend a vacation through utilization of the army's own facilities: 5600 out of approximately 33,600 children.[124] This means further, however, that only every three or four years is the opportunity for spending a vacation at an inexpensive and well-supplied vacation spot run by the army available to the professional cadre and their families; the rest of the time they must find expensive and less satisfactory solutions for their vacation problems. Moreover, since the facilities that are available have no provision whatsoever for those with three or more children (only twenty-four rooms are available at the military vacation spots for couples with three children in the entire country!), and since by law most professional cadres are not allowed to leave the country for Western vacations, a large number of the professional members of the military do not spend their times away from the garrison even during their vacations.[125]

As a result of the various problems mentioned above, it is interesting to observe that the military authorities are beginning to be seriously concerned about the alienation of the military, about their alienation from community life, about their lack of participation in community affairs, and about their increasing concern for material goods such as cars, vacation homes, condominiums and so forth.[126] These signs are all signs of turning inward, away from the community--and coupled with the serious problems of alcoholism, suicide, divorce, all of which are very high in the military--they represent a serious concern for the military authorities.[127]

There is, of course, no doubt that the "good life" is still good for the officers, somewhat less good for the NCOs, and for the vast majority of draftees not good at all. The having-to-go-to-the-army syndrome is far stronger than the volunteer syndrome among the young people drafted, most of whom regard the service as a waste of their time. Even among the members of the elite border guard units, the conscripts' lack of enthusiasm is clearly felt.[128]

The nonuniformed part of the military service that operates under the Ministry of Interior, and police officers engaged in military tasks, of course, fall into different categories. In Hungary, unlike the other socialist states of the region, there are today no uniformed security police personnel; the early terror administered by the infamous AVO, which was abolished during the Hungarian revolution of 1956, makes the presence of such a force generally unacceptable to the population as a whole. It is clear, however, that there are among the members of the Ministry of Interior specially designated individuals with military rank whose salaries are twice as high as those of similar ranks in the army. Such individuals do gain a far greater amount of prestige and income, but we know far too little about their performance and role to be able to draw successful conclusions.

The opposite side of the coin of the good life--and thus the negative side of reliability and commitment to the regime--is fear of the army and its corps, both fear of losing prestige and position should the regime lose in a conflict and fear of positioning themselves in the wrong camp, and once again being on the side of the loser. The experience of 1956--especially the brutal hanging and murder of AGO officers by angry mobs on the streets of Budapest--weighs very heavily still on the minds of individual officers, especially those detached to the Ministry of Interior, and it has been one of the reasons why uniformed security forces (aside from those of the Border Guard) have not been instituted as permanent, visible, uniformed organizations. At the same time, even if these events are still shown in the training courses for young officers in the military schools, their brutality assumes a historical perspective and, in a curious way, serves opposite goals from those they were intended to serve: the showing of these pictures and events illustrates what happens to those who return to Stalinist methods of rule, rather than reinforcing the fear component.

The fear that the USSR would lose a war and leave is less strong than the fear that the USSR would win even greater control over the military in case the recalcitrant Hungarian army performed less than admirably under combat circumstances. The close integration of the upper echelons of the command structure with their Soviet counterparts, stands in stark contrast to the professional, independent, rather nationalistic élan of the low ranking officers, the professional NCOs, and certainly the draftees. For the upper echelons, privileges, power, and possibilities for personal and professional advancement are all tied to their role within the

Warsaw Pact and the fear of the potential loss of these inducements would compel them to be eager supporters of the Pact in fulfilling their duties as defined by the mandates of Moscow, within the limits accepted by the party leadership. For the low ranking officer, for the NCOs, and for the professional low-level cadre and recruits, these benefits are not as visible and both their innate sense of nationalism and their training in "socialist patriotism" imply a closer connection to Hungarian national interests and a rejection of Moscow's presence as nothing but a form of national occupation: they perceive the Soviet garrisons, even today, as occupying armies.

But even the upper echelon's devotion to Moscow is tempered by certain historical limitations and these limits are carefully mapped out and reinforced by the party. During the fall of 1980 and the winter of 1980-81, for instance, the party leadership sent the message out to the generals: without party orders, do not commit Hungarian troops for an operation against Poland, and do everything you can to convince the Soviets not to invade. The use of even the best staffed elite units against Poland would lead to far more disasterous consequences than did the Hungarian participation in the Czechoslovak invasion of 1968 and the political leadership has been aware of this problem: the political control over the military so far has been adequate to insure military compliance.

POLITICAL SOCIALIZATION

The goals of political socialization for the armed forces have been clearly delineated in Hungarian political literature. Although they were codified later on, as early as 1958 the following main themes had emerged: (1) defense of the fatherland and its connection with the building of socialism and securing peace; (2) the connection between the strength and wealth of Hungary and the efficiency of defense activity; (3) teaching of defense activities in the schools and the necessity of instilling a moral-political world view in the population; (4) fight against "imperialist ideology, nationalism, 'atomic fatalism,' passivism, the neutrality;" and (5) "... achieving the conscious recognition of the necessity of the Warsaw Treaty Organization, inculcating the belief in the invincibility of the forces of the socialist camp, making the armed forces more popular among the people."[129]

On the draftee level today the political socialization work is handled almost exclusively by the Communist Youth League (KISs). Here, in simple seminars and political education lectures, the attempt is made to inculcate a "Marxist-Leninist world view in the members of the armed forces."[130] They are taught "national pride, socialist patriotism and internationalism," with the emphasis on national pride and national values.[131]

On the professional officer level the political socialization work is carried on through the colleges, the academy, and the unified system of officers schools. In the colleges and the academy, political education consists of inculcating those political values that contribute to training the officers as a leading part of the professional military personnel of a socialist army: moral-ethical education as a socialist officer; the army officer as a member of socialist society; the role of the army officer in accepting directives of the party; the role of ideology and specifically the importance of Marxism-Leninism; the concept of socialist democracy; the role of the military in building socialism; national pride; socialist patriotism; and socialist internationalism.[132]

For the modern army officer, political education thus falls into two different categories. On the one hand, the military is regarded as fulfilling part of a domestic process. It contributes to the building of socialism by utilizing draftees in the construction of the material bases of society. Following party directives, the army attempts to inculcate the Marxist-Leninist worldview within the army, specifically emphasizing the necessity of productive labor performed by members of the armed forces. Thus, in a sense, the purpose of political education is training people to accept the army as a legitimate part and productive unit of society. On the other hand, political education also emphasizes the necessity of combating the notions of separatism, isolation from society, and the concept of superiority over other state organs. The army, hence, is required to fight against its natural tendency of Bonapartism, and the army officers must continue to inculcate the importance of civilian party leadership.

Is it possible to resolve the conflict between the concept of partiinost ("party mindedness," e.g., maintaining values advocated by the party) and the necessity of upholding modern managerial values? Are the two values inherently contradictory? This topic evokes contrasting opinions. It seems to this observer that the main thrust of party education in the military has been to emphasize the concept of partiinost in theory while stressing modern management in practice. Yet it would be foolish to assume that the modern army officer possesses either type of rigid mentality. For the fact remains that even the modern managerial technician must operate within the framework of partiinost, utilizing the language of Marxism-Leninism and thereby mitigating the most serious conflicts. In noncombat situations the conflict is far less visible. Where the efficiency of the army in combat situations is the determining factor, party mindedness and party supremacy remain no more than theoretical constructs. The professional military officer knows the language of the party and of the social system. Utilizing that language and the theoretical constructs taught to him earlier, he applies the framework toward the beneficial technological upgrading of his modern combat unit.

The army is supposed to instill values of national pride and socialist patriotism in the members of the armed forces as well as the seemingly contrasting value of socialist internationalism. Several serious problems are posed to the political education process in this respect. First and foremost, the very composition of the armed forces represents a high coalescence of nationalist values. As discussed above, both the officers corps and the draftees are recruited largely from the workers and peasant strata of society where the value of nationalism has always been the greatest. Unlike the 1950s, the current instilling of national pride and glorification of the nation's heritage--values deemed necessary for the creation of attitudes conducive to national defense--results in the fact that the army, at the present time, can be probably regarded as the most patriotic and nationalist pressure group within society. Although its nationalism is presently focused on the rather narrow issue of the ethnic Hungarians in Transylvania, it is still a nationalism which the party must try to contain.

This nationalism must be contrasted in the mind of the Hungarian army officer with the tasks of socialist internationalism, presenting an obvious conflict of values. The memories of 1956 are weakening. The participation by the Hungarian armed forces in the joint exercises of the Warsaw Pact forces were intended to heighten the personal commitment of its members to the concept of socialist internationalism and to anti-imperialist sentiments. But the fact that the armed forces of the WTO countries have been utilized only against one another in combat--notably the unwilling and unfortunate participation of Hungary in the invasion of Czechoslovakia in 1968--tends to re-emphasize the importance of nationalism as contrasted to the continually changing interpretation of the theory of socialist internationalism. According to one Hungarian army officer interviewed by the author, "it is easier to emphasize such permanent values as national tradition, than to explain the fine points of socialist internationalism in regard to the invasion of Czechoslovakia or in reference to the application of the theory of socialist internationalism in our relationship with Romania and Yugoslavia." In short, the new Hungarian army and its officers can be regarded as far more reliable inculcators of values connected with the defense of the nation than as unconditional advocates of the loving affection that should be exhibited toward the fraternal socialist states.

It should also be noted that Hungary is probably the only state in the region that has a real irredentist claim on Czechoslovakia, Yugoslavia, and notably on Romania. While the treatment of Hungarians living in the territory of Yugoslavia is good, and in Czechoslovakia is barely acceptable, the treatment of some two million Magyars by the Romanian authorities is clearly one that borders on at least cultural genocide.[133] The Soviets, of course, have tried to exploit this feeling by egging the Hungarians on in order to put pressure on Romania's independent policies, and, clearly, the Kádár regime's very legitimacy is weakened by its inability to ameliorate the rough treatment meted out to the minorities in general and to the Hungarian minority in particular in Romania. It is clear that the external-offensive reliability of the Hungarian army in combat against Romanian forces would be very high; the small size of the army, compared to that of the Romanian army, and its projected mission makes it unlikely that Hungary--even with Soviet acquiescence and support--would be allowed to operate independently against Romania. The scenario advanced by some that Hungary's troops would be used to put pressure on Romania in case of a general war in order to secure safe conduct passage for Soviet troops on land along the Black Sea seems a plausible, though highly unlikely, scenario and the Romanian leadership is confident that it would fail to scare Romania into such an acquiescence.

After Tito's death there was some tentative political pressure put on the Hungarian leadership to engage in hostile propaganda aimed at stirring up nationalism among the Hungarian citizenry in general toward the Magyar population of the Vojvodina and among the Magyar population in the Vojvodina toward their Hungarian homeland. These efforts were at best tentative and totally unsuccessful for two reasons: (1) the Magyar population in the Vojvodina lives a freer and a better life than their compatriots in Hungary and the people on both sides of the border are well aware of this; (2) the Hungarian political and military leadership realized, wisely, that it would be a no-win situation, even if Yugoslavia disintegrated after Tito's death and thus did everything possible to stay out of the conflict and to convince the Soviets of the danger of any adventurism that might result from a miscalculation of American might and determination.

SITUATIONAL ELEMENT AND MISSION

From the preceding it seems to be clear that the mission of the Hungarian army in any full-scale war with the West--and their use is not very likely under any other circumstances in offensive combat situations--lies in the realm of three possible scenarios:

1. The use of the army against Romania as a pressure point and a threat vis-a-vis Transylvania, in order to permit Soviet troops to pass through the territory of Romania on their way to the south. Given the distance such travel from the Odessa-Kishinev area to the Mildye (Turkey) zone would encompass, and given the nature of the road system and the relative ease and relative safety of troop transfer from Odessa to Turkey through the use of surface ships, such a projected use seems to be unlikely and unsuccessful;
2. The use of the army in order to secure the Vojvodina as part of "historic Hungary" in a general conflict in which Yugoslavia's neutrality would be violated, is a part of the general mission of the armed forces. Just as in the early 1950s,[134] the securing of Subotica and Novi-Sad seems to be a possible target of opportunity and well within the capability of the Hungarian army, provided the Soviet army would be sufficient to overcome the regular Yugoslav army's defenses. The disposition of forces in the region and the location of the vast majority of the Hungarian army in Transdanubia seems to make this scenario, however, of secondary consideration, both because of the expected strong resistance from the Yugoslav army and the Yugoslav population and because of possible Soviet plans to neutralize Yugoslavia.
3. The most likely scenario involves the use of the Hungarian army for the purpose of assisting in an offensive aimed at the opening of a Soviet-WTO presence near Trieste. Such a move would tie down the Italian army and navy as a combat force, and would project Soviet power onto the Mediterranean. While one can certainly expect determined opposition from the Yugoslavs, the relatively small area to be occupied, the relative ease with which the salient could be protected, and the possibility of continuous reinforcements through Hungary would make this scenario the most likely. The enormous number of military engineer exercises

and the large number of water crossings as part of the military exercises tend to indicate this as a part of the mission.[135]

SUMMARY

How reliable then is the Hungarian army? In internal matters it is clear that it is a very useful instrument in the hands of the party. Where internal defensive activities are concerned, the party can count on the army to defend it against attacks, as long as the present policies of the regime relating to both the depoliticization of public life and the extension of public economic welfare to the population at large continues to prevail. Due to the general satisfaction of the army officers and professional military personnel with their position, prestige, and remuneration, even in a general revolt similar to 1956, the army at worst will remain neutral and, in my view, it would come to the defense of a beleaguered leadership. The chances for internal-offensive activities of the army, a generalized coup against the party, are close to nil.

Moreover, the army would also perform well in a defensive-external situation, given just about any scenario. It would protect the national borders against just about any enemy from the West, and the East. The potentiality of Soviet invasion presents us with the only problemmatical scenario; against Romanian, Yugoslav, Czech or German troops the Hungarian army would perform well. Against a possible Soviet invasion--whether utilizing Soviet forces currently located in Hungary or those stationed elsewhere--Hungarian efforts would be hampered greatly. The Soviet control over the command, communication, and intelligence functions, as well as over the air defenses of Hungary, are so overwhelming that only limited, subdivision level, resistance can be expected.

As far as the external-offensive reliability of the Hungarian army is concerned, it must be examined in a situational setting because the findings are highly differentiated. In spite of the preparations for such a goal as presented above in point number three, the reliability of the army in an offensive scenario toward Trieste remains somewhat problematical. In a lightening thrust, in which the Yugoslavs are compelled to fold, initial enthusiasm among the officer corps and among a minority of the recruits perhaps can be built up; that enthusiasm would wane very rapidly, especially if the Yugoslavs put up strong resistance and if NATO made it clear that it will not give up, but will fight for every inch of Soviet-occupied territory. While the Hungarian army, sandwiched between Soviet units already stationed in Hungary, which can be rapidly reinforced by additional large complements, would have no option but to follow Soviet orders, any doubts cast on chances for Soviet success would decrease that offensive reliability by leaps and bounds, especially on the recruit, lower-level professional military cadre, and NCO levels. Their performance under such circumstances would be closely watched on the part of the Soviets, who would have a major concern with the political reliability of the Hungarian ground forces. Only in assisting with and providing air defenses would the Hungarian air force component of the military be reliable; if their view here is that the territory of Hungary is being protected, the air force would be proud to assist in this mission. The use of pilots in external-offensive combat is considerably more problematical, and the fact that the Soviet leadership has begun to supply the air force with more up-to-date equipment can be viewed as recognition of this vulnerability.

NOTES

1. István Nemeskürty, Requiem egy hadseregért (Budapest: Gondolat, 1968), especially chapter 1.

2. For the relating documents see László Zsigmond, ed., Magyarország a második világháboruban (Budapest: Kossuth, 1959); for German documents see György Ránki et.al., eds., A Wilhelmstrasse és Magyarország (Budapest: Kossuth, 1968).

3. Nemeskürty, Requiem egy hadseregért.

4. Ránki, A Wilhelmstrasse, p. 620.

5. Ibid., p. 625.

6. Zsigmond, Magyarország, 2nd ed., 1961, p. 411 and Nemeskurty, Requiem.

7. Zsigmond, Magyarország (1961), p. 411.

8. György Ránki, 1944 március 19 (Budapest: Kossuth, 1968).

9. For the best summary see Béla Király, "Hungary's Army Under the Soviets," East Europe 1 (1958).

10. Zoltán Vas, Viszontagságos életem (Budapest: Magveto, 1980), pp. 430-36.

11. Király, "Hungary's Army," pp. 9-10.

12. The dates for the introduction of Soviet style ranks and decorations were 7 November 1951 and 15 March 1950 respectively.

13. For an interesting view of the dual command structure see Dale Herspring, "The CPSU and the Military," Problems of Communism (March-April 1976).

14. On the developments that foreshadowed the Sovietization of the army see Károly Munk, "A hadsereg helyzete az 1945-ös választások után," Hadtörténelmi Közlemények 1 (1961).

15. Király, "Hungary's Army," p. 12.

16. Bėla Kirȧly, "Honvėds unter Sowjetbefehl," Hinter dem Eisernen Vorhang 5 (1958).

17. Lȧszlo Hives, "Bokor Pėter elvtȧrs," Szabad Ifjusȧg, 25 January 1952.

18. Szabad Nėp, 25 May 1954.

19. On Malėter see Endre Marton, Forbidden Sky (Boston: Little, Brown, 1971), pp. 145-51.

20. Kirȧly, "Hungary's Army," p. 3.

21. Istvȧn Szent-Miklosy, "Political Trends in the Hungarian Army, 1945-1956" (Santa Monica: Rand, 1957).

22. On the army colleges, see Gosztony, Zur Geschichte, pp. 130 and 180.

23. J.M. Mackintosh, Strategy and Tactics of Soviet Foreign Policy (New York and London: Oxford University Press, 1963), p. 171. David Irving, in his despicable book, Uprising (London: Hodder and Stoughton, 1981)--the central thesis of which is that a main motor of the 1956 revolution was the anti-Semitism of the Hungarians --tries to minimize the defeat of the Soviet soliders. This, of course, is not surprising; what is surprising is that Irving, as he claims, has been extraordinarily successful in getting hitherto untouchable sources to cooperate with him, including General Batov, the former Commander of the Carpathian Military District. While the Russians have not even allowed Hungarian historians to interview men of Batov's stature, they somehow allowed Irving to get to this man. Rather surprising. Irving's documentation, however, is so uneven and so biased that few serious scholars will take his work and certainly not his documentation at face value.

24. On the role of the army during the revolt see Peter Gosztonyi, "A magyar nėphadsereg a forradalomban," Magyar vȧltozȧsok, 1948-1978 (Bėcs: Integratio, 1979), pp. 36-59. For the best English language study on the subject see: Bėla Kirȧly, "Hungary's Army: Its Part in the Revolt," East Europe 6 (1958), has argued that the only organized battles were fought at Nagykovȧcsi on 13 November 1956, by the troops under his command, and by elements of the Piliscsaba mechanized division who fought Soviet tank units on the outskirts of Budapest effectively; the army, however, was not ordered by Prime Minister Imre Nagy to fight. Nagy, in fact, when asked by General Kirȧly what the army should do, has simply stated: "Thank you for your report, Comrade General." Author's Interview with Bėla Kirȧly.

25. Radio Nyiregyhȧza, 1715 h., 31 October 1956.

26. Keljko Micunoviċ, Moscow Diary (New York: Doubleday, 1980), pp. 133-34; Irving seems to imply that the decision not to intervene was made, probably, on 29 October 1956 by the Politburo in Moscow. On the following day, 30 October 1956, news of the massacre of the ȦVH contingent in Budapest reached Moscow and seems to have prompted the reversal. Uprising, pp. 394-95; the

plain fact, of course, is that Soviet troop movements were continuous and there was no way to sort out when one unit or another was actually ordered to occupy Hungary; nonetheless, all indications seem to point to 30 October or the early morning hours of 31 October 1956. On the role of the army during the second intervention see Zoltán Sztáray, "A néphadsereg és a forradalom," Uj Látohatár 5 (1961).

27. Pál Darnoy, "Ungarn als Mitgliedstaat des Warschauer Paktsystems," Wehrkunde 11 (1956).

28. Az MSzMP honvédelmi politikájárol (Budapest: Zrinyi, 1974), p. 26.

29. For the full text of the declaration see Ibid., pp. 64-65. For some Hungarian evaluations of the role of the army during and immediately after the revolution see "A Magyar Néphadsereg szerepe az ellenforradalom idöszakában és harca a munkás-paraszt hatalom védelméért," Katonai Szemle 2 (1957); Peter Gosztony, "Zur Geschichte des ungarischen nationalen Wiederstandes in der Anfangsperiode des Kadar-Regimes," Osteuropa 10-11 (1968); Károly Munk, "A hadsereg pártirányitásának megszilárditását biztosito néhány fontos 1956-1957-ben hozott intézkedésröl," Honvédelem 6 (1966); Peter Gosztony, "Der Ungarische Volksaufstand, 1956" in Gosztony, ed., Aufstande unten dem roten Stern (Bonn: Hohwacht, 1979); Michael Csizmás, "Die ungarische Volksarmee nach der Revolution," Österreichische Militärische Zeitschrift 2 (1967): p. 34.

30. Az MSzMP, p. 27.

31. János Kádár, Szilárd népi hatalom: független Magyarország (Budapest: Kossuth, 1958), p. 101; Árpád Szabo, A Magyar Honvéd Forradalmi Karhatalom tevékenységének néhany kérdéseröl, (Budapest: Zrinyi, 1966).

32. "A hadsereg pártirányitásának," p. 11.

33. "A katona köszöntése," Magyar Nemzet, 29 September 1966; Jenö Halmai, "Die Ungarische Volksarmee seit 1956," Wehrwissenschaftlische Rundschau 10 (1958).

34. The Military Balance, 1980-1981, p. 96. For the new defense law replacing Law No. 1 (1976) see Law No. 5 (1980), Article 38 amended, Magyar Közlöny (24 December 1980), p. 1388.

35. Pravda, 8 December 1978.

36. During the giant military parade in 1980 there were thirty-eight T-72s and 122 amphibious tanks shown on the streets of Budapest (eyewitness reports).

37. Néphadsereg, 13 May 1978; for a remarkably frank discussion emphasizing this capability see Haditechnikai Szemle 3 (1977): 73-83.

38. Lt. Col. Dr. A. Juhász and A. Szécsi, A társadalom és a hadsereg (Budapest: Zrinyi, 1978). Cf. Lt. Col. Anna Töröcsik (Mrs. Almási), "A katonai

szolgálatra valo alkalmatlanság értékelése," in Károly Molnár, ed., Az egyén és a hadsereg, (Budapest: Zrinyi, 1975).

39. Cpt. Jozsef Malomsoki and Major György Szücs, "A sorköteles fiatalok néhány demográfiai jellemzöje, és azok hatása a katonai nevelésre," in Molnár, Az egyén és a hadsereg, p. 32.

40. See Defense Minister Lajos Czinege in Népszabadság, 23 September 1979.

41. Magyar Hirlap, 17 January 1980.

42. Népszabadság, 13 October 1979.

43. Dr. Károly Ozsváth, Érzelmi feszültségek a katonai szolgálatban (Budapest: Zrinyi, 1978), p. 33.

44. S.M. Shtemenko, "Boevoe bratstvo," Krasnaia Zvezda, 24 January 1970.

45. Az MSzMP KB 1968 februári ülésének és VIII. Kongresszusának Jegyzökönyve (Budapest: Kossuth, 1963), p. 428; and Mit kell tudni a háborurol és a korszerü hadseregekröl? (Budapest: Kossuth, 1973), p. 219.

46. Az MSzMP X. Kongresszusának Jegyzökönyve (Budapest: Kossuth, 1970), p. 168; XI. Kongresszus (1975), p. 519; XII. Kongresszus, p. 191.

47. A honvédelmi nevelés alapjai (Budapest: Zrinyi, 1972), p. 17.

48. Ibid., p. 48.

49. Interview with General Király.

50. Néphadsereg, 2 April 1978; 18 March 1978; 13 May 1978; and Lobogó, 27 September 1979, for the latest documentation.

51. Mit kell tudni a hadseregröl, p. 203.

52. Honvédelmi nevelés (Budapest: Tankönyvkiado, 1977), especially p. 19.

53. In over a dozen officer interviews conducted by this author in Hungary during 1970, 1975, and 1979 the above mission has been generally confirmed and re-confirmed.

54. Micunovic, Moscow Diary, pp. 153-54.

55. György Kiss, Jegyzetek az elsö évekröl (Budapest: Gondolat, 1976), p. 307; Lajos Illés, ed., Örökös örségben (Budapest: Zrinyi, 1976), p. 107.

56. Micunovic, Moscow Diary, p. 154.

57. For scathing indictments of Farkas, see Vas, Viszontagságos életem, pp. 625-29; and Király, "Hungary's Army," pp. 8-10.

58. Király, "Hungary's Army," pp. 7-9.

59. One of the instruments of control were the "political-intelligence," or "D" officers, whose tasks were espionage, counterintelligence, and political investigation. They were, from the very beginning however, distinctly separated in function from the orientation officers; the function of the latter was political education and re-education and corresponded most closely to the current function of the political control

in the post-1956 army. Király, "Hungary's Army," pp. 5-6.

60. István Sterl, "A Varsoi Szerzödés szervezetének fejlödése," Néphadsereg 37 (1970).

61. "A Magyar Néphadsereg szerepe az ellenforradalom idöszakában és harca a munkásparaszt hatalom védelmeéert," Katonai Szemle 2 (1957) and János Berecz, Ellenforradalom tollal és fegyverrel (Budapest: Kossuth, 1969) give interesting accounts of the official post-1956 view on the role of the army in 1956 and in the period shortly after the defeat of the Revolution.

62. This is not to say that men like Lajos Czinege, Gyula Uszta, István Szabo, Pál Ilku, and others who were trained in Moscow, who have had extensive ties to the Communist elites and were steeped in political activity, did not side with the regime and with the Communist-Muscovite faction. The fact, however, was that the professional army cadre below that of the top general officers, was proven to be unreliable from the Soviet perspective. See Király, "Hungary's Army" pp. 12-15.

63. Az MSzMP honvédelmi politikája, p. 26.

64. Frigyes Puja, Miért van szükség a Varsoi Szerzödésre? (Budapest: Kossuth, 1970).

65. Mit kell tudni a háborurol és a korszerü hadseregröl? (Budapest: Kossuth, 1973), p. 206. Csizmás lists several staff exercises held on the territory of Hungary in 1967 and 1971; he also includes in his list the 1968 and 1969 Soviet-Hungarian exercises held in the territory of Hungary. Der Warschauer Pakt, pp. 68-71.

66. Jones, "The Warsaw Pact," pp. 12-19; Mit kell tudni, pp. 205-08; Csizmás, Der Warschauer Pakt, pp. 68-71.

67. Mit kell tudni, p. 206; Csizmás, Der Warschauer Pakt, pp. 68-71.

68. Mit kell tudni, p. 107.

69. Magyar Hirlap. 11 September 1979; Népszava, 13 April 1980.

70. Jones, "The Warsaw Pact," p. 21. On the Soviet academies see V.G. Kulikov, ed., Akademiia general'nogo shtaba (Moscow: Voennizdat., 1976).

71. The Military Balance, 1980-1981, p. 110.

72. Néphadsereg, 20 May 1978.

73. Pártépités (Budapest: Kossuth, 1972), p. 79.

74. Néphadsereg, 20 May 1978.

75. Népszabadság, 23 September 1979.

76. László Szabo, "Hivatásuk: katonatiszt," Népszabadság, 20 August 1977.

77. J. Sz., "Hazát védö hivatás," Népszava, 8 August 1978.

78. Lt. Col. István Matuszka, "A politikai aktivitás fejlesztésének néhány kérdése," in Molnár, ed., Az egyén és a hadsereg, p. 293.

79. Honvédelmröl, nevelöknek (Budapest: Zrinyi, 1975), p. 150.

80. Gábor Gombos, "A pártszervezetek a Pajzs-'79 gyakorlat sikereért," Pártélet 7 (1979), 74-77.

81. Károly Kutika, "Számitunk a KISz-esekre,az Ifjugárdistákra," Ifju Kommunista (December, 1970), 21.

82. Honvédelemröl, nevelöknek, p. 157.

83. Ibid., p. 146.

84. "Uj hadsereg született," Magyar Hirlap, 27 January 1980.

85. Lt. Col. János Pallagi, "A sorállomány politikai oktatásárol," in Molnár, ed., Az egyén és a hadsereg, p. 112.

86. Magyar Hirlap, 18 June 1978.

87. 1 November 1974.

88. Twenty kilometers (Article 4, paragraph 1).

89. Sixty centimeters (Article 9).

90. Magyar Közlöny, 1 November 1974, pp. 889-96.

91. Ifju Kommunista, 9 September 1979, especially pp. 11-13.

92. On the paramilitary organizations in Hungary see Peter Gosztony, "Die Paramilitärische Organisationen in Ungarn," in Gosztony, ed., Paramilitärische Organisationen in Sowjetblock (Bonn-Bad Godesberg: Hohwacht, 1977), pp. 295-331.

93. A Magyar Szocialista Munkáspárt XII. kongresszusa (Budapest: Kossuth, 1980), p. 34.

94. Jozsef Földi, Világnézeti, politikai oktatás és nevelés a tiszthelyetteskèpzés emelt szintü rendszerében (Budapest: Zrinyi, 1977), pp. 13-16.

95. For a summary of defense education see Ivan Volgyes, "Political Socialization in Hungary," in Ivan Volgyes, ed., Comparative Political Socialization (New York: Praeger, 1975), pp. 92-131 and by the same author "The Political and Professional Perspectives of the Hungarian Armed Forces," Journal of Political and Military Sociology 2 (1977): 285-87.

96. Ernö Keserü, "Honvédelmi munka a Kölcsey Ferenc gimnáziumban," Magyar Nemzet, 4 September 1964.

97. Béla Földeáki, "Sorozás idejen," Veszprém megyei Naplo, 14 September 1961.

98. Békés megyei Népujság, 27 September 1962.

99. László Révész, Mililitärische Ausbildung in Osteuropa (Bern: SOI, 1975), for extensive treatment of the problem.

100. It is interesting to note that political instruction also plays major roles in the training of the NCOs on the professional level. After a recruit joins and volunteers for NCO training, out of 250 hours, only 25 hours are spent on military instruction qua instruction and 66 hours spent discussing current problems of the Hungarian labor movement and socialist construction; the topic relating to international events is taught in

45 hours, partly political works are analyzed in 60 hours and questions of Weltanschauung and ethics receive 54 hours worth of treatment. In spite of previous efforts on the high-school level, fully "82 percent of all conscripts possess average or less than average political knowledge," which necessitates the social science portion of instruction to be exceedingly heavily concentrated on political topics. Földi, Vilàgnèzeti, pp. 70, 55; for draftee training proper see: K.A. Gy., "Tanrend a kikèpzötàborban," Magyar Hirlap, 27 January 1974 and Làszlo Szabo, "Tanulo katonàk között," Nèpszabadsàg, 27 April 1967.

101. "Egyetemre Kèszülö fiatalok a hadseregben," Magyar Hirlap, 3 March 1971.

102. "Szeptemberi interju," Hevesi Nèpujsàg, 26 September 1971.

103. Similar programs also have upgraded instruction at the other colleges listed earlier; since the Kossuth is the most important training institution we shall concentrate here on its curriculum.

104. bicsek--"Leszerelö katonafiatalok," Tolna megyei Nèpujsàg, 21 September 1975.

105. Jànos Botyànszki, "Hivatàsuk a haza vèdelme," Bèkès megyei Nèpujsàg, 24 December 1972.

106. Istvàn Bertalan, "Fehèr nègyszög a zubbonyon," Nèphadsereg, 4 May 1968.

107. For the social breakdown of the NCOs see Földi, Vilàgnèzeti.

108. The basic studies on the subject have been conducted by Lt. Col. Istvàn Gruber, "A Katonai Föiskolàra jelentkezett fiatalok pàlyamotivàltsàga," in Kàroly Molnàr, Tanulmànyok a katonai nevelès köréböl (Budapest: Zrinyi, 1973), pp. 162-97; Gruber, "A honvèdelmi nevelès hatèkonysàgàrol a tisztjelöltek felvèteli vizsgàjànak ès személyisègvizsgàlatànak alapjàn," in Molnàr, ed., Az egyèn ès a hadsereg, pp. 240-61; Antal Forgàcs, "A honvèdelmi nevelès idöszerü kèrdèsei," in Tanulmànyok a katonai nevelès köréböl (Budapest: Zrinyi, 1968), pp. 370-88.

109. Istvàn Gruber, "A Katonai," p. 163.

110. Ibid., p. 164.

111. Istvàn Gruber, "A honvèdelmi nevelès," p. 157.

112. Istvàn Gruber, "A Katonai," p. 177.

113. Ibid.

114. Ibid., p. 179.

115. Ibid.

116. Istvàn Gruber, "A honvèdelmi nevelès," p. 246; Sàndor Palkò, "Tisztjelöltek között," Nèpszabadsàg, 24 June 1979, and "Tisztavatàs utàn a laktanyàban," (Nèpszava, 13 April 1980; Andràs Faragò, "Ki szuletik katonànak?"), Magyar Ifjusàg, 2 February 1979; Jòzsef Kònya, "Egy katonatiszt karrierje'," Nèpszabadsàg, 19 August 1978.

117. Lt. Cols. Richárd Bézi, Károly Molnár, Béla Simon, "Hivatás és magánélet," in Molnár, Az egyén és a hadsereg, p. 212.

118. "A katona köszöntése," Magyar Nemzet, 29 September 1966.

119. Bézi et.al., "Hivatás és magánélet," pp. 204-05.

120. Statisztikai Zsebkönyv, 1978 (Budapest: Statisztikai Kiado, 1978), p. 150 and Keserü, "Nagy tapasztalat." For earlier pay-scales see Gosztony, Zur Geschichte, pp. 180, 182.

121. "Tisztavatás után," Néphadsereg, 14 September 1978; Cf. Imre Tarján, "A katonai pályaválasztást befolyásoló egyes motivumokrol," Honvédelem, 6 (1970); "Ankét a fiatal tisztek csapatszolgálatba valo beilleszkedéséröl," Honvédségi Szemle 7 (1972).

122. Bézi et.al., "Hivatás és magánélet, pp. 224-25.

123. Ibid., pp. 222-23. It is also true, however, that extremely luxurious apartment complexes have been built in Budapest for senior-level military officers in various parts of the capital. Two such complexes are located on Vérhalom utca in the luxurious IInd District of Budapest, the first on the corner of Szemlöhegy utca, the second on the corner of Vérhalom tér.

124. Ibid., p. 234.

125. Ibid.

126. Ibid., pp. 216-17. The authors cited also make the startling statement on these pages that the "vast majority of the NCOs do not participate in any forum of public life."

127. For a startling article see Lajos Körmendi, "Az ápolonö," Mozgo Világ (December 1980), 16-17; cf. the best serious study by Lt. Col. Károly Molnár, "A polgári lakosság és a katonák öngyilkosságaniak eltérö tendenciái a XIX. es. XX. században," in Molnár, Az egyén és a hadsereg, pp. 328-87.

128. Magyar Nemzet, 18 June 1978; Ifju Kommunista 9 (1979); Elemér Czák and Ákos Mester, "Kupé a hálokocsiban," Élet és Irodalom, 27 December 1980.

129. Az MSzMP honvédelmi politikája, pp. 141-43.

130. István Kaczur, "A tábornok meg a fiu," Csongrád megyei Hirlap, 24 May 1969.

131. Lajos Kónya, "Emberformáló évek," Dolgozók Lapja, 20 May 1966.

132. Volgyes, "Political Socialization," p. 125.

133. Ivan Volgyes, "Szabad-e sirni a Kápátok alatt?" Irodalmi Ujság (March-April 1979); for full documentation see Volgyes, "Problems of Nationalities and the Magyars in Hungary and in Eastern Europe," Crossroads (Winter-Spring 1981), 127-48.

134. In fact, in 1951 General Király was told by Col. Voloshin, strategic adviser to the Hungarian

General Staff, that "... Hungary has one enemy: Yugoslavia. Consequently, the only military geography you need to teach (them) is that of Yugoslavia. Every soldier should know that in detail." Király, "Hungary's Army Under the Soviets," p. 13.

135. See for instance, Haditechnikai Szemle 3 (1977); Néphadsereg, 23 July 1977; Népszabadság, 20 August 1977; Néphadsereg, 18 March 1978; 2 April 1978 and 13 May 1978.

8
Martial Law and the Reliability of the Polish Military

Jan B. de Weydenthal

INTRODUCTION

On 13 December 1981, Polish authorities declared a "state of war" in their country, a term used in Polish legal parlance to describe martial law. The immediate effect of the declaration was a dramatic change in Poland's internal political situation. It introduced massive administrative measures aimed at restricting civil liberties and transferring the execution of power into the hands of the military. A new political authority, the Military Council of National Salvation, consisting of 20 senior military officers and chaired by General Wojciech Jaruzelski, was established. Effective control over the operations conducted by state administrative, economic, and educational agencies was assumed by military commissars, who were charged with responsibility to supervise the implementation of the council's directives. All those developments suggested that the military had emerged as the key element of the system of rule. Broader implications for both the existing political system and the population, however, remain unclear.

By now it is commonplace to assert that martial law both transformed the character of the country's public life and changed the nature of its political system. In some respects, this assertion is undeniably correct, particularly with regard to a major alteration in the style, the extent, and the substance of popular participation in politics. Through the first eight months of martial law, the situation was characterized by rigid centralization of decision-making, far-reaching restrictions on the activity of social groups and public

---

Jan B. de Weydenthal (Ph.D., Political Science, University of Notre Dame) is Senior Analyst in the Radio Free Europe Research Department (Munich, Federal Republic of Germany).

associations, and almost absolute limitation on the ways in which the public can influence the process of policy formation. More important, many of these traits, while described as temporary by the leadership, may well be permanent since the authorities appear determined to reserve for themselves the exclusive prerogative to set the direction of the country's evolution. The release of some political detainees in July 1982 did not alter that determination.

The issue of change in the nature of the political system seems more complex, however, and fundamentally elusive. The main argument in support of such change rests upon the assertion that the imposition of martial law, and the situation produced by that operation, both resulted from and contributed to the dramatic ascendency of the military over all other institutions of the system. Evidence for this development has been seen in the actual mechanics of implementing martial law by uniformed troops, in the militarization of all, or almost all, visible aspects of public life, and in the assumption of major decision-making positions by military personnel. The obvious implication is that the military as an institution has replaced other institutions, such as the communist party and the government, in their operational and political functions. In short, the argument claims that the essence of the Polish change is not so much a procedural transformation, in the sense of changing the rules of the political game, as a structural one, in which the very bases of the game have been considerably modified.

Few could deny the conceptual attraction of this argument and certainly no one would underestimate the significance of such a development if it actually occurred. At the same time, there is a need to raise questions regarding the extent of military involvement in and control over the unfolding evolution of Polish politics. From the standpoint of both Warsaw Pact and NATO planners, moreover, there is a need to assess how the political involvement of the Polish military affects its reliability as a Soviet ally.

THE MECHANICS OF MARTIAL LAW

One of the most persistent assertions made about the operational aspects of the imposition of martial law has been that they were executed by troops of the regular armed forces in conjunction with police units. This assertion might be misleading. As the months pass since the fateful days of mid-December 1981 and more information on the events that took place then becomes available, it is increasingly clear that the actual role of regular soldiers in quelling social protests was relatively limited, that many army units did not take part in the operations, and that troops frequently were used for purposes other than that of dealing with the population and the workers. Indeed, it appears that the main role in suppressing active resistance was played by security organizations, such as the paramilitary services and the special police units. In this sense, the imposition of the "state of war" could be regarded as basically an operation conducted by the security apparatus rather than the military forces.

The Polish regular military forces consist, according to reliable estimates,[1] of some 319,500 men, of which 187,000 are conscripts. They serve in four separate branches: the ground forces (210,000 men of which 154,000 are conscripts, 18 divisions in three military districts), the navy (22,500 men of which 6,000 are conscripts), the air force and the air defense forces (combined force of 87,000 of which 27,000 are conscripts). In addition, the regular forces include units of the Military Security Service (WSW) (military counterintelligence, as well as the military police force); the size of these units is difficult to establish inasmuch as they include troops from all four branches.

Since the mid-1960s, the regular forces have been designated as the "operational army."[2] Their primary mission has been to prepare for action outside Poland and to fulfill tasks in both defensive and offensive operations. Commanded directly by the Minister of National Defense, the "operational army" is included in the Joint Armed Forces of the Warsaw Pact. The executive command over the operational troops has rested in the hands of the Chief of the General Staff, a function performed since January 1973 by General Florian Siwicki, and the Chief Inspector for Training, a position occupied since 1971 by General Eugeniusz Molczyk. Both generals have been Deputy Ministers of National Defense and the latter has served as Deputy Commander-in-Chief of the Warsaw Pact Joint Armed Forces.

The paramilitary services include units of the Internal Defense Forces (WOW), the Border Protection Forces (WOP), and the territorial defense troops. All those units number about 72,000[3] and have since 1965 been subordinated to the Chief Enspectorate for the Defense of National Territory, a body headed since March 1971 by General Tadeusz Tuczapski, who has also held the position of a Deputy Minister of National Defense. The stated mission of the paramilitary services is to insure armed resistance against the hypothetical penetration of Poland by enemy forces, owing to which function the Chief Inspector for the Defense of National Territory also controls some units of the air defense forces, as well as to protect the stability of the state against the danger of internal upheavals.[4] To fulfill the latter task the commander of the paramilitary services has always cooperated with the Ministry of Internal Affairs. Indeed, all paramilitary services were controlled until 1965 by the Ministry of Internal Affairs alone. Even after that, the division of administrative and political responsiblities between the military and the civilian agencies of the government with respect to the operations and functions of the services was never fully clarified; it appears, in fact, that the Minister of Internal Affairs has preserved considerable authority and effective control over those units.

The formal role of securing internal peace has been performed by a relatively large police force. Its estimated strength is about 200,000 men and women, including some 20,000 to 25,000 special riot police (Motorized Detachments of the Citizens' Police, ZOMO).[5] They are supported by the Voluntary Police Reserve (ORMO) of some 370,000. All those units are directly controlled by the Ministry of Internal Affairs, which also has its own separate security force of at least two divisions, the so-called Vistula Divisions, to be used for special purposes in maintaining internal order.

It is still difficult to determine how many men, and from which formations, took part in the imposition of martial law; it is certain, however,that some regular military units remained in their quarters during the entire operation. This was indirectly confirmed by Colonel Zdzislaw Malina, a ranking officer involved in the work of the military administration, who said in an interview with the official party daily that only "part of our armed forces had to move out of their quarters to restore order in the country."[6] Moreover, the role of those regular troops that took an active part in the implementation of martial law appears to have been relatively innocuous: they enforced the curfew, patrolled the streets, guarded roads and bridges, and marked their uniformed presence.[7]

This operational restraint obviously was related to the leadership's broader considerations of military preparedness; no responsible military commander would allow the complete deployment of the available personnel for essentially nonmilitary tasks; the requirements of defensive readiness preclude that. Furthermore, it turned out that there was no apparent need for any mass deployment of regular troops as the level of active opposition to the imposition of martial law was relatively limited and concentrated in selected industrial centers. In this regard, a scenario in which the reliability of regular troops for domestic coercion could be tested did not materialize.

The brunt of the "dirty work" was taken up by the security bodies, the paramilitary services, and the police. According to numerous eyewitness reports about actions undertaken against striking workers during the first days of martial law at Silesian mines as well as coastal cities and other urban centers,[8] internal security paramilitary troops and the police, particularly the riot police units (ZOMO), played the crucial role in breaking the workers' resistance. It was they who surrounded the factories with tanks, crashed through walls, and assaulted the protestors. It was also they who shot at the demonstrators and were held responsible, at least in the public mind, for killings and tortures. It was they, too, who carried out mass detentions and arrests of both presumed and real opponents of martial law.

This role was explicitly acknowledged by Minister of Internal Affairs General Czeslaw Kiszczak, who extended to "the police and the security forces as well as to the soldiers of the Border Protection Forces and the ministry's special units and the ORMO" words of special appreciation for their efforts to ensure "peace in the fatherland and the full normalization of life."[9] Members of those units subsequently were decorated with medals and distinctions;[10] there has been no public indication that similar honors were bestowed upon regular soldiers or units of the "operational army."

The apparent effort by the authorities to limit the involvement of regular soldiers in "civilian" operations seems to reflect several considerations. The most obvious is a possible concern about the reliability of regular troops in carrying out orders in a scenario of internal political repression. There had been persistent rumors, both in the country and among foreign observers, that Polish soldiers would refrain from shooting at protesting civilians. This has always been a debatable question, since the experience of two earlier instances of military intervention in domestic political troubles, the suppression of a workers' revolt in Poznan in June 1956 and the pacification of several coastal cities in December 1970, failed to provide clear evidence of the soldiers' attitudes.

There is, for example, considerable evidence that regular troops fired at and killed civilian protestors both in Poznan in 1956 and in Gdynia and Szczecin during 1970.[11] It is also true, however, that some regular military units ordered to action in Poznan not only refrained from shooting at the demonstrating crowds, but actually joined the protestors.[12] Similarly, there have been indications that some troops, and even some officers, resented orders to put down public protests in 1970 by force and tried to limit their involvement in the operation to essentially passive functions.[13] Against this background, one is tempted to speculate that the leadership could have been hesitant to test soldiers' political loyalty since the outcome of such a test was uncertain.[14] Such a presumption of uncertainty appears particularly justified in view of the social and political situation prevailing at the end of 1981, when the very foundations of a communist party system seemed to be crumbling under the pressure of popular demands for change. Even if one assumes that the soldiers were relatively isolated from civilian concerns and activities, owing to military separateness and organizational discipline, it is unlikely that they remained immune to the influences of society at large--a point introduced in Dan Nelson's chapter in this volume. It is obvious that this point was never lost on the political and military leaders as they prepared for and then implemented martial law.

Another consideration was that of avoiding a "post-operational" trauma that might affect military morale and discipline once the pacifying activities were terminated and public life had returned to its usual pattern. There have been several reports that such feelings of guilt and shame emerged in military units following the events of 1956 and 1970. Conscious of their lasting and negative repercussions for military cohesion and thereby reliability for future operations, the authorities appear to have decided to restrict them to the absolute minimum and to take precautions not to expose soldiers needlessly.

Finally, there must have been purely political considerations as well. Until recently, and particularly during the continuing crisis of 1980-1981, the military enjoyed a relatively high standing in the public perception of various institutions, trailing only behind the Church and Solidarity in opinion polls.[15] There is no doubt that this standing has been skillfully used by the authorities during and since the imposition of martial law, which they have presented in the form of a military endeavor to create the foundations for "a return to peace, discipline , order, and hard work." By the same token, authorities were wary of not ruining the military's reputation and public standing--attributed that could prove useful in the future.

The mechanics of the coup therefore provide a picture of an intricate political ploy. By restraining the military's actual involvement in the operation itself, in which the main role was played by the security forces, the authorities appear to have attempted both to preserve the integrity of the troops and to insure that the image of the national army would not be irreparably damaged, both crucial for mobilization potential. At the same time, by proclaiming the imposition of martial law as a quintessentially military action, the authorities seem to have been attempting to remove the ultimate onus from the security forces, which could later be presented to the public not as the instigators of martial law but the mere executors of orders. In this way,no one would bear the responsibility, at least not the entire one, while both bodies could be charged with only partial blame.

THE MILITARIZATION OF THE STATE

The imposition of martial law has produced a curiously hybrid form of government, in which new decision-making bodies have been both superimposed upon and enmeshed with the long-established administrative structures. The stated objective of this development is to streamline the government's work and to "create operational guarantees that will make it possible to regain discipline and conformity to the law."[16] Its immediate effects, however, have been institutional confusion and administrative chaos. It is obvious that the current arrangement cannot continue for long since it undermines the very basis of the government's authority and weakens its effectiveness. That much has been recognized by the authorities themselves, who repeatedly assert that such a system is only temporary. Nonetheless, it is unclear when and how changes will be made.

The most important new body that has emerged within the framework of the current regime is the Military Council of National Salvation. Set up in 13 December 1981 on its own initiative, without any discernible legal basis but claiming for itself a mandate derived from the support of "the Polish armed forces,"[17] the council has clearly and effectively ruled the country ever since the imposition of martial law.

Even so, due to the circumstances of its emergence and to the manner of its operations, the council's institutional role in the system remains enigmatic. Its members seem to exercise the highest power, issuing declarations and instructions that are binding for all other institutions. At the same time, the council has defined itself as "a temporary body that will operate only until the situation stabilizes."[18] While hardly explanatory, the assertion of temporariness only complicates the problem of institutional stabilization and creates serious doubts as to who will exercise authority once the council is dissolved.

Equally confusing has been the council's assurance, made at the time of its public emergence and never modified, that its activity "does not undermine the competence of, and does not replace, any bodies of (civilian) authority in performing their work." One might here inquire about the political status of the authoritative messages that in any other circumstances would be issued by constitutionally defined state bodies.

The Military Council of National Salvation is formally neither a policy-making nor an executive body and has consciously adopted the role of a policy-inspiring as well as policy-coordinating center. This was specifically asserted in its initial declaration, which included both general statements on foreign and domestic policies and explicit promises to streamline the operations of various state bodies throughout the country.

To insure administrative compliance with its "inspirational" and "coordinating" instructions, the council has activated a network of commissars, all of them military officers, whose duty has been to "supervise directly the activity of...state administration (and other institutions) in matters related to the security and defense preparedness of the country."[19] It is still impossible to ascertain exactly how many officers have become commissars, but their estimated number runs into thousands. Some of the commissars were recruited from among retired military personnel as well as reserve officers. Others, particularly those operating in factories and smaller communities, were chosen from among the commanders of the so-called "military task forces" that had been created at the end of October 1981. Then, the officially announced mission of those groups, which were initially dispatched to more than 2,000 communes and small towns and subsequently were sent to large factories and industrial centers, had been to streamline the work of local state administrators and to "improve production effectiveness."[20] Now, with the benefit of hindsight, it is apparent that their main task was to prepare a contingency plan for the imposition of martial law. Even so, the obvious change in the functions of the task forces in the aftermath of the imposition of martial law has not entailed the termination of their work; they continue to maintain a ubiquitous presence throughout the country.

This situation could suggest that the military authorities and military personnel have taken over the levers of both decision-making and administrative supervision, replacing the appropriate state bodies. At the same time, it must be noted that the new military bodies have preserved strong institutional links with the established formal structures of the government. These links have been maintained, above all, through the presence of General Wojciech Jaruzelski at the head of both the Military Council of National Salvation and the government's hierarchy. General Jaruzelski has been Minister of National Defense since April 1968 and has served since February 1981 as the country's prime minister as well.

Such links have also been demonstrated by the fact that four members of the council (Generals Florian Siwicki, Tadeusz Tuczapski, Eugeniusz Molczyk, and Jozef Baryla) are Deputy Ministers of Defense, three (Generals Czeslaw Kiszczak, Tadeusz Hupalowski, and Czeslaw Piotrowski) hold civilian positions in the government,[21] and one (General Michal Janiszewski) is the director of the prime minister's civilian cabinet. The operational implications of this linkage should not, perhaps, be exaggerated. But immediate institutional effects could be serious, since the dual membership in the council and the civilian government creates potential differences between particular administrative branches of the government, in which some ministers acquire additional leverage and others lose importance and influence.

It must also be noted that the commissars, while watching over the fulfillment of the military council's instructions, operate formally as representatives of the national Committee for the Country's Defense, a body defined in the 1967 Law on Universal Military Service as the principal administrative agency of government in war conditions. Although strongly influenced by military elements, this committee has never been conceived of as a purely military institution. Instead, it was envisaged in the law as an operational committee of the Council of Ministers, presided over by the Prime Minister and comprising other officials designated by the Council of Ministers.[22] The committee, which was to act as a collegial body, would maintain a network of provincial defense committees, each of them including regional civilian administrators, party secretaries, police commanders, and military representatives.

These provisions have been in force in Poland ever since the imposition of martial law. In addition to his many other functions, General Jaruzelski has become the head of the national committee. No precise information about the other members of that body is available, but it could be presumed that it includes several government officials as well as senior military officers. The provincial defense committees are presided over by the respective voivods (provincial chief administrators appointed by the prime minister), with chiefs of provincial military staffs acting as deputy chairmen on an *ex officio* basis. To insure that the work of the committees conforms to orders from above, several civilian voivods in particularly sensitive areas have been replaced by military officers. Those areas include parts of the coastal region (Gdansk, Elblag, Koszalin), Silesia (Katowice), and parts of central Poland (Kalisz, Radom, Tarnobrzeg, Zielona Gora). In addition, military officers took over positions as chairmen of local people's councils in several other cities.

The alleged goal of all those regulations has been greater administrative efficiency. There is no evidence to suggest, however, that such efficiency has been achieved. Instead, the immediate result of the new arrangement has been a multiplication of control mechanisms over the activity of various state agencies, factories, and educational as well as cultural establishments. This control is now executed through at least three separate, but interlocking, channels. The first is the usual administrative or managerial control of each institution by specific state agencies, such as the Supreme Chamber of Control attached to the Sejm (parliament). The second is exercised by officials selected to sit on the local defense committees. Finally,the additional controlling functions rest in the hands of the military commissars, and they remain directly linked with the national committee. The commissars are empowered to "supervise directly the work of the committees as well as local bodies of state administration...and observe whether the decisions taken by the committees correspond with those of the supreme authorities, the Military Council of National Salvation, and the national Committee for the Defense of the Country."[23]

There is no doubt that the entire picture of double and triple control is confusing. Yet the stated function of the committees, and through them the entire controlling machinery, is still to "stabilize, in the conditions of the state of war, the social, political, and economic situation." Furthermore, as if to indicate that the current pattern of administrative and institutional development is likely to continue for some time, an authoritative spokesman for the national committee indicated in early 1982 that "one has to realize that any progress in the gradual removal of the (main features of) the state of war will...depend only on the extent of stabilization of social and economic life."[24]

There is no need to speculate about the efficiency and the effectiveness of the countless administrative officials, managers, workers, scientists, teachers, and artists as their activities are constantly interfered with, supervised, and controlled by various civilian and uniformed agents of the ruling establishment. Any assessment will have to await the results of their efforts. In the meantime, one cannot escape the impression that the militarization of major economic and administrative institutions--their employees are regarded as "mobilized" into the armed forces for the duration of martial law--testify to the authorities' fundamental distrust of the public.

The long-term effects of this development could be serious in that they are likely to affect the prospects for some future "normalization" of public life. The purpose of this "normalization" is to provide conditions in which the key political institutions,such as the party and the government, could function in a fully authoritative fashion. This was indicated by General Jaruzelski when he announced the imposition of martial law on December 13; it has also been repeatedly asserted in various statements and proclamations by other military and political leaders. But it has always been obvious, and acknowledged by the leadership itself, that to succeed in "normalizing" the operations of the system, public support, or at least acquiescence, would be necessary. Such acquiescence would be much more difficult to achieve in the current situation, in which the pervasive control will weigh heavily on public morale. In the process, the very ability of the authorities to insure the unforced compliance of the population with their policies, an element that is indispensable in fulfilling the basic requirements of government and a nation's military reliability, is certain to be severely damaged.

THE MILITARY AND THE PARTY

Conventional wisdom now holds that the imposition and the maintenance of martial law effectively have eclipsed the role of the communist party in the Polish system of government. A political institution asserting for itself the right to set the direction for social and economic life, the party appears to have been forced to retreat into relative obscurity with the levers of power controlled by the military and the security bodies. Even so, any predictions about the future role and status of the party must be made with the greatest caution, since the chances of its political regeneration are still strong.

There is, of course, considerable evidence that martial law has had an adverse effect on the party, particularly on its local organizations and the rank-and-file membership. Numerous party bodies in factories, offices, and universities have been dissolved, while in other institutions and agencies the activity of the party has been curtailed. There have also been indications that considerable numbers of ordinary party members have left the organization, either in protest against the imposition of martial law or because they have lost any hope of improvement in the party's operations in the future.[25] There is reason to believe that this phenomenon has acquired national proportions and affected both manual workers and intellectuals, administrative employees and artists, and even some high-ranking members of the party's professional staff.[26] There is little doubt that the communist organization is experiencing real difficulties. The question remains, however, whether those difficulties were, in fact, prompted by the military rule and whether its maintenance continues to weaken the party and its role within the system.

Here the answer, admittedly tentative,is negative. To support this contention, it is necessary to recall that the party had developed serious problems, both in its organizational behavior and its political appeal, a long time before the imposition of martial law. What is certain, of course, is that the forced turnaround in the country's political life provoked by the military intervention has not made the situation in the party any better. It is equally obvious, however, that this development did not initiate any new process of internal disintegration; it merely accelerated and reinforced the existing trends. This appears particularly true of the decline in the membership, a process that has been going on for more than a year.

In addition, while most attention has been focused on organizational aspects of the party's difficulties, the crucial problem faced by the Communists is, and has long been, that of self-perception. This problem is related directly to the broad social and political developments that have taken place in Poland during recent months and could be summed up in a single phenomenon: pluralization. As new social organizations and institutions, claiming full operational and conceptual autonomy, such as Solidarity and various youth and professional movements, have emerged, the position of the party and its role in the system have dramatically changed; it has come to be regarded by the public simply as another body--admittedly with rather special prerogatives--but basically comparable to others. More important still, this assessment of the party's role has begun to be accepted by large numbers of party members themselves, who with increasing frequency have argued for a redefinition of its programs and demanded changes in its internal statutes. The net result of all these trends has been a drastic decline in the once general acceptance of the "leading role" of the party within the system.

There is no doubt that the party leaders fully realized the long-term implications of the development. They have also repeatedly warned on numerous occasions preceding the imposition of martial law that the leadership would not accept the institutionalization of an arrangement in which independent social groups would acquire permanent recognition of their autonomy within the system of government. Waning party prestige, however, meant that no measure, short of widespread suppression, could reverse the trend toward democratization. The imposition of martial law did just that.

This fact, in itself, has created new opportunities for the party to embark upon a road toward some sort of new beginning. It will certainly be an uphill struggle, requiring major efforts to develop long-term programs of political activity so as to regain some degree of internal cohesion as well as to insure public compliance with the party's directives. There is still no clear sign that such programs are in the offing, however, a fact which testifies to the magnitude of the political malaise. Instead, the main emphasis in current activities has been on purges, personnel reshuffles, and propaganda campaigns designed to inculcate in the party's rank-and-file membership and the population a conviction of the finality and the inevitability of "socialist normalization."

In all these activities, the involvement of the military has not only been openly acknowledged, but also widely publicized. For example, hardly a week has passed since the imposition of martial law without detailed reports in the media about investigations undertaken by military prosecutors against presumed or real opponents of martial law and about sentences passed by military courts in case involving such opponents. Indeed, it seems that the entire Polish judicial system has been put under the direct control of military commissars, who have been empowered to direct legal proceedings and supervise its implementation.[27] On a more general plane, it has certainly not escaped public attention that a military officer, General Michal Janiszewski, instituted the practice of requiring state employees to sign a pledge of loyalty to the system. That requirement, combined with a normal renunciation of membership in Solidarity, was introduced on 17 December 1981.[28] Any state employee refusing to sign the pledge was to be removed from his/her position. Finally, there have been recurring press reports that local military officials, both commissars and recently appointed administrators, have been the prime movers in conducting purges of personnel employed in social, cultural, and economic life.[29] No exact figures related to that process are available; there is little doubt, however, that the brunt of the action has been directed at all those who displayed some degree of either support for or understanding of the public movement toward autonomy.

A closely related development has been the expanding military influence over recruitment in both the party and the higher echelons of the state administration. This development was perhaps inevitable following the election of General Wojciech Jaruzelski as the party's first secretary in mid-October 1981. It acquired institutional momentum, however, with the appointment, on 28 October 1981, of General Tadeusz Dziekan as head of the Central Committee's Cadres Department, a party agency supervising personnel matters and recruitment policies within the entire organization. Commenting on the department's work since November 1981, Dziekan's deputy, Colonel Jerzy Wojcik, recently noted that more than 2,000 changes have been made within the state administrative leadership, while "rotations and changes" have affected more than 5,000 employees of the party's apparatus, of whom 670 have retired and 3,500 have been moved to positions outside the organization's professional staff.[30] In mid-1981, the party's apparatus consisted of 17,166 fulltime employees.[31]

The military presence and military influence have

also emerged as major factors in shaping the character of the propaganda activities undertaken by the current political leadership. This was particularly obvious, of course, in the first days and weeks of martial law, when Poland's television viewers saw only uniformed speakers, when Zolnierz Wolnosci, the daily paper published by the Main Political Administration of the armed forces, set the tone for press reporting and commentaries, and when the public was inundated by countless military communiques and proclamations. In time, such visible aspects of martial rule gradually disappeared, only to give way to some subtler but equally important changes. The most obvious of them is the continuing militarization of the media, a situation in which journalists and editors are bound by military discipline and are subjected to military control exercised by commissars attached to the networks, agencies, and newspapers. The other change was marked by the dissolution of the journalists' union, a step formally implemented through a decision of the newly appointed Mayor of Warsaw, General Mieczyslaw Debicki. Taken together, those measures, combined with the sharpening of censorship, drastically curtailed press freedom, inhibited journalists, and created the basis for a fundamental containment of the media.

No one can deny that the growing military involvement in Poland's politics is likely to have a major impact upon the character of the country's public life and the military as well. Some of these repercussions, already apparent, have a symbolic quality. Here the most obvious is the aura of toughness, discipline, and firmness, attributes frequently associated with the military profession. The entrance of uniformed officials onto the political arena has created an impression in the public mind and among observers that the arena itself has changed and become more stable, something that civilian politicians had longed to achieve and failed to accomplish.

The other element is more practical and, in the long run, perhaps more important. There is little doubt that the enhancement of the military's political presence has also entailed a considerable influx of representatives of the armed forces into positions that otherwise would be occupied by civilian politicians. This has been most evident at the level of the party's highest leadership, in which General Wojciech Jaruzelski occupies the top post as the Central Committee's first secretary, while two other military officers, Generals Czeslaw Kiszczak and Florian Siwicki, are deputy Politburo members. Less obvious, but politically very significant, has been the progressive penetration of lower party bodies by military personnel. Numerous officers have been either elected or appointed as party secretaries in various provinces--this has been particularly noticeable in the major industrial centers of Silesia and the coastal region--and many others have recently been coopted to local committees in towns, factories, and administrative agencies. The scope of this development is still difficult to assess, yet its political meaning is clear. Within the party organization has emerged a new cohesive group defined through common experience, easy identification, and a strong esprit de corps.

Whether this heralds a permanent modification of domination by civilian politicians is still uncertain. In part, this uncertainty reflects a continuing lack of information about the way decisions are made within the leadership, in general, and about the actual relationship between the new military bodies, such as the Military Council of National Salvation, and the party's Politburo and the Secretariat, in particular. There are, moreover, grounds to believe that some civilian party leaders have not only preserved considerable influence over the decision-making process but might have actually helped in both preparing and then maintaining the state of martial law. Few could doubt, for example, that the task of implementing martial law required long months of intensive training and preparation. It is inconceivable that the civilian political leadership was not aware of these activities. Indeed, it is more than likely that it abetted the military preparations and encouraged their implementation. There is also evidence that the highest party leadership was instrumental in creating the conditions for purges and personnel changes. In fact, the framework of those developments was provided through a special, still secret, instruction issued by the party's Politburo a few days before the imposition of martial law.[32]

Equally important is the attitude of the current military leaders to the party's role and functions. A retrospective glance at recent Polish political history could be helpful on this point. Commenting on the role of the military in quelling workers' protests in the coastal cities in December 1970, General Wojciech Jaruzelski, then a deputy Politburo member and Minister of National Defense, told the workers in Szczecin a few weeks later that the decision to use troops--although made by the political leadership--had been faithfully implemented because "do you want an army...that would take over power for itself, that would change the authorities in a manner (similar to that of) Latin American of Africa? (An army) that would (refuse to follow) this or that decision taken by (the country's) legally elected leadership and would abolish that leadership? No! Our Polish soldier will always defend people's power, whatever it may be, will always defend the party."[33] There is no reason to assume that General Jaruzelski, the current first secretary of the party as well as Prime Minister and Minister of National Defense, thinks differently today, although he seems to prefer a uniform and the military functions of armed forces supreme commander and head of the Military Council of National Salvation rather than being identified with either the party or the government over which he presides.[34]

There is also no reason to assume that the attitudes of other members of the military establishment, particularly those members who recently have assumed political roles, are any different. Although there is no firm evidence one way or the other, several indications have emerged during martial law that provide ground for some tentative conclusions. Above all, according to voluminous press reports on the military's activities in various areas of public life, the officers and soldiers involved in this work were invariably either members of the party or its youth appendages. Although this may be construed as simply another propaganda ploy, it should not be surprising, since 85 percent of the entire officer corps in the Polish armed forces has been reported to be party members.[35] More important seems to be the claim that the "tone" for political work conducted by the military has been set by experienced party activitists in the armed forces, veteran "party members in uniform."[36] These, in all probability, consist of senior staff officers--it is, indeed, striking that no operational, "line"commanders have been included in the various military councils or among the commissars--party secretaries, political officers, and other officials of the Main Political Administration of the armed forces. Due to their administrative functions or political roles, those people have long been more closely related to the party apparatus than to ordinary soldiers in the field.

At the same time, it has been clear for some time that political work among military had its own organizational and ideological characteristics. Relatively isolated from society and subjected to their own rules and disciplinary codes, the armed forces have provided a comparatively easy and conflict-free element for political indoctrination. Whether this activity has produced the desired effect of making the soldiers immune from nomilitary political and ideological influences, and thus enhancing their reliability, is doubtful.[37] There is no doubt, however, that the organizational cohesion of the party and its executive bodies in the military has been largely unaffected by the decay and progressive disarray that has plagued the civilian party. This, more than anything else, explains the recent growth of political and organizational influence exercised by "party members in uniform" in the country, and particularly within the party.

Viewed from this perspective, the militarization of political life does not necessarily imply any structural transformation within the system, in the sense of the ascendancy of the military over other authoritative bodies. Rather, it may mean that a specific branch of the system's establishment, functionally separate from the other branches but fully integrated into the system's ideological and political framework, has emerged as the main instrument in enforcing public compliance with the leadership's policies. In some ways, the current situation appears related to that of the early 1950s, when the security forces largely replaced the party's regular bodies "as the principal factor in shaping the flow of centrally induced social and economic activities."[38] There is no need to recall here that the experience of the 1950s led to a major turmoil within the system and a drastic downgrading of the security apparatus, which, after being thoroughly purged, was turned into a mere instrument for party and government leaders to control the public. But then, such reminders from the past could and should also be taken seriously into consideration by the current military leadership.

PROSPECTS FOR MILITARY RELIABILITY

What, then, are the consequences of developments discussed above for the military itself, particularly with respect to its self-identity and reliability? Indeed, major and potentially significant changes affecting the armed forces are regarded widely as both necessary and inevitable. Issues about which there is less agreement are the character, conditions, pace, and scope of these changes' implementation.

The most obvious change will involve a shift in the composition of the military leadership. This is, of course, a direct result of the recent influx of military personnel into positions within the party and government hierarchies. Increasingly preoccupied with the fulfillment of essentially civilian political tasks, those officers will have to limit or abandon military responsibilities. Their functions in the military will be taken over by others, perhaps younger and obviously less experienced officers.

The effect of this shift both upon the military as an institution and on its reliability for internal or external use under varying scenarios is not clear. It can be argued, for example, that such a personnel shift would make little or no immediate difference. Incoming commanders would, after all, have been thoroughly trained by the departing officers and they would be likely to possess characteristics--political as well as ideological and behavioral--similar to those of their predecessors. Furthermore, there is a strong possibility that the new appointees would not only maintain a cooperative relationship with the political authorities, a typical feature of military-civilian relations in Poland over the years, but that their loyalty to the current leadership might be much greater than that of those they replaced to previous leaders since they would owe their advancement to that leadership alone. This, in turn, would serve to preserve the basic continuity of the armed forces' political and institutional identity while enhancing their reliability in defending the existing system. For domestic use, then, such a transfer of military command due to the army's entry into politics may upgrade mobilization potential and thereby reliability.

Notwithstanding this effect, one cannot preclude the possibility that the new commanding group--one must talk of a "group" here, considering the large number of officers who are likely to replace those who have become involved in civilian operations and structures--could be pushed toward an active self-assertion in the relationship, especially where its own interests are at stake. Such interests include a degree of institutional autonomy within the system, a clearly delineated structure of command that rests on the principle of authority exercised by the officers in charge, and concern over professional preparedness and operational modernization that rely upon different standards than those set for the civilian areas of the system. Indeed, a preoccupation with these interests has long provided the grounds for the institutional distinctiveness of the military in comparison with other organizations and agencies operating on the Polish political scene; there is no reason to suggest that the future situation will be any different, regardless of the personal characteristics of the top political leaders.

This point has certainly not been lost on General Jaruzelski and his associates as they prepare themselves and the armed forces for a change of command. The pace of this change has been, until now, very slow. This is particularly striking with regard to senior positions in the military's political sector as well as in the staffs, in which there was little movement even while it is clear that many officers from those bodies have already taken up full-time posts in either the party or the state apparatus. Such slowness of pace could be justified, perhaps, by the pressing requirements of martial law, in which the tasks of both implementing the decisions of the leadership and coordinating the activities of various civilian agencies are fulfilled by active or mobilized members of the armed forces. And yet, the continuing maintenance of the military trappings of martial law as a means to an orderly transition could, instead, contribute to tensions within the officer corps. Potential conflicts may be stimulated between those officers who stay with the troops and those who move on to the political arena and to alienate the armed forces from the leadership that purports to represent and symbolize them.

To make matters worse, there is a growing likelihood that the conditions of martial law will remain for some time; while the name could change, and some detainees may be released, the failure of current leadership to accomplish its stated mission to create stability, order, and legitimacy for the existing system may perpetuate de facto martial law. As the years pass since December 13, 1981, it has become obvious that the authority of the ruling establishment remains as questionable, if not more so, as before, since it continues to express itself through the use of police force rather than any form of popular support. Despite a flurry of promises by political leaders and repeated propagandistic assurances about the government's inevitable future success, no major new policies have been introduced and no new departures in decision-making have been made. There is a growing realization among many observers and large sectors of the Polish population that no improvement in either economic or social conditions has been achieved and that the leadership is drifting without any discernible sense of direction.[39]

There is also considerable evidence that a public spirit of defiance against martial law, its leaders, and its regulations is very much alive. It is, of course, true that many social organizations, particularly the labor unions and numerous formerly autonomous bodies, have been deprived of the right to conduct their statutory activities. Even so, there have been recurrent reports of localized protests, brief strikes, and demonstrations in various parts of Poland. A relatively large network of conspiratorial groups opposed to martial law has already been set up throughout the country, and the spirit of defiance has been reinforced by the proliferation of underground papers and periodicals as well as by the emergence of several broadcasting outlets, which operate clandestinely in major cities and industrial centers.[40]

In many ways, this situation is not surprising. Strains between the institutional system and the population, as well as the internal decay of the power structure, were of such intensity and long standing that no attempt at partial improvement, including the militarization of public life, could mitigate them for long. Indeed, one might justifiably wonder whether the military's stated objective of rebuilding order and legitimacy for the government was not impossible from the start. If so, one could inquire whether current policy of militarization of the regime, through the implantation of military personnel into various civilian bodies and the identification of the system's values and operation with those of the armed forces, would not produce effects detrimental to the morale and the effectiveness of the military itself. Were this process of decay within the armed forces to begin or be accelerated by martial law, then reliability would decline as intervention continues.

For some time, and particularly during the last four years or so, the military has enjoyed a reputation as the only body within the system that was both competent and effective in conducting its work. This reputation was established not so much on the basis of what the military actually did, however, as on the public assumption that it kept apart from other institutions and their activities. The military, therefore, was not blamed for the mistakes, failures, and debacles associated by the public with the performance of the political leaders of both the party and the government; it was not seen as corrupt in the way the party was or bureaucratized as the government was. Whether such an image of honesty, effectiveness, and orderliness corresponded to reality is a moot point; its net effect, however, was a widespread respect for the armed forces and its leaders, an attitude that clearly contributed toward building the military's morale and its self-confidence.

This situation is bound to change under the impact of the current political and economic circumstances. While the initial performance of the military leaders during the imposition of martial law could arguably be regarded as providing testimony of their tactical skills and operational efficiency, their subsequent activities have given little or no reason for satisfaction. Indeed, their performance seems no different from that of their civilian predecessors. Politically, no perceptible change has occurred, and the very existence of such military bodies as the Military Council of National Salvation and the network of controlling commissars seemed to undermine the authority of other institutions within the system further rather than stabilizing their functions. Economically, a similar lack of improvement must be noted, while there are numerous indications that the production, distribution, and consumption of goods as well as foreign trade have rapidly deteriorated. The end result of these developments is progressive public disillusionment with the military's capability to provide an effective government, combined with a measure of contempt for its leadership. As the military's "image" tarnishes, it will become more and more difficult for Jaruzelski or his successors to be assured of full compliance or willful obedience among Polish citizens.

More serious still could be the effects on the

armed forces themselves. No information about this is available yet. There is some doubt, however, whether the poor performance of the political leadership, particularly since it includes so many military officers and identifies itself so closely with the military institution, will be conducive to either strengthening or even preserving the soldiers' morale and their self-confidence. The lowering of these, in turn, will have an almost inevitably adverse effect upon the armed forces utility and reliability to defend authority at home and to serve as an effective ally in the Warsaw Pact.

NOTES

1. The International Institute for Strategic Studies, The Military Balance 1981-1982, London, 1981, pp. 20-21. Hereafter quoted as The Military Balance.

2. For details see A. Ross Johnson, "The Polish Military," in A. Ross Johnson, Robert W. Dean, Alexander Alexiev, East European Military Establishments: The Warsaw Pact Northern Tier, R-2417/1-AF/FF, The Rand Corporation, December 1980, pp. 31-33. Hereafter quoted as Johnson.

3. The Military Balance, p. 21.

4. Johnson, pp. 33-37.

5. The Military Balance, p. 21; see also Drew Middleton in The New York Times, 5 January 1981.

6. Trybuna Ludu, 23 December 1981.

7. See reports in Zolnierz Wolnosci, a daily paper published by the Main Political Administration of the Polish armed forces, 15-20 January 1981 and thereafter. This was also confirmed in numerous reports printed in the Western press.

8. See Information Centre for Polish Affairs, (U.K.), Uncensored Poland News Bulletin, London, No. 2 (5 February 1982), pp. 15-18, and No. 3 (6 March 1982) pp. 10-15. These bulletins include reports published in underground papers circulating in Poland.

9. Trybuna Ludu, 2-3 January 1982.

10. For example, see a report in Glos Wybrzeza (Gdansk), 17 January 1982.

11. For details on the Poznan operation see Jaroslaw Maciejewski and Zofia Trojanowicz, eds., Poznanski Czerwiec 1956, Poznan, 1981. This recently published book includes detailed reports based on eyewitness testimony, documents, and chronological presentations; see also Ewa Wacowska, "Poznan 1956," in Poznan 1956/Grudzien 1970, Paris, 1971, pp. 153-216. For reports on the situation in December 1970 see Kazimierz Zamorski in ibid., pp. 19-65; also Barbara Seidler, "Gdansk-Gdynia: Grudzien-Luty," Zycie Literackie (Cracow), 21 February 1971 as well as a

special edition of Glos Wolny, a mimeographed paper published by students of Warsaw University, containing documents and materials used at a session held at the university, "Grudzien 1970," 17 January 1981.

12. Evidence of cooperation between the protesters in Poznan and regular soldiers, particularly those from the Higher Armored Troop Officers School in Golecin (suberb of Poznan) who were sent first to pacify the revolt, has come from numerous eyewitness reports. Those reports have been published in Maciejewski and Trojanowicz, op.cit.; See also an interview with Jan Sandorski, one of the contributors to that book, as published in a mimeographed edition of Solidarnosc (Gdansk), No. 22/52, 26 June 1981, esp. p. 7, in which he expressed concern over the fate of those soldiers who had joined the protesters. See also articles on the subject in Slowo Powszechne, 12-14 June 1981 and Fakty, 6 June 1981. Units of regular troops used in suppressing the revolt included IV Army Corps (Armored) from the Silesian Military District and X Armored Division from Wroclaw. By contrast, security troops (Internal Security Corps, KBW) were involved only on a limited scale.

13. Those indications have been provided through sporadic reports and occasional eyewitness testimonies. See, in particular, an article in Za i Przeciw (Warsaw), 13 December 1981 as well as a testimony by a former soldier in Glos Wolny, 17 January 1981. No documentary evidence on the matter is available.

14. Such a speculation appears particularly justified in view of the military's reported hesitation to become involved in any action against striking workers in June 1976. The workers struck then in protest against a government decision to raise prices of meat and food; in view of that protest, the authorities rescinded their decision shortly after it had been announced. Subsequently, it was reported by some Western observers that at the root of the authorities' reversal had been a warning from Minister of National Defense General Wojciech Jaruzelski that the Polish soldiers would not shoot at the Polish workers. This, in turn, was seen as an indication that the Polish military was determined to stay aloof of internal political conflicts even at the risk of undermining the authority of the party and government leaderships. Such an interpretation, however, might have been mistaken. Without disputing the authenticity of Jaruzelski's remark, one could and should inquire whether it reflected the general's preference for moderation in politics or whether it merely amounted to an admission that the army had not been sufficiently prepared to secure an effective suppression of the population's protests. In light of the recent experience of the military intervention in

December 1981 such an enquiry is not without foundation. Here, one may be reminded that during a party meeting in Gdansk at the end of August 1980, another high-ranking military officer, Admiral Ludwik Janczyszyn, was also reported to have said that the military would do nothing to sever its ties with society and the workers. Admiral Janczyszyn eventually became a member of the Military Council of National Salvation and has emerged since the imposition of martial law as one of the most active and outspoken supporters of the military intervention.

15. Kultura (Warsaw), 21 June 1981. No breakdown of percentages was given.

16. See Jaruzelski's speech announcing the imposition of martial law as broadcast by Radio Warsaw, 13 December 1981; also Trybuna Ludu, 14 December 1981.

17. See the declaration of the council issued on 13 December 1981 and broadcast by the radio and television networks. The text was also published in Trybuna Ludu, 14 December 1981.

18. Ibid.

19. Trybuna Ludu, 2-3 January 1982.

20. The announcement of the group's objectives was made by General Tadeusz Hupalowski, Minister of Administration, Local Economy, and Protection of the Environment, in a speech broadcast by Radio Warsaw on 25 October 1981.

21. Ministers of Internal Affairs; Administration, Local Economy, and the Protection of the Environment; and Mining and Energy, respectively.

22. A revised text of the law on military service was published in Dziennik Ustaw, an official government publication, 6 August 1979, pp. 235-276.

23. Trybuna Ludu, 2-3 January 1982.

24. Ibid.

25. According to information provided by a Central Committee Secretary and deputy Politburo member Wlodzimierz Mokrzyszczak and broadcast by Radio Warsaw on 12 June 1982, 660,000 members left the party during the period from June 1980 to May 1982, including more than 205,000 since 13 December 1981. Mokrzyszczak said that in June 1982 the party's membership was about 2,488,000; these figures are not firm, however, as there is reason to believe that the exodus from the party exceeded the number provided by the secretary.

26. See Bernard Guetta in Le Monde, 4 January 1982 reporting on some of the individuals who left the party, including a deputy head of the Central Committee's Cultural Department, Michal Jagiello.

27. See a statement made by Colonel Henryk Kostrzewa, a military commissar charged with the supervision of the country's judicial system, in which he gave detailed instructions to all provincial judges about who should be tried by the courts and what the

proper attitude of judges under the conditions of martial law should be. The statement was published in Le Monde, 3 February 1982.

28. The text of General Janiszewski's instruction, issued in the form of a circular letter addressed to all state institutions, was published in Le Monde, 25 January 1982.

29. See, for example, interviews with such military officials published by Sztandar Mlodych, 15 March 1982, and Polityka, 29 May 1982.

30. Zycie Warszawy, 25 June 1982.

31. Nowe Drogi, August 1981, p. 99.

32. A reference to the instruction was made in Trybuna Ludu, 2 February 1982; see also Jozef Cegla, "December, February, and then...," Polityka, 6 March 1982.

33. This is an excerpt from a taped speech delivered by General Wojciech Jaruzelski at a meeting between the party leadership and workers in Szczecin on 24 January 1971. The tape of the discussions at the meeting were transcribed and published in Ewa Wacowska, ed. Rewolta Szczecinska i jej znaczenie. Paris, 1971, p. 135.

34. This situation may soon change. Meeting with Leonid Brezhnev in the Crimea on August 16, Jaruzelski wore civilian clothes rather than his customary military uniform. Reporting the event, neither TASS (the Soviet press agency) nor PAP (the Polish press agency) have mentioned the Polish leader's military rank. Both agencies carefully refrained from acknowledging Jaruzelski's chairmanship of the Military Council of National Salvation. Instead, his status was reduced to that of the Polish party's first secretary and the government's prime minister.

35. Johnson, p. 201.

36. See Stanislaw Reperowicz in Trybuna Ludu, 23-24 January 1982.

37. Public opinion surveys conducted among soldiers during 1979 and 1980 showed that religious beliefs were not only strong, but also markedly increased in spite of a strong atheist propaganda campaign conducted by the political instructors. Similarly, soldiers were said to have supported the prospects of another visit by the Pope to Poland. See Jozef Czerwinski's articles in Argumenty, 6 December 1982 and 18-24 April 1982.

38. Jan B. de Weydenthal, The Communists of Poland, Stanford, California, 1978, pp. 69-71.

39. According to official statistics, sold production in the socialized industry declined during the first six months of 1982 by 7.8 percent in comparison with the same period of 1981, the purchase of slaughter animals was lower by 7.9 percent, transport fell by 13.9 percent, investments decreased by 28 percent, exports

increased by 0.9 percent and imports were down by 20.9 percent. Poland's debt to socialist countries was at the level of 3.1 billion rubles and to the West at US dollars 24.5 billion. The standard of living decreased by about 25 percent. See PAP, 26 July 1982.

40. The best and probably most accurate assessment of the political situation in the aftermath of the imposition of martial law was provided in a secret speech of a military commissar at the Polish Radio and Television, who was reported to have told the loyal party activists there that "the situation remains complex...complicated and it is still extremely difficult to predict how it will develop in the coming months." He went on to say that the party was still unable to take over the political direction of the country, that martial law "is likely to last for years," and that political opposition to the existing system, particularly from Solidarity, is in the process of "organizing itself." The speech was published in Le Monde, 15 April 1982; subsequent pronouncements and actions of the established leadership suggest that not much has changed in the ensuing months.

9
Romania

Walter M. Bacon, Jr.

INTRODUCTION

Even if one employs the useful concept of "mobilization potential," the reliability of the Romanian armed forces in "coalition warfare" is difficult to assess. First, one must contend with the general problem of the dearth of relevant and reliable information, exacerbated in the Romanian case by Bucharest's reluctance to publish data pertaining to recent economic failures.[1] Second, one must address the thorny issue of how well, indeed, if, the Romanian armed forces, trained for a decade-and-a-half in the priorities of "people's war," could be integrated into Warsaw Pact plans and operations for a Central European campaign.[2] And third, given the unanimity of Western analysts on the "patent" unreliability of the Romanian armed forces in an East-West armed confrontation, the very question may be moot.[3]

With these considerable caveats in mind, this chapter will attempt a tentative evaluation of Romania's "mobilization potential." First, however, a brief description of the causes and development of Romania's divergent military policy is in order.

A "NATIONAL COURSE"

While there exists considerable scholarly debate concerning the precise date of the onset of Romania's "national course," there is general agreement about its initial causes. The Romanian leadership, believing the country's best opportunities for rapid economic development lay in emulation of the Soviet Stalinist model, rejected Khrushchev's attempts to integrate the bloc's

---

Walter M. Bacon, Jr. is an Associate Professor of Political Science, University of Nebraska at Omaha. He received his doctorate from the Graduate School of International Studies, University of Denver.

economies in the late 1950s and early 1960s. To have complied with Soviet plans for an international socialist division of labor would have, in Ronald Linden's well turned phrase, perpetuated Romania's status as the bloc's "breadbasket and gas station."[4] Exploiting the Soviet Union's preoccupation with the intensifying Sino-Soviet split and encouraged by the West's willingness to supplant bloc financing of extensive industrialization, the leadership declared its commitment to national priorities in April 1964.

Deviations from bloc norms were most apparent in interparty relations and foreign policy: the Romanian Communist Party (RCP) remained neutral in the Sino-Soviet dispute, retained party contacts with the Albanian Party of Labor, intensified relations with the League of Yugoslav Communists, supported Dubcek's leadership of the Czechoslovak party, and advocated Eurocommunist autonomy; Romania anticipated bloc recognition of the Federal Republic of Germany by establishing formal diplomatic ties in 1967, retained cordial relations with Israel after the 1967 War, condemned the Warsaw Pact invasion of Czechoslovakia, established close economic relations with the West, defined itself as a Third World state, and took "unSoviet" positions on a number of international issues. At the same time Romania maintained its membership in bloc organizations, such as the Warsaw Pact (WTO) and the Council of Mutual Economic Assistance (CMEA), using its access to their decision-making bodies to thwart the Soviet Union's hegemonistic designs. Robert Farlow has cogently designated Romania's Janus-like posture as a policy of "partial alignment."[5]

The assertion of autonomously defined goals evoked the deep-seated nationalism of the Romanian people who, despite the Draconian sacrifices required by Stalinist developmental priorities, appeared to support the regime. Domestically, the desatellitization process effected a rebirth of national pride, manifested in derussification of culture and history and in an unfortunate but predictable discrimination toward Romania's minorities, particularly its two million Hungarians. Notwithstanding the legitimizing policies of General Secretary Nicolae Ceausescu, the leadership remained wholeheartedly Stalinist in its methods of social, political and economic control. As economic problems multiplied during the 1970s, culminating in an inability to meet debt payments in 1981-82 and severe shortfalls in planned output, the social decompression of the 1960s all but ceased, leaving Romania the most rigidly orthodox state within the Soviet bloc. Dissent was effectively suppressed and incipient pluralism stopped dead in its tracks.

Domestic orthodoxy was not only dictated by

Stalinist logic but it also defused the Soviet Union's best excuse for direct intervention in Romanian affairs. Ceausescu's Romania was neither Dubcek's Czechoslovakia nor Kania's Poland. There was no danger of a loss of party control. The regime exploited the support generated by its nationalist policies by arguing that orthodoxy was Romania's best insurance against "fraternal assistance." For a decade that trade-off was sufficient to stifle both potential demands and logical needs for domestic reform. More recently, however, the privations visited upon the Romanian people by their uncompromisingly Stalinist leader have overextended his nationalist legitimacy.[6]

Both the domestic priorities and the foreign policy consequences of Romanian Stalinism as well as international circumstances argued for a reorientation of military policy and doctrine. With planned rates of capital accumulation around 30 percent and the priorities of extensive development, the expense of maintaining a Soviet-model technology-intensive force posture was illogical. Romanian leaders thus sought and found a military policy stressing the centrality of the individual combatant. Costs per effective were reduced substantially and the military's proportional claims on the state budget were cut.[7] Although some Romanian authors would argue that such a policy shift was implicit in the decisions of the Ninth Congress of the RCP (1965), i.e., the official opening of the "Ceausescu era," Romanian military policy and doctrine--aside from a gradual institutional distancing from the Warsaw Pact--remained congruent with those of its allies until 1968.[8] Since the Warsaw Pact invasion of Czechoslovakia and the unmistakable but unannounced designation of similar "fraternal assistance" as the foremost military threat to its national sovereignty and independence, Romania has adopted a "people's war" doctrine and has implemented the consequent changes in force structure. "The struggle of the entire people" ("lupta intregului popor") involves mobilizing the maximum number of effectives, both regular armed forces and paramilitary soldiers, for a defensive struggle on Romanian territory.

The regular armed forces consist of two tank divisions (each of 11,000 men and 325 tanks, mostly older "T 54/55s"); eight motorized rifle divisions (13,000 men, 266 tanks); three alpine brigades; a number of artillery, missile, antitank and antiaircraft units; the militarized units of the Ministry of Internal Affairs (apx. 20,000 men); a 7,000 man navy equipt with small river and coastal defense craft; and, a 34,000 man air force with 328 combat aircraft, the majority of which are MiG-21s. Reserves total 365,000 effectives.[9] The primary component of the paramilitary forces are the Patriotic Guards, formed immediately after the invasion of Czechoslovakia and currently numbering 700,000. Patriotic Guard groups are composed of volunteers from economic units and are commanded by reserve officers and NCOs. They are equipped with light weapons only and are directly subordinated to the RCP Central Committee.[10] Other paramilitary formations include detachments of youth receiving military training and local civil defense units. If, in the unlikely event that provisions of the 1972 Defense Law were implemented maximally, almost all adults would participate in a defensive people's war. In such a scenario, Romania could conceivably field between 4,700,000 and 6,250,000 fighters.[11]

The missions, equipment and training of both the armed forces and the paramilitary organizations reflect the essentially defensive character of Romania's military doctrine. While the standing armed forces structurally resemble those of other Warsaw Pact armies, the Romanian literature stresses defensive mobility and the capacity of independent actions.[12] For example, Romania fields three alpine brigades--Bulgaria is the only other East European state with a similar unit--the mission and training of which indicates their use in the Carpathians which might well serve as the national redoubt in the event of an invasion. Ivan Volgyes has noted the incompatibility of Romanian equipment with its use in offensive operations outside Romania.[13] Joint exercises with the Patriotic Guards are emphasized in the Romania press.[14] The Guards themselves are given training and weapons in keeping with their mission of disrupting communications and logistics in hit-and-run attacks behind enemy lines.[15] In sum, Romania's military posture is designed both as a deterrent and as an effective defense against substantial invading forces with technical superiority. By creating a credible force which would make an enemy occupation long and costly, Romania hopes to persuade potential aggressors that the costs of an invasion would outweigh its benefits. In the event of invasion, Romanian regular and irregular units are equipped and trained to mitigate an enemy's superior firepower and technology.

AN ASSESSMENT OF MOBILIZATION POTENTIAL

"Mobilization potential" is said by Daniel N. Nelson to depend on five sets of variables: the scenario of hostility; the degree of systemic integration; domestic socio-economic conditions; domestic political conditions; and, military preparedness. Within the informational restraints initially mentioned, each set of variables will be addressed in turn.

Nicolae Ceausescu, the Supreme Commander of the Romanian armed forces, has clearly stated the purely territorial defensive mission of the Romanian armed forces.

> ...our strategic objective is to defend our country and we do not aim at getting out of our boundaries...[16]

> ...our army has the mission to defend the homeland... (and) our army does not aim, in any way, to take action against other peoples but exclusively has the mission to secure the people's peaceful work, to defend the integrity and sovereignty of the homeland...[17]

Despite Bucharest's frequent protestations of commitment to the defensive obligations incurred as a member of the Warsaw Pact,[18] Western analysts and Romanian authors doubt the utility of the Romanian armed forces outside Romania.[19] These analyses posit that the statutory limitations placed upon the use of the Romanian armed forces, their weaponry and logistical infrastructure, and their training all but preclude their use in an East-West armed confrontation outside of Romania. However, within the context of intramural defensive operations, the Romanian regular and paramilitary forces deployed against either traditional enemies (i.e., Russians, Hungarians and Bulgarians) or invading Western forces might, if countermeasures were not undertaken, prove to be formidable. Their political reliability, equipment and training appear to be appropriate given the analogous preparations of other recent successful national resistance movements.

The armed forces of the Socialist Republic of Romania are the least systemically integrated of any member of the Warsaw Pact. First, their military doctrine differs radically from those of their allies. In fact, authoritative Romanian sources decry the doctrinal "mutation" caused by uncritical adoption of Soviet norms before 1965.[20] "The struggle of the entire people," on the other hand, is praised for its historical and ideological legitimacy.[21]

Second, since 1968 Romania has decreased its dependence on Soviet and bloc equipment by diffusing its foreign sources of weaponry and by building up a small armaments industry of its own which manufactures military products uniquely suited to its doctrine. Romania has purchased aviation equipment from Great Britain (small transports) and France (helicopters) and has, with Yugoslavia, developed a multipurpose fighter aircraft. The Romanian navy has purchased Chinese attack craft.[22] The army has procured modified T-55 tanks from Israel and has even raised the possibility of buying F-5 aircraft from the United States.[23] Operating under licenses and with domestic designs, Romania produces a wide variety of military equipment, from complex systems to rifles.[24] By 1975, Romania was producing 66 percent of its military equipment needs and, as a result, has become an exporter of arms.[25] Arms produced in Romania are mission-specific and would, therefore, be of little use in the most often contemplated scenarios of East-West confrontation.[26] Domestic sources for equipment used by the Romanian armed forces not only increase the combat efficiency of those forces in the missions assigned to them, but they also decrease dependence on the Soviet Union, cut the outflow of foreign exchange, and aid in the development of spinoff technologies.

Third, integration is hampered by Romania's reluctance to participate, in all but symbolic ways, in Warsaw Pact activities. Since 1963, Romania has permitted only map room joint exercises on Romanian territory and has sent small contingents to major Pact war games.[27] While Ceausescu politely receives representatives of the United Armed Forces of the Warsaw Pact, there is no indication that Romania ever ratified the 1973 convention which established that body.[28] Ceausescu's position on the integration of command functions and his ambivalent attitude about Romania's relationship with the Pact were underscored in his defiant speeches following the November 1978 meeting of the Political Consultative Committee in Moscow.

> ...in keeping with this consistent policy of our Party and State, we will continue developing collaboration with the armies of the Warsaw Pact countries. But we desire this collaboration to rely on the socialist principles of relations among states, hence among armies too, on the principles of equality and respect for each one's independence,...by starting from the fact that each national army can only be under the command of the respective Party and State bodies, which are the only ones to have the right to commit the army to any kind of action. Nobody else can do it! Never will we admit that the Romanian army should be committed to any military action by anybody else, except by ourselves, except our people![29]

Ceausescu has also moved decisively to reduce Soviet penetration of the Romanian armed forces by training Romanian military officers exclusively in Romania, by elevating loyal officers to command positions, and by discontinuing intelligence cooperation with the GRU.[30] And fourth, it is important to remember that not only do the Romanians resist systemic integration but also the Soviets allow them to do so. In the Soviets' perception, Romania must be seen as the European Warsaw Pact state of the least importance: it borders on no

NATO member-state and is logistically unimportant for the most likely theatres of operations in north central Europe such as the North German Plain or Fulda Gap. Romanian hindering of a southern front was recently mitigated by the establishment of an Odessa-Varna ferry service with heavy load capacities capable of bypassing the land route of supply through Romanian territory.[31]

The third variable defining "mobilization potential" is domestic socio-economic conditions. Once boasting Europe's fastest growing economy, Romania in the 1980s is experiencing severe economic difficulties, the result of mismanagement, irrational investment priorities, over-indebtedness, natural calamities, and international political and economic circumstances.[32]

These difficulties have led to a retreat from the overly ambitious goals elaborated at the Twelfth RCP Congress (1979) and to a freezing of military expenditures at their 1982 level through 1985.[33] More importantly, economic decline has seriously undermined the legitimacy of the Ceausescu regime which had retained popular support for its Stalinist policies with a mixture of assertive nationalism and a rising standard of living. Rationing of food and energy and a virtual freeze on salaries have given pause to even the most ardent nationalists. Economically caused social discontent is exacerbated by minority problems, intensified internal security measures, a personality cult of ludicrous proportions, and the public's perception of widespread official corruption.

While socio-economic problems afflict other Warsaw Pact member-states, they are particularly dysfunctional for Romania's military posture since both its deterrent and defensive value depend on the degree of support the regime can elicit from its part-time soldiers. On the other hand, one might argue that the impact of economic hard times on the Romanian military would be less than the other Warsaw Pact member-states because of the cost efficiency of Romania's military forces. Still, in a military posture which continues to emphasize the value of the individual combatant over his access to sophisticated weaponry and which underscores the relationship of economic development to defensive capacity, Romania's economic problems cannot but undermine morale and material capabilities.[34]

Despite economic setbacks, the Romanian polity appears to be relatively stable. Nicolae Ceausescu has ruled, with no overt challenges to his authority, since 1965. His leadership style is, like Stalin's, autocratic and his personal imprint may be perceived in most party and state policies, including military policy. Romanian sources identify him as the author of the doctrine of "the struggle of the entire people," a credit to be expected in Ceausescu's highly personalist regime but one, it would seem, with some justification.[35] It was, after all, Ceausescu who made the decision in 1968 which necessitated the formulation of a new military doctrine and who initially announced every military policy change of the last fifteen years.

His personal involvement with military policy has produced both political benefits and risks. In the early 1970s, when Ceausescu's popularity may have been at its peak, his association with the new military doctrine lent it legitimacy and offset the frustration of older officers who resented both their loss of functional exclusivity and their new role in the national economy.[36] Ceausescu gradually purged the older generation of command personnel, many of whom retained ties to the Soviet military, and replaced them with officers who had assisted him in formulating the new doctrine and, thus, had a stake in its maintenance.[37] In early 1983, however, resentment over the freeze in military expenditures, the lack of material incentives for military professionals, the greater role assigned to military personnel in the economy, and the rapid antiquation of weapons systems may have lead to serious challenges to Ceausescu's authority within the military. The Western press reported two military plots against Ceausescu and the Romanian press mounted a campaign glorifying Ceausescu as a military leader.[38] Independent confirmation of a January 1983 plot has been received by this author. According to usually reliable Romanian sources, the chief conspirator was the young and very popular commander of the army's airborne unit. Rumors of his and his co-conspirators' executions were widespread during 1983.

The alleged anti-Ceausescu conspiracies among the military are not only symptoms of one elite's dissatisfaction but also a reflection of a general malaise among Romanians who have had to bear the burden of the regime's inadequate response to the economic crisis. Ceausescu seems particularly reluctant to undertake meaningful economic reforms, instead accelerating the pace of cadre rotation, intensifying the cult of personality, and calling for still greater material sacrifices for the sake of the homeland. The well of nationalist legitimacy for Ceausescu's Stalinist regime may be dry. As one Bucharest intellectual complained to this author, "You can neither eat nationalist rhetoric nor can you light your apartment with it."

The last of the five variables is military preparedness. Military spending, an awkward and perhaps inappropriate gauge of preparedness, remains frozen for the years 1983-1985 at the 1982 level of 10,773,000,000 lei, or 3.2 percent of government expenditures and about 1½ percent of GNP (1982). While the absolute 1982 figure represents a 3.3 percent increase over the 10,480,000,000 lei expended in 1981, the proportional figures for both budgetary outlays and GNP, as well as expenditures per capita and per full-time effective, are the lowest for any European member-state of the Warsaw Pact.[39] Some expenditures for arms research and development and for training of the Patriotic Guards, the Youth Receiving Military Training and Civil Defense units might well be hidden in other parts of the state budget. More importantly, the absolutely and relatively low projected military budgets preclude modernization or replacement of Romania's largely antiquated military hardware, much of which is of 1960s vintage (e.g., the bulk of the army's tanks and the air force's fighter/interceptor squadrons). Budgetary constraints may have also delayed production and deployment of the Romanian-Yugoslav "Orao" multipurpose aircraft. Predictably, Ceausescu's response to anticipated military resentment caused by the cutbacks has been to urge more efficient use of existing material and a greater patriotic commitment on the part of soliders.[40]

Perhaps more so than a conventional military posture, a "people's war" defense and deterrent depends on the credibility of the armed forces' training. In case of invasion, Romania's regular armed forces can, at best, hope to delay a superior enemy's advance and thus purchase enough time to effect general mobilization, to establish a defense in depth, and to begin disruptive tactics behind enemy lines. However, the capacity to rapidly mobilize depends on the organizational efficacy of training.[41] Training has been effected negatively by the economic crisis both in terms of the economies imposed on resources used in exercises and in terms of the greater amount of time that has been allotted to the military's "self-provisioning" activities.[42] A perpetual concern is the cooperation of all elements of the defense system. In virtually every statement he has made on military matters, General Secretary Ceausescu has urged both the military and the paramilitary "activ" to intensify cooperative training.[43] These continual exhortations for better cooperation may indicate residual resistance on the part of the regular army to delegate the desired amount of combat responsibilities to the paramilitary forces. Such cooperation must be perceived as in place and effective if the military posture is to have the desired effect upon potential aggressors.

CONCLUSION

What conclusions may be drawn from the available data and their analysis? First, it is difficult to argue with most Western analysts who view Romania's value to the Warsaw Pact in an East-West armed conflict as minimal. The force structure, training, and lack of integration in Pact command institutions of the Romanian armed forces all but preclude their initial participation in coalition warfare beyond the frontiers of Romania. Because the RCP leadership has insisted on the free exercise of its sovereign authority over the Romanian armed forces, one cannot even be sure that it would recognize a "casus foederis" unless a Pact ally were directly attacked by a Western state.

Second, it is equally as difficult to escape the conclusion that Romania is genuinely determined to resist any attack on its territory with all the meagre resources at its disposal. The question of the efficacy of Romania's resistance remains. Certainly, recent economic and political difficulties undermine the credibility of Romania's defenses.

Third, Ceausescu's legitimacy among military professionals, and thus their support for his military doctrine, is under strain. The only realistic alternative to Romania's current defense posture would be a return to "full alignment," an option that might prove attractive to a number of military professionals because of the lure of a high-technology military profile. Ceausescu may have been attempting to defuse the attraction of that option by calling for greater cooperation with the Pact in his March 1983 speech to the military "activ."[44]

In sum, Romania's "mobilization potential" for defense of its territory remains relatively high while its "mobilization potential" for use in coalitional warfare outside its frontiers is probably lower than that of any other European Warsaw Pact member-state.

NOTES

1. Not only did the Central Statistical Directorate revise its reporting base in 1981, but it also halved the amount of data published in its official yearbook. Compare the 1981 yearbook's 734 pages to the 1982 yearbook's 363 pages. Anuarul statistic al Republicii Socialiste Romania 1981 and 1982 (Bucharest: Directia Centrala de Statistica, 1982 and 1983). See also, Radio Free Europe Research, Romania Situation Report 11, 29 June 1983, pp. 17-20. (Hereafter cited as RFE, Romania/Situation Report number, date, pages.)

2. See Arie Chaplin, "The 'Popular War' Doctrine in Romanian Defense Policy," East European Quarterly, XVII, 3 (Fall 1983), pp. 267-282; David P. Burke, "The Defense Policy of Romania" in Douglas J. Murray and Paul R. Viotti (eds.), The Defense Policies of Nations: A Comparative Study (Baltimore and London: The Johns Hopkins University Press, 1982), pp. 323-341; and, Aurel Braun, "The Yugoslav/Romanian Concept of People's War," Canadian Defense Quarterly, VII, 1 (Summer 1977), pp. 39-43.

3. E.g. Christopher D. Jones, Soviet Influence in

Eastern Europe: Political Autonomy and the Warsaw Pact (New York: Praeger, 1981), passim; Alex Alexiev, "Romania and the Warsaw Pact: The Defense Policy of a Reluctant Ally" (Santa Monica: Rand, 1979), P 6270, pp. 22-23; A. Ross Johnson, "The Warsaw Pact: Soviet Military Policy in Eastern Europe" (Santa Monica: Rand, 1981), P 6583, pp. 4n, 19, and 30-34; Dionise Ghermani, Die nationale Souveranitatspolitik der SR Rumanian, Vol. I, Im Rahmen des sowjetischen Bundnissystems (Munich: R. Oldenbourg Verlag, 1981), pp. 154-168; and, Ivan Volgyes, The Political Reliability of the Warsaw Pact Armies: The Southern Tier (Durham, N.C.: Duke Press Policy Studies, 1982), pp. 41-59.

4. Ronald Haly Linden, Bear and Foxes: The International Relations of the East European States, 1965-1969 (Boulder, Colorado: East European Quarterly, 1979), p. 201.

5. Robert L. Farlow, "Romania and the Policy of Partial Alignment," in James A. Kuhlman (ed.), The Foreign Policies of Eastern Europe: Domestic and International Determinants (Leyden: A. W. Sijthoff, 1978), pp. 191-207.

6. For two excellent analyses of Romania's foreign policy and its domestic linkages see Jeanne Kirk Laux, "Socialism, Nationalism and Underdevelopment: Research on Romanian Foreign Policy Making," in Hannes Adomeit et al. (eds.), Foreign Policy Making in Communist Countries: A Comparative Approach (London: Saxon House, 1979), pp. 49-78; "The Limits of Autonomy: Romania in the 1980's," in East European Economic Assessment: A Compendium of Papers Submitted to the Joint Economic Committee, Congress of the United States, Pt. 2, Regional Assessments (Washington: Government Printing Office, 1981), pp. 107-127. For recent internal and foreign policy developments, see Robert L. Farlow, "Romania: Problems of Independence and Development," in Milorad M. Drachkovitch (ed.), East Central Europe: Yesterday, Today, Tomorrow (Stanford: Hoover Institution Press, 1982), pp. 327-348.

7. See Walter M. Bacon, Jr., "Romanian Military Policy in the 1980s" in Daniel N. Nelson (ed.), Romania in the 1980s (Boulder, Colorado: Westview Press, 1981), pp. 209-211.

8. For the 1965 argument see Lt. Gen. Dr. Constantin Olteanu, "Doctrina militara a Romaniei socialiste, fundamentata si elaborata de tovarasul Nicolae Ceausescu" in Lt. Gen. Dr. Ilie Ceausescu (ed.), File din istoria militara a poporului roman, studii, Vol. 10 (Bucharest: Editura militara, 1982), pp. 477ff.

9. Georges Marey, "The Army of the Socialist Republic of Romania" Est et Ouest, January, 1979, pp. 15-21 in JPRS #72881, pp. 166-7; Robert W. Clawson and Lawrence S. Kaplan (eds.), The Warsaw Pact: Political

Purpose and Military Means (Wilmington, Delaware: Scholarly Resources Inc., 1982), p. 159; The Military Balance 1982-1983 (London: International Institute for Strategic Studies, 1982), p. 23.

10. See Robert R. King, "Die paramilitarischen Organisationen in Rumanien" in Peter Gosztony (ed.), Paramilitarische Organisationen im Sowjetblock (Bonn-Bad Godesberg: Hohwacht, 1977), pp. 226-8; Cols. Leonida Loghin and Alexandru Petricean, Garzile patriotice din Romania (Bucharest: Editura militara, 1974), pp. 128-32; and, Gen. Ion Coman et al., Apararea nationala in conceptia Partidului Comunist Roman (Bucharest: Editura militara, 1982), pp. 232-4.

11. For the provisions in question see Apararea nationala a Romaniei socialiste. Documente, 1965-1977 (Bucharest: Editura militara, 1978), pp. 527-554. For the number of effectives calculated, see Col. Gen. Dr. Constantin Olteanu, The Romanian Armed Power Concept: A Historical Approach (Bucharest: Military Publishing House, 1982), pp. 319 and 321.

12. E.g., Lt. Gen. Dr. Ilie Ceausescu, The Entire People's War for the Homeland's Defence with the Romanians (Bucharest: Military Publishing House, 1980), p. 319; Coman et al., Apararea nationala, pp. 201-2.

13. Volgyes, Political Reliability, pp. 47-8.

14. E.g., Scinteia, July 23, 1982, p. 1.

15. Lt. Gen. Dr. Ilie Ceausescu, Entire People's War, pp. 321-4. General Ceausescu has written an entire book on the tactics and doctrine of harassing an occupying army. Hartuirea in actiunile de lupta duse in razboiul intregului popor pentru apararea patriei (Bucharest: Editura militara, 1981).

16. Nicolae Ceausescu, Romania on the Way of Building Up the Multilaterally Developed Socialist Society, Vol. 13 (Bucharest: Meridiane Publishing House, 1978), p. 418, speech of October 1, 1976.

17. Nicolae Ceausescu, Romania on the Way of Building Up the Multilaterally Developed Socialist Society, Vol. 17 (Bucharest: Meridiane Publishing House, 1981), pp. 77, speech of September 16, 1978.

18. Ibid., p. 79.

19. E.g., Volgyes, Political Reliability, pp. 58-9; Clawson and Kaplan, Warsaw Pact, p. 160; Ivan Sylvian, "Romania" in Teresa Rakowska-Harmstone et al., Warsaw Pact: The Question of Cohesion, Phase I (Ottawa: Canadian Department of National Defence, Operational Research and Analysis Establishment, ORAE Extra-Mural Paper No. 19, 1980), p. 223; Alexiev, "Romania and the Warsaw Pact," p. 23; and Dale R. Herspring and Ivan Volgyes, "Political Reliability in the Eastern European Warsaw Pact Armies" Armed Forces and Society, VI, 2 (Winter 1980), p. 289, table 3. For authoritative Romanian statements see Olteanu, "Doctrina militara",

pp. 491-3; and, Coman et al., Apararea nationala, p. 126.

20. E.g., Olteanu, The Romanian Armed Power Concept, pp. 301-314.

21. For a concise statement of the historical legitimacy inherent in both Olteanu's and Gen. Ceausescu's recent histories, see Ilie Ceausescu, "Lupta intregului popor pentru apararea patriei-constanta a istoriei romanesti de peste doua milenii," Anale de istorie, XXVI, 5 (1980), pp. 23-36.

22. For details see Walter M. Bacon, Jr., "The Military and the Party in Romania" in Dale R. Herspring and Ivan Volgyes (eds.), Civil-Military Relations in Communist Systems (Boulder, Colorado: Westview Press, 1978), p. 169.

23. Clawson and Kaplan, Warsaw Pact, pp. 223-4.

24. RFE, Romania/Situation Report 4, 7 March 1983, pp. 8-11.

25. Col. Gen. Vasile Ionel, "Politica Partidului Comunist Roman de dezvoltare a productiei proprii de technica militara" in Al. Gh. Savu (ed.), Armata Republicu Socialiste Romania: traditii si contemporaneitate (Bucharest: Editura militara, 1975), p. 146; and RFE, Romania/Situation Report 3, 19 February 1983, p. 21.

26. Coman et al., Apararea nationala, p. 211; Olteanu, "Doctrina militara," pp. 497-8.

27. Jones, Soviet Influence in Eastern Europe, pp. 117-8; Ghermani, Souveranitatspolitik, p. 162.

28. Jones, Soviet Influence in Eastern Europe, p. 134. For the most recent visit of the command personnel of the United Armed Forces, Marshal Kulikov and Gen. Gribkov, see Scinteia, December 7, 1982, p. 1.

29. Ceausescu, Romania on the Way, Vol. 17, pp. 230-1, speech of November 27, 1978.

30. Jones, Soviet Influence in Eastern Europe, pp. 207-210; and, Alexiev, "Romania and the Warsaw Pact," p. 17.

31. Clawson and Kaplan, Warsaw Pact, p. 58.

32. For a litany of 1982's economic failures see Walter M. Bacon, Jr., "Romania" in Robert Wesson (ed.), Yearbook on International Communist Affairs 1983 (Stanford: Hoover Institution Press, 1983), pp. 328-330, and 331-2. For an overview of the better days see Andreas C. Tsantis and Roy Pepper, Romania: The Industrialization of an Agrarian Economy Under Socialist Planning (Washington: The World Bank, 1979).

33. Scinteia, March 5, 1983, p. 3.

34. For explicit statements of these relationships see Coman et al., Apararea nationala, pp. 131-137 and 169-186; and Lt. Gen. Gheorghe Gomoiu et al., Factorii pe care intemeiaza capacitatea de aparare a patriei (Bucharest: Editura militara, 1981), pp. 22-53 & 123-139.

35. See Col. Gen. Vasile Milea, "Tovarasul Nicolae Ceausescu, fondatorul doctrinei militare a Romaniei socialiste," Viata militara, XXXV, 1 (January 1983), pp. 14-15; and, Nicolae Ceausescu, Apararea nationala a Republicii Socialiste Romania, culegere de texte (Bucharest: Editura militara, 1983).

36. For speculation on this resentment see Bacon, "The Military and the Party," pp. 170-4; and, Walter M. Bacon, Jr., "Civil-Military Relations in Romania," Studies in Comparative Communism, XI, 3 (Autumn 1978), pp. 245-9.

37. A good example of such an officer is Colonel General Constantin Olteanu, in 1983 Minister of Defense, who in 1974 was but a colonel and military historian.

38. RFE, Romania/Situation Report 3, 19 February 1983, pp. 8-12.

39. RFE, Romania/Situation Report 1, 21 January 1982; and, The Military Balance 1982-1983, p. 124. For a historical overview of absolute and comparative expenditures see Bacon, "Military Policy," pp. 209-10.

40. Scinteia, March 5, 1983, p. 3.

41. Gomoiu et al., Factorii, p. 161-2.

42. Gen. Olteanu hinted at these difficulties in his speeches to the Central Committee plenum in June, 1982, and to the RCP National Conference in December 1982. Scinteia, June 3, 1982, p. 6 and December 18, 1982, p. 8.

43. E.g., Ibid., October 11, 1980, p. 3 and March 5, 1983, p. 3. An entire book was published recently on army-Patriotic Guards cooperation. Ibid., April 6, 1982, p. 4.

44. Scinteia, March 5, 1983, pp. 1 and 3.

Conclusion

Daniel N. Nelson

Analyses presented in this volume cannot, nor should they, set to rest debates about the reliability of East European military forces. Conditions about which contributors have written will change as will our interpretations. Certainly, there is much in the foregoing chapters which reflects diverse views about conceptualizing and measuring reliability (e.g., the views of Ivan Volgyes as contrasted with my own in Chapter 1). Because of likely contextual changes (new regimes, economic crises, international tensions, etc.) and the need for further refinements in our empirical indicators, the work of authors here should prompt continued reassessments of WTO reliability.

Having said as much, however, articles in this volume reflect our best judgments of East European military reliability circa the mid-1980s. Through a project such as this, using both broadly comparative and nation-specific perspectives, we have not eliminated uncertainty about the response of Warsaw Pact forces to combat, but we have lessened the imprecision with which the term reliability has thus far been employed.

No knowledgeable observer, Soviet or Western, is likely to expect that all forces available in East European militaries would be used to maximum effect in combat. A consistent finding in this volume is the high probability that the mobilization potentials of Soviet allies would face serious impediments were hostilities to occur. Frequently, the point was made throughout these chapters that the type of conflict, i.e., against whom and for what rationale, and length of hostilities are critical components in gauging reliability. Yet, even when scenario of hostilities and the duration of conflict were excluded from consideration, as my contribution suggested, other empirically-based indicators imply that only the GDR and Bulgaria exhibit WTO integration, socioeconomic and political conditions and military infrastructure which warrant the adjective "reliable". When scenario and duration are considered as well, the GDR (argues Krisch) may have difficulty in convincing its population to engage in offensive operations in the Federal Republic of Germany. The Bulgarian military, if confronted with NATO resolve and effective Yugoslav resistance, might resort to a putsch--a route Ivan Volgyes sees as historically plausible in that case.

All other cases reveal even greater cause to doubt the reliable performance of East European forces. Of Czechoslovakia's military, Condoleezza Rice writes that a moral-political "malaise...continues to haunt the CLA", and points to the "legacy of doubt about its ability to defend" the nation. For Poland, Jan de Weydenthal indicates that the influx of military personnel into all walks of politics and administration during martial law may make the armed forces vulnerable to many strains from which it previously had been insulated. As the Jaruzelski regime fails to resolve Poland's dilemmas, the military acquires many of the same problems of public support which Gierek, Kania and their predecessors had faced. Its relatively positive image now tarnished, the morale and effectiveness of the Polish military may be weakened in de Weydenthal's view. Hungarian forces, generally content with Kadar's policies and the position of the military, would be reliable in internal and defensive modes according to Ivan Volgyes. But without a quick "lightening like thrust", Volgyes anticipates that Hungarian forces would be unlikely to endure prolonged hostilities (which, in modern warfare, could imply a very short duration). Romania's minimal role in any East-West conflict is noted by Walter Bacon, Jr. The low level of support for Ceaușescu, combined with economic difficulties since the late 1970s, mean that Romania's mobilization potential for Soviet military endeavors is virtually non-existent. Romania's potential to defend <u>against</u> Soviet invasion, as mentioned by Bacon and other contributors, may be higher due to a large paramilitary force and a doctrine calling for resistance via a guerilla-type "struggle of the entire people".

Reliable Soviet allies are, then, few in communist Europe. <u>Only</u> the German Democratic Republic exhibits consistently a high level of systemic integration, a developed and productive economy, political control and military preparation to serve as an adjunct to Soviet interests were hostilities to occur in Europe. Only the GDR's forces are seen by contributors as unreliable if confronted by <u>Soviet</u> military action against them. Aggregate indicators cited in Chapter 1, as well as Henry Krisch's case study, identify the components of mobilization potential in East Germany. Krisch adds detail about factors as diverse as fuel dependency, the complete party (SED) penetration of the officer corps, military professionalism, and military ethos of German (especially Prussian) history, the adamant political control asserted by the SED and, of course, the massive presence of Soviet troops.

But from the standpoint of Moscow, even this "most reliable" ally with serious military potential has a bothersome record of political unrest and a persistent, disaffected minority which clusters under the Lutheran Church. Given past controversies about conscientious objection and growing debate about nuclear weapons, Marshall Kulikov and his colleagues cannot be sanguine about East European resolve in scenarios of conflict which imply great manpower and material losses in the GDR.

The Soviets know, to be sure, of these limitations on their allies' military performance. Soviet forces stationed in Eastern Europe, Byelorussia and the Ukraine are sufficient to be ominous without the addition of East European divisions. But the security of the USSR, and their ability to effect decisive victory if East-West hostilities were to explode in Europe, would be far simpler were the Warsaw Pact an assured instrument.

That the USSR has learned to live with an alliance in which, as Robin Remington discussed, interests of East European members are voiced, and Soviet plans (e.g., regarding increases in military budgets) are no longer automatically implemented, implies a Soviet desire to maintain the WTO. In an effort to encourage alliance cohesion, the USSR perhaps employs the "carrot" of modernization programs and deliveries of advanced weapons systems. The "stick" of Soviet military intervention, although still present, is no longer the unilateral threat it was in the 1950s. Much of the Soviet effort to ensure reliable allies, instead, lies in the realm of political indoctrination as discussed by Christopher Jones. Through the interlocking main political administrations of Warsaw Pact militaries, the Soviets hope to foster an attitudinal loyalty sufficient to withstand the stress of combat. Winning the "hearts and minds" of East European armed forces, however, may not be an entirely successful campaign and would not, in any case, do much to insulate these allies from the disintegration of domestic socioeconomic and political conditions or from inherent weaknesses in military preparedness. Were the scenario less than optimal and the duration more than the "quick, lightening thrust" to which several contributors alluded, attitudinal loyalty within the military would not compensate for a regime's inability to mobilize manpower and material resources from the nation as a whole.

These observations lead me to a conclusion with which not all contributors to this volume would agree. After almost thirty years, I think it is fair to regard the Warsaw Pact as more a symbol of Soviet weakness than of Soviet strength. It has now become an entity fraught with indications that communist party regimes cannot be assured of their own militaries. The USSR's principal ally, in terms of raw military potential, is Poland. In the aftermath of two years in which the Polish United Workers' Party ceased to govern, and two more years of martial law in which the Polish military squandered the trust it had held in order to administer repression, no WTO military commander could rest well thinking of depending on the resolve of that nation's army. The USSR's most reliable ally with notable military strength is the GDR, a state with many political uncertainties despite the SED's assiduous effort to assert its control. In short, there is little about which Moscow or East European rulers can be fully assured in the Warsaw Pact.

Western (i.e, NATO) planners ought not, of course, prepare only for what appears most probable from aggregate or case-study analyses. "Worst case analysis" must still guide the military planner. Precisely what constitutes such a worst-case, however, is a debate in which analyses from this volume may play a role.

Index

DATE DUE

261-2500

Printed in USA